My Quests for Hope and Meaning

My Quests for Hope and Meaning

AN AUTOBIOGRAPHY

Rosemary Radford Ruether

CASCADE *Books* · Eugene, Oregon

MY QUESTS FOR HOPE AND MEANING
An Autobiography

Cascade Books
An Imprint of Wipf and Stock Publishers
199 W. 8th Ave., Suite 3
Eugene, OR 97401

www.wipfandstock.com

ISBN 13: 978-1-62032-712-8

Cataloging-in-Publication data:

Ruether, Rosemary Radford.

My quests for hope and meaning : an autobiography / Rosemary Radford Ruether ; Foreword by Renny Golden.

xiv + 196 p.; 23 cm—Includes bibliographical references.

ISBN 13: 978-1-62032-712-8

1. Ruether, Rosemary Radford. 2. Theologians—United States—Biography. I. Golden, Renny. II. Title.

BX4827 R83 2013

Manufactured in the USA

Contents

Foreword

The Chispa Carrier: Rosemary Radford Ruether

Renny Golden

She came to the prison with hidden keys. The way forward,
she said, is behind us. With only a spoon of history she
gutted a tunnel that ran below the plazas of Prince after Prince.

We sat waiting behind bars; mouldy histories, slop theologies
In mush bowls shoved under cell doors. Eat this or starve.
We prayed for deliverance we could not name.

We imagined her walking through deserts, our prophet
Searching the sand for bones, poring through ancient scripts,
Gospels, archeologies, the dank stacks of basement libraries.

Reliquaries with their throb of real blood, archives.
We rattled the bars with questions: Can she pick locks?
Can the past be more than our requiem? She kept digging:

Turned over rocks until truth slithered forth, a sacred
Snake that remembered the hour of women.
It was our singing, she said, that opened the tombs.

Everything rising from the Hidden, desert in bloom,
Purple cholla, fingers of scarlet ocotillo, feathered dahlias.

Releasing their clutch of sleep. This rising of women
Is what she wrote for, the fire she lit again and again,

Carrying the chispa in her own blistered hands.

The spirit of foremothers trudging beside us, luminous
Where we pull the song wagons over gutted paths.
We are her legacy, a choir of wild women intoning a Magnificat.

Acknowledgments

I thank Margaret Hover, Mary Gindhart, and Theresa Wilson for reading and discussing chapter 2. I thank Zayn Kassam and Santiago Slabotsky for stimulating feedback on chapter 3. I thank Dean Freudenberger for reading and comments on chapter 6. I thank Dick Bunce for feedback on chapter 5. And as always I thank Herman Ruether for comments on the book as a whole.

Introduction

The Human Construction of Hope and Meaning

Religion is a human construction. To say this is simply to say that all human culture is a human construction. Scientists creating mathematical systems to explain the workings of the universe and charting its emergence from a "big bang" are doing human construction of meaning. Humans create culture in its extraordinarily variegated expressions. What culture is about is creating hope and meaning. It is about affirming that new life can rise from the constant threat of death, that we can create something that continues to affirm love, delight, beauty and comfort, even as death carries off the finite beings that presently exist.

For many humans, especially Christians (Buddhists would be less surprised), the statement that religion is a human creation will be seen as bad news, as an assertion that religious belief is meaningless and groundless. This is because humans, especially Christians, tend to denigrate themselves. They see themselves as sinful, very inadequate, even "totally depraved," to quote Calvin's famous phrase. But this claim of total human inadequacy is actually a way of generating another power that can be totally adequate, namely, God, who is all good, true, and powerful and will provide the adequacy that we lack. I think that humans are indeed inadequate, but not totally inadequate. We cannot become infallible and inerrant. We cannot escape our finitude. But we can do better at creating finite moments of goodness by taking responsibility for what we do.

In our affirmations of life in the face of death, humans do not simply engage in specious gestures. They do in fact create new life. Humans, through their affirmations of meaning and hope, produce endless new realities by which life is carried forward; diseases cured; better food production created and shared; beauty celebrated in art and music; children educated; communities that care for each other brought together; nature shaped into gardens of flowers; and great libraries assembled, by which humans can continue to remember their own past creations. By imagining a God who cares, we do indeed becoming more caring. We also do many stupid and evil things as well, like making war in the name of ending war. But we constantly struggle to do better, to create better and more lasting expressions of good life. Humans are hope and meaning creators.

This book is about some of my own quests for hope and meaning. It is also an effort to explain how I got where I am in my intellectual journey, how I was shaped by my family, my social context, my educational experiences, to raise the questions and issues that have characterized my thought. In chapter 1, "Growing Up in Matricentric Enclaves," I discuss the female-centered patterns of my family as I experienced it (as the youngest daughter in my family). I also reflect on the female-centered patterns of the community that surrounded me: my mother's female friends and my female colleagues. I show how these matricentric enclaves helped ground and shape my movement into women's history and feminist theory.

In chapter 2 "Catholicism: Critiquing, Expanding, Staying," I look at the kind of Catholicism I received from my mother—a Catholicism at once spiritually and intellectually serious, and critical of superficial dogmatism. I trace the expanding circles of my experience of religion: my father's Episcopalianism, my great-aunt's and sister's Russian Orthodoxy, my mother's friends' Quakerism, my uncle's roots in Judaism. I show the increasing frustration of progressive Catholics like myself with Vatican leadership that has sought to undermine and repress the reform efforts of Vatican II, but also why the feminist and liberation movements that have shaped post-Vatican II Catholicism remain my primary community of affiliation, shaping a Catholicism that is ecumenical and interfaith.

In chapter 3, "The Warring Children of Abraham: Jews, Christians, and Muslims," I turn to my concerns with the interrelationship of the three monotheistic faiths, sparked in my childhood by my relation to my Jewish Uncle David. I recount the terrible histories of Christian hostility to Judaism, as well as to Islam, their anti-Semitism and Islamophobia. I also discuss how Judaism has seen Gentiles, and how Islam has seen Judaism and Christianity. I then look at recent efforts, particularly in my own community and theological school in Claremont, California, to shape a community of theological education and life together for Jews, Christians, and Muslims, as well as for those of some other religions.

In chapter 4, "Explorations of Religion: Beyond Monotheism," I show how I began to move beyond the Christian and monotheistic tradition of religion in college through an interest in Greek and ancient Near Eastern paganism, sparked by my entrance into classical studies and through reading authors such as Walter Otto, who took Homeric religion seriously as a religious worldview. I show how this interest in premonotheist paganism has continued in my recent writings in response to feminist quests for a prepatriarchal religion. I go on to discuss my participation in Buddhist-Christian dialogue and the importance of Buddhism for shaping some key aspects of my theological thought about the self and ultimate reality. Finally I address recent writings on the "new atheism" and its failures to address progressive religion.

Chapter 5, "Crisis of the Mental Health System: Mind, Brain, and the Finite Self," turns to my and my family's experiences of my son's mental illness. I discuss the failures of the mental health system to create an adequate community for recovery of the mentally ill, and the challenges of recent literature questioning the biomedical model of mental illness. This literature particularly raises disturbing questions about how the reliance of the present mental health system on psychotropic medication may be actually expanding the numbers and worsening the condition of the mentally ill. I ask how these crises and challenges are raising in a new way questions of how the mind and brain are related to each other in the construction of the self.

Chapter 6, "Ecology, Feminism and Spirituality for a Livable Planet," focuses on what I see as the most critical challenge of our day, namely, the crises of our planetary ecosystem. I draw particularly on Bill McKibben's challenging new book, *Earth: Making Life on a Tough New Planet*. In this book McKibben argues that the worsening of the ecosystem through rising temperature, more chaotic weather, acid oceans, melting ice caps and rising sea levels is not a "future threat" that will happen if we don't cut our fossil fuel emissions. It is already happening.

This destruction will get worse if we continue to pour these emissions into the atmosphere, but we already have a permanently altered planet that has changed the possibilities of our global system of life from what it had been for ten thousand years. In this chapter I explore ecofeminist responses to these patterns of domination of nature and of women, and their recommendations for change. I look at how new agricultural and energy systems are beginning to suggest a way of living in this "tough new planet."

I conclude by asking what kind of spirituality can motivate and support this more sustainable way of living together in this new situation.

I include at the end of this book a complete bibliography of my writings: book publications, chapters in books, and articles in journals and magazines from 1963 to 2011. Researchers on my work have often asked me for a bibliography. Including my bibliography in this autobiography will provide this.

1

Growing Up in Matricentric Enclaves

I grew up in series of matricentric enclaves led by intelligent, articulate, and self-confident women. This reality has something to do with my assumption, for as long as I can remember, that I was an autonomous person and could do whatever I wanted. Both my mother's family and that of my father were clearly patriarchal, although not oppressively so. But these patterns seemed far away, not impinging on my immediate world. For me, as a child, my male ancestors were present in swords, in combat ribbons and photos hanging the wall, but they were dead or away at war. The immediate references of my world were my mother, my aunt Mary, who came to live with us and help my mother manage after my father died when I was twelve, and my two older sisters, Bequita and Manette.

I realized many years later that my experience of my family, and particularly of my mother, was significantly different from that of my older sister Bequita. In 1992 I wrote an article titled "A Wise Woman: Mothered by One Touched by Wisdom's Spirit"[1] on my mother, in which I spoke of my feelings of being unconditionally affirmed by my mother. When I was a child she and I used to play a game at night in bed about what I should do when I grew up. Mother would canvas various professions (teacher, lawyer, doctor, etc.). I realized later that she never mentioned wife and mother. She herself and several of her best friends married late, in their thirties and even forties, after having jobs and interesting travel. She met my father in her early twenties on a boat coming from Europe, but they married only seven years later. She assumed that I would eventually marry, but only after college and travel. (She herself went to Elmira for college from 1912 to 1916.)

1. *Christian Century*, February 17, 1993.

Marriage and children did not seem to define the center who she thought I should be.

My sister Bequita, born in 1932, was four years older than I, and (I realized much later) experienced my mother very differently from the way I did. My father was much more of a presence in the family in her childhood. She was nine when he left for Europe in World War II, while I was only four. She was a pretty, vivacious teenager when our family lived in Athens, Greece, in 1947 and 1948, and attracted boyfriends, particularly American sailors posted there. When we returned to our family home in Washington DC after my father's death, with my mother shouldering the task of raising the three of us alone, she saw my sister Bequita as a "handful" and feared she would "run off" with an inappropriate male. Thus my sister experienced my mother as distrusting her, fearful that she would misbehave. I as the baby, and more a student than a dater in high school and college, experienced more unconditional trust from my mother. Fears about our developing sexuality was a major problem for my mother, a fear focused on my sister Bequita. When my sister read my article on my mother in 1993, she said to me, "That wasn't my experience of mother. I experienced her as mistrusting me, and that was a very painful part of my life."

This difference of our position in the family led to a poignant moment in the later relationship between myself, my sister Bequita, and my mother. Bequita married into a military family shortly after finishing college in 1954. She quickly produced three sons and adopted a fairly conservative view of her role as full-time wife and mother. When I married in 1957 in the last year of college, had a baby when I graduated from college, and determined that I would combine graduate studies with marriage and motherhood, my sister wrote me a polemical letter rebuking me for not devoting myself to full-time domestic life. She was then living with my mother in La Jolla with her children, while her husband was away at war. If I had received this letter, the two of us would probably have been deeply alienated for some years. But I never got this letter. My mother, realizing what my sister was writing, hid the letter in her desk. Did she tell my sister she would mail it and then not do so? I don't know.

I found the letter only when my mother died in 1978, twenty years later. I came across it cleaning my mother's desk while clearing her house. I smiled when I discovered it, trying to imagine the dynamic going on between Bequita and my mother. I did not tell my sister I found it. No need to remind her of this moment in our past. By this time her life and our relationship had greatly changed. Her boys by then were grown, her husband retired from the military and soon dead. She had broken away from subservience and had done an MA in biblical studies, taking her place in a network of progressive Catholic nuns as a teacher and spiritual director in her own right. We had become intellectual colleagues and friends.

Childhood in Washington DC: 1936–1952

For me, then, my family was much more of a matricentric enclave than it was for my older sisters. There I moved as youngest daughter enjoying a sense of affirmation in a world governed by my mother, who seemed to assume that whatever I wanted to do would be good. My father, who I remember as very kindly toward me, teaching me to be the map reader on a trip to his family enclave in Virginia when I was ten, was only briefly present in my life. Absent during the war, he returned for a year in 1945–46, only to leave soon thereafter to become head engineer for the American Mission for Aid to Greece. There he was in charge of restoring the railroad system and clearing the Corinth Canal trashed by Nazis as they left the country in 1945. My sisters, my mother, and I joined him there in 1947–48. But Manette and Bequita went off to France and Switzerland to school, accompanied by my mother. I was left alone with my father when he suddenly took ill and died in October 1948. My sisters remained in school that year, while my mother and I returned home to Washington.

Thus our family home returned to being what it had been for most of my childhood: a realm governed by my mother, now with the added presence of my aunt Mary, who moved in with us. Aunt Mary was a social worker and had a job in a Mormon orphanage. My mother also sought employment to pay our bills. She brushed up her accounting and secretarial skills from premarital days and got a job with a real estate agent a few doors from our home on 1524 31st street in Georgetown, Washington DC. Thus my two mothers carried the load of family life through their work and home management. At the end of that school year my sisters returned from Europe. We were then a female community of five. Bequita, then eighteen, became the "boy" in the family, hanging out the windows of our three-story townhouse to install the storm windows and doing other such housekeeping feats beyond capacity of the other four of us.

Manette had been sent to Sweetbriar College in Virginia where Southern belles arrived with their own horses (my father's choice; she hated it), and had spent a year in Montpelier University in the south of France, becoming fluent in French. Back home, she signed up at American University to study political science. She followed the diplomatic bent of the family, returning to Europe with the State Department for several years after finishing college, before moving to the San Francisco area where she found employment with the State of California. She never married. In later life she indulged her bent for water, boats, and music by buying and living in a houseboat in Sausalito, California, surrounded by a catamaran sailboat, a rowboat, and several kayaks, and playing music with local groups on several instruments. She did an MA in French, writing her thesis on Jacques Cousteau and Antonie de Saint Exupery.

Meanwhile (in 1948) I returned to the Catholic grade school, Dunblane Hall, where I had studied before we left for Athens, and then went on to their high school, Immaculata. This too was a matricentric enclave in a patriarchal world, an all-female world of nuns and girls. Although male clerics were in exclusive control of the realm of priests, they appeared only as distant figures in chasubles with their backs to us when we filed into the chapel for Mass. I don't remember ever talking to one of them during my whole Catholic schooling. Nuns were in charge of all aspects of our school, as principal, teachers, and sometimes playmates who took their turns at bat in baseball and joined us on sleds during snowy days.

Even the liturgical highlight of our school year was exclusively female. This was May Day celebrated on or near May 1 each year. Several weeks were devoted to preparing for this event. Hours of time out from classes were given to practicing the songs and procession. Each grade-school class wore a different-colored sash over white dresses and carried matching flowers. A leading student in the eighth grade was selected to crown Mary Queen of the May. Our large, tree-lined campus was the scene of a winding march of students from all grades that culminated in assembling around Mary's statue as she was crowned with a flowery chaplet, while we all sang "Oh Mary, we crown thee with flowers today: Queen of the Angels, Queen of the May." Mary was our goddess in this drama; Christ, God the Father, or priests nowhere to be seen.

Our sisters (the nuns) were affirmative of females. They even hinted that girls were better than boys; perhaps smarter students, certainly better at keeping our shirts tucked in. I remember "my nuns" as good teachers who gave me the writing skills that would hold me in good stead for my future academic career. When I went in for debating and won the title as top debater for the District of Colombia on the topic of the American Constitution and its amendments, the nuns were there in the front row cheering and enveloping me in the ample folds of their habits in a big hug. Years later I received an invitation to the "motherhouse" (in Indiana) of the Sisters of Providence who ran our school. They had turned their land into an ecojustice center devoted to concerns for the proper care for the earth. They wanted me to speak on the subject. There I discovered my former third- and fourth-grade teacher, Sister Grace, now restored to her original name, who was retired. I realized with a start that when she was my beloved teacher, she was only in her early twenties. At that time she seemed ageless.

La Jolla, California: 1952–1957

In 1952 my mother got a chance to escape the dark world of the Radford house in Georgetown and return to her native California. Helen Marston Beardsley came to visit us in Washington. She and mother had met each other at San Diego High School around 1910 and were lifelong friends. Helen was the daughter of George Marston, San Diego city founder. Marston came to San Diego in 1870 at the age of twenty and founded Marstons, which became the leading dry goods department store in that city. He became deeply interested in city planning and contributed funds and land for the building of Balboa Park, the cultural and recreational center for San Diego still today.

Helen, his youngest daughter, was born in 1892. She became committed to civil rights and peace, and founded the San Diego chapter of the Women's International League for Peace and Freedom (WILPF) in 1923 and the San Diego chapter of the American Civil Liberties Union (ACLU) in 1933. She worked in the settlement movement in New York and Chicago and was a friend and colleague of Jane Addams. She also taught in progressive schools in San Diego, particularly concerning herself with rights of the Mexican population. She was part of a delegation of the ACLU and WILPF that went to Imperial Valley, California, to enforce a federal injunction that gave the farmworkers the right to assemble. Although driven out of town by a growers union, she returned several times to Imperial Valley to support the farmworkers union's efforts. Helen was an active Socialist in the 1930s and the secretary of the local Socialist party.[2]

2. See the webpage: http://helenmarston.tripod.com/.

Helen had built herself a small house in La Jolla, California, in the 30s, which was available since she was then married and living in Pasadena. She invited my mother to occupy it until my mother could buy a house of her own. My mother was delighted and quickly set to work clearing the Radford home in Washington and putting it on the market. In the summer of 1952 I, my sister Bequita, who had just earned her driving license, our mother, and the family dog, Badger, got in our family car and drove to California. We moved into Helen's little house a block from the beach in La Jolla, jamming our heavy furniture from a town house in Washington into this summer cottage.

Mother soon found nearby a suitable three-bedroom house with a garden, where she lived for the rest of her life. I attended La Jolla High School to finish my last two years of high school. Here I became involved in writing for the high school newspaper and soon found myself appointed its editor. I and a creative staff prided ourselves on running a first-class paper that succeeded in "scooping" school elections: that is, having the paper printed and back at school, with headlines announcing the winners by the close of school hours on election days.

Our paper generated one moment of controversy. A local retired admiral found our editorial opinions threatening and complained to our high school principal that he found our paper "communist"—this in the McCarthy era of 1954. The principal called us in to tell us this, going on to say that we should not worry because he supported us. What the admiral found communist was never clear to me. I had written an editorial criticizing the commercialization of Christmas, and perhaps that was it. But we all felt proud of ourselves. (Wow, we're communist!)

In La Jolla I found myself in another even more stimulating matricentric enclave, consisting of my mother and her network of female friends. This group of women, mostly single or widows, in female-headed households, were involved in cultural activities and social concerns. Central among these women was Helen Marston Beardsley. Helen, although in her seventies in the 1960s, was still very involved in peace and civil rights, demonstrating against nuclear testing and the Vietnam War and in behalf of the farmworkers. This included supporting young men who became war resisters after joining the military and having been treated particularly badly by the armed services.

On several occasions Helen invited me to come with her to these antiwar and pro-farmworkers demonstrations, thus beginning my political education. On one occasion, when I went with her to the trial of antiwar resisters in the military, I noticed in the front row of supporters the famous rabbi Abraham Joshua Heschel.[3] During the Nixon administration a list of people the president regarded as his key enemies was leaked to the press.[4] Helen Marston Beardsley's name was on it. I still remember my mother and her female friends laughing together and exclaiming, "We are so proud of Helen. She made the enemies list!"

Scripps College and Claremont Graduate School: 1954–1965

In 1954 I graduated from La Jolla High School and received a four-year scholarship to go to Scripps College in Claremont, California. This was a school that seemed very suitable to me. It was a women's college, which I liked. Male students were nearby at Pomona College and what was then called Claremont Men's College. But having women as the primary group of fellow students felt empowering to me. It was also a school with a large commitment to the teaching of applied arts, painting and sculpture. I had been involved in studying painting since grade school, working in several media, both oil and watercolor. I wanted to continue this work for a possible career as an artist. Scripps was also strong in the humanities, which also suited me. It occupies a beautiful campus of flowering gardens and fruit trees. I flourished there for four years. My future writing, based on an excellent background in humanistic culture, is well rooted in the integrated humanities education that I got from Scripps College.

I did not, however, continue to major in the applied arts. Instead I found myself drawn more to the spoken and written word, a draw that led to future work as a teacher and writer. Classicist Robert Palmer, who taught the courses in history and ancient culture in the curriculum, drew me into his group of select students whom he groomed to study the Greek and Latin classics. I found myself fascinated by this world of classical antiquity. Painting as an interest faded away as a possible future career and became a leisure-time activity (which I still cultivate by painting watercolors during travels). I was being shaped to be an intellectual. Palmer assumed that his

---

3. Abraham Joshua Heschel (1907–1972) was the most famous American rabbi of his generation through his accessible writing and antiwar activism.

4. Nixon's enemies list started by naming his political enemies but expanded to include hundreds of names of progressives he came to see as opponents.

best students would go on to doctoral work, although this only gradually became clear.

In those heady and naïve days of women's-college education there was no career counseling or talk of how to prepare yourself for a future career. The immediate agenda was the excitement of understanding ideas, moving into the great world of the human cultural legacy for its own sake, not to *do* something to make a living! I don't regret that. It was a privilege to be able to become a explorer of ideas for their own value, without having to ask what we were going to do.

Although Scripps was a women's college with a student body of three hundred bright and creative women, at that time it was not feminist. I became very bonded to my core group of women friends, five of whom moved to live together in the tower of Browning Hall (three single and one double room and a big porch on the third floor of this housing unit). This enabled me to continue my experience of living in a female-centered core community, although I didn't have the consciousness to name it that way then. But the hierarchy of the school as a whole was very male dominated. All the professors were male, with the exception of three women, two of whom were wives of male professors and all of whom taught languages. One of them, Franciszka Merlan, was a Polish Jew who had a PhD in philosophy and was the wife of renowned Austrian Jewish philosopher Philip Merlan. He taught philosophy and modern European intellectual history. She taught German. It didn't occur to anyone—students or faculty—to imagine that she might teach a course in philosophy.

This arrangement carried an implicit message. Women were secondary teachers, just as teaching language was a secondary subject. Powerful men, like our very articulate and authoritative male professors, taught ideas. Women taught you how to read ideas in languages other than English. In those days that meant French and German; if you weren't a serious scholar, Spanish. Greek was available at Pomona College. I soon found myself going there to be able to read Greek classics, as well as doing French and German at Scripps College.

At that time it never occurred to me to take Spanish. I had already been well socialized from high school to regard Spanish as an unscholarly language, even though my mother was born in Mexico, was bilingual, and loved Spanish. (Yet she shared some of the same linguistic bias and never suggested I might learn Spanish.) It was only in my thirties that I realized how I had been wrongly deprived of what should have been my linguistic heritage. Then I began to go to Mexico and Guatemala to study Spanish so I could read the blossoming writings of Latin American liberation and feminist theology. Fortunately the sexism of Scripps College faculty has greatly changed today, with the school boasting many strong female professors, female presidents, and lively work in women's subjects.

Feminism didn't exist as an idea in the 1950s, as far as I knew at the time. If the word *feminist* was ever pronounced, it was as a slur word. I remember in my sophomore year I became involved in a rather mild campaign to make our discussion groups in Humanities II more meaningful. When I passed the French teacher, Madame Glenn, in the hall, she shook her finger at me and said, "Watch out. You will become a feminist!" I remember being surprised and wondering, what is a feminist? But I didn't pause to explore this question at that time. It would only be ten years later, when this idea was reborn in a new feminist movement, that I would realize that I had been a feminist implicitly all along, as were my mother and her friends, like Helen Marston Beardsley, a socialist feminist from the 1930s.

In 1958, one year married and with a baby daughter, I was stubbornly pursuing my love of learning and insisting on going on for graduate work. I refused instinctively to accept the implied dominant message of my society and church that I should bury my head in diapers and frequent childbearing and drop out of school; but I lacked any name for myself, such as *feminist*, to justify this instinct. My mother too had no language to protect my desire for continued study from my sister's guilt-tripping polemic, and she responded to it by quietly hiding my sister's letter to me. Yet continue to study I did, even with two more children, before I figured out how to master contraception.

By 1965, with three children under seven, I had done an MA in Roman history (with a thesis on the lineage of a leading Roman political clan) and a PhD in classics and patristics (with a thesis on the literary and philosophical thought of Cappadocian church father Gregory Nazianzus). I was also writing a book on ecclesiology, published as *The Church against Itself*. I was ready to become a professor. Although long self-affirming as a female, I had not yet become consciously feminist. I still used androcentric language. No one then discussed inclusive language. Yet my original title for my book on ecclesiology had been *The Church against Herself*. My editor at Herder and Herder did not like this use of the feminine for the Church and insisted on using *Itself*. One wonders in retrospect what it would have meant to keep the *Herself*.

I was happy at my survival, with a completed dissertation, so imagine my surprise when, with a third baby on my hip, I turned in my painfully typed doctoral manuscript (no computers in those days) to Robert Palmer, who had mentored me from being a freshman undergraduate through a completed PhD. Instead of congratulating me, he grumbled that I was letting him down by going off to teach, somewhere else, rather than remaining as his permanent teaching assistant. I was stunned! Did this man really think I had done a PhD to continue for the rest of my life as his teaching assistant in Humanities I! Did he perhaps, despite his pressing me to do doctoral work, never really imagine that I could grow up to be his peer! This incident was my final confrontation with the deep patriarchalism of Scripps' male faculty of the 1950s and '60s.

I resisted the impulse to throw my thesis at him. I could not afford to offend him at that point. Instead I quietly went off, thesis in hand and baby on hip, to find a way to turn in my thesis another way. During the oral on my thesis, yet another implicit clash with Palmer took place. He started the oral by asking me in a preemptory fashion why it was that I had used the nineteenth-century Migne Greek text of Gregory, rather than the new Greek text by Werner Jaeger.[5] I was shocked to realize that Palmer, as a classicist who did not read patristics, did not know the difference between Gregory Nazianzus and Gregory Nyssa! Again, this was no time to expose the ignorance a professor who was had the power to pass or fail my doctoral work. I muttered quietly that the nineteenth-century Migne text was the latest source for Gregory Nazianzus's work. Palmer quieted down.

I somehow made it successfully through the oral on my doctoral thesis despite Palmer, and also despite the sexual harassment I was experiencing from the Irish priest who had read Gregory Nazianzus in Greek with me. I never talked with Palmer again. This is sad, for I owed him much for my education. But these incidents made clear his limitations. As for the Irish priest, who also tried to trip me up in the oral exam, he had backed off trying to persuade me to run off with him. Rather he turned to trying to save himself by becoming a Benedictine monk, after receiving shock treatment in the mental ward of a hospital. I had survived these assaults and was on the verge of moving to Washington DC, where both I and my husband, Herman Ruether, would take up teaching positions. At that time

---

5. Werner Jaeger sought to make a complete text of the writings of Gregory Nyssa. He began this project before World War I. The first volume appeared under Berolina: Apud Weidmannos in 1921. The tenth volume appeared posthumously in 2009.

I had several published articles and was about to have to my credit the publication of two books. But meanwhile I had another challenge to face: the legacy of American racism in Mississippi.

Mississippi Summer, 1965

During my graduate years at Claremont I had become involved in the ecumenical chaplaincies of the Claremont Colleges. Civil rights for African Americans was the central issue of their activism, and I was drawn into this work. In the spring of 1965 they put together a delegation of students, faculty, and chaplains to go the Mississippi to work with the Delta Ministry, a network of Christian groups working on civil rights issues in this state. I volunteered to join. My husband, Herman, was in India at the time, working on research for his doctoral thesis on the Khilafat (Muslim nationalist) movement and its relation to Gandhi in the 1940s.

My mother agreed to have our three children live with her in La Jolla while I went to Mississippi. She used to enjoy telling a story about this. She was picking out groceries while my daughter sat in a shopping cart in the grocery store. A man passing by, and not seeing any young mother nearby, leaned over and said to my daughter, "Where is your mother, little girl?" My daughter replied pertly: "My mother is in Mississippi and my daddy is in India." Needless to say, the man was very surprised; my mother was amused.

The summer in Mississippi would be no joke for me. It was in many ways a turning point in my own self-awareness. The previous Mississippi summer, of 1964, had been a violent one. Three civil rights workers, James Cheney, a Congress of Racial Equality (CORE) leader from Mississippi, and Michael Schwerner and Andrew Goodman, from New York, had gone missing, and their bodies were later found shot and buried. They had been murdered by Mississippi Klansmen. We who were going to Mississippi were aware that we too might encounter hostility and perhaps violence from hostile Whites. I remember thinking about this possible violence as we drove to Mississippi in an old, battered car. The thought occurred to me that I too might get killed. It was the first moment in my life that I remember thinking about dying. I had three young children and was in no way eager to become a martyr. It was an important moment as I weighed the possibility of death against doing the right thing. I determined that I must go on.

The Watts riot in Los Angeles also took place during six days in August of that summer. We heard about it while we were in Mississippi and wondered about the appropriateness of what we were doing. Why were a bunch of Los Angelenes in Mississippi working on racial injustice when our own city was on fire from racial injustice? We felt a little foolish and realized that when we returned we would need to address our own city's treatment of the Black people of Watts, whom we knew nothing about.

In the summer of 1965 the Delta Ministry, along with a number of other civil rights projects, were located at the campus of Mt. Beulah, in Hinds County near Edwards, Mississippi, on the southwest side of the state, a former Black college that had closed in about 1954.[6] We were lodged in the former dorm rooms. A few weeks before we arrived, a group of Ku Klux Klansmen had driven through the campus one night shooting at the windows of the buildings. No one had been hurt, but the Beulah organizers had set up a night vigil, served by a rotating committee, to guard against such an incident in the future. If such night riders appeared again, the watch group were to ring a bell, and everyone was to dive under their beds to protect themselves from bullets coming through windows. This seemed pathetically inadequate protection, but I duly took my place in the night vigils, acutely aware of our vulnerability in a world of open war between civil rights workers and White racists.

Our group attended worship at a local Black Baptist church, who welcomed us kindly. The minister did admonish us to dress well for church. The Black people here, he pointed out to us, wear their Sunday best for church, often the only "good" outfit they own. We demean them if we come in jeans, he said—a helpful lesson for us young Whites from Los Angeles. I remember a sermon in which the pastor instructed his people on registering to vote, a key activity with which we were there to help. He compared his people to dogs who had been beaten and tied up for many years. When suddenly the rope was cut and they were free, it took them a while to realize they were free and to break away. So too Blacks of Mississippi needed to learn to act on being free and to break the habits formed by their long experience of domination. The people nodded.

One Sunday a group of us, Black and White, decided to try to attend a White Baptist church. As we approached, we heard the windows banging shut. A delegation of church leaders met us at the door with a printed

6. This college was run from 1875 to 1952 by the United Christian Missionary Society under the name of the Southern Christian Institute.

statement to the effect that God had decreed the separation of the races, and humans were not to change these god-given patterns. We were not allowed to enter, and went back to our Black church, duly warned.

Some of our group decided that their project for the summer was to build a swimming pool on campus, since the local town pool was for Whites only. This seemed a little Californian to me. A group of my fellow students did succeed in building a pool that summer, but I understand that it was never actually opened. Water for it was not accessible. In any case, my choice for work was to volunteer with the Mississippi Child Development Group (MCDG), a statewide organization running Head Start programs for Black Mississippi preschoolers.

Head Start was major idea in the U.S. at that time, and federal money was available for it. But the program had been criticized for spending most of the money on the bureaucrats and not getting much to the grass roots. "Feeding the horses to feed the pigeons," (i.e., the grain got to the pigeons through the excrement of the horses) was the way one critic referred to it. The MCDG wanted to get most of the money to the local community, by organizing them to run the Head Start programs themselves. Thereby they also hoped to help them build a community organization that they could use to do other things they needed, like getting a water system.

I and a Black woman community organizer from Brooklyn took on the task of driving around the state visiting Head Start centers to collect information about what they were doing. This was a powerful experience for me. In one Head Start center the children (four- and five-year-olds) had been given paints and large papers to depict their experiences. They had then been asked describe what they had painted, and their accounts had been written on their paintings. Their stories were vivid expressions of their experiences of racial oppression. They also spoke of family members who went "North" for better opportunities. "The man" was the phrase used for oppressive Whites. These young children were extraordinarily articulate in explaining the vivid images by which they portrayed their reality.

As my friend and I drove around the state, we kept a careful watch for white men in trucks with guns positioned on the back window. We knew that such Whites were accustomed to stop a car containing Whites and Blacks together and beating them up or worse, so we were vulnerable. We also heard during our travels that the nearby town of Bogalusa, in the northeast corner of Louisiana, was being besieged by the Ku Klux Klan. We decided to drive across the state line to check it out. We were well received by the town leaders, who took us to a church to one of the rallies (that were going on nightly) to organize the people to resist the Klan-enforced White domination of the city. We were given beds for the night and spent long hours around a kitchen table hearing the stories of the townfolk. The Deacons for Defense and Justice had set up an armed defense system in Bogalusa. We experienced a Black militancy not found among the more subdued rural Blacks in Mississippi.

After these experiences my friend and I drove back to our base at Beulah. I remember sitting in a bedroom with my friend as she brushed her hair. Facing a mirror and with her back to me, she said quietly, "I have always hated White people." I immediately felt a warm glow. I realized that our adventures together had broken through historical enmity to a beginning of personal friendship. After that summer I lost touch with her. I wonder what she did after that summer.

My summer in Mississippi was a decisive turning point for me. For the first time I got a glimpse of what White America looked and felt like from the side of Black people. I realized that this was a very different world from that shaped by and for Whites like me. I gradually came to realize that this is true, not only in the U.S., but also throughout the world. You only begin to glimpse the full reality of a society if you locate yourself in the disadvantaged sector and look at it from that context. I have since sought to understand several other societies: Israel-Palestine from 1980 to today, Nicaragua in the '80s, South Africa under apartheid in 1989, among others. In each case I have sought to live in the oppressed community, even if briefly, to gain some insight of what the society looks like from the other side.

Minette Lall, an African American from LA whom I met that summer, and I did remain lifetime friends. We decided that when we returned to Claremont, we had to contact people working in Watts to learn more about it and do something there. We contacted several clergy working for justice in Watts, and they gave us information and advice. For some reason that I can't remember, we decided to put on a Christmas party in a church in 1965 for Watts people. We collected a lot of donations and assembled refreshments, presents, and decorations. As we drove into Watts on Christmas Eve for the party, we noticed Christmas tree stands that had been abandoned and stopped to pick up as many trees as we could to further decorate the church.

A local Black leader had volunteered to be the Santa Claus to give out the presents in suitable attire. The party took off with gusto. Every present was scooped up, as well as all the food, the trees, and other decorations. When the party was over and the church barren of gifts and decorations, Santa Claus told us with chagrin that someone had also lifted his wallet from his back pocket! We felt a little silly, but, oh, well. Clearly Watts people knew how to take whatever outside guilt-givers brought in, even if a little more wealth got redistributed than intended.

Howard University, School of Religion: 1966–1976

Later that summer, I, Herman Ruether, and our three children moved to Washington DC to take up a new life. He had a job at the School of Government and Public Administration and the Center for South and South-East Asian Studies at American University. I had secured two classes: one in church history at George Washington University and one in historical theology at the School of Religion at the historically Black Howard University. The next year, 1966, the School of Religion offered me a full-time position, which I happily accepted, teaching there for ten years.

The School of Religion was then located in a smallish three-story building inside the campus of Howard University. The library, classrooms, and faculty and administration offices were all located in that one building. I had an office in a small room in the basement next to the boiler room. Two other Whites taught in the school beside myself, but the faculty was predominately Black (They preferred the term *Negro* and flinched at the word *Black*.) The student body was almost all of dark complexion, but internationally so. Most were African Americans, but we also had Caribbean Blacks, Africans, and dark-skinned folk from places like India. It was a socially rich community.

I came to Howard at the beginning of a new stage of the civil rights movement. In June of 1966 Stokley Carmichael proclaimed the need for "Black power." Many Whites who saw themselves as supporters of Black civil rights were shocked at the new militancy. Martin Luther King's strategy of nonviolence was seen as being rejected by a Black separatism they could not support. I did not share this White fear of Black power. Having been in Bogalusa, where I saw organized Black defense against the Klan, I was critical of the implied paternalism of many White liberals who assumed that Blacks should be grateful to receive their rights from Whites based on their good behavior. This dependency needed to be rejected. Blacks needed to affirm their own autonomy and organize their own power to take their place as equals in American society.

James Cone, a young Black theologian, was claiming a Black theology rooted in black power.[7] My colleagues at Howard, socialized in the language of moderation of the "Negro" middle class, were uncomfortable with this militant language. I found myself in the odd position of introducing black theology to my students at the Howard School of Religion. I wrote articles defending the appropriateness of Black theology. The goal was the achievement of full humanity of all racial-ethnic people, but in the US American context this meant passing through a stage of radical rejection of the legacy of White racism that claimed Whiteness as normative humanness. In this context Whiteness becomes the symbol of evil and oppression, Blackness the metaphor for liberation. This is the way Cone was using the symbols of Whiteness and Blackness.

In the late '60s and early '70s I became aware of racism and oppression as international or global systems, rooted in European colonialism. Colonized groups worldwide were seeking their liberation, while the United States was intervening around the world, seeking to shore up colonial dependency and to become itself the new colonial imperial power. I learned about the new militancy of Latin American resistance to oppression in groups such as the Golconda movement in Colombia, and the involvement of priests such as Camilo Torres in wars of resistance. The 1968 Latin American Bishops Conference at Medellin took liberation into the heart of the vision of the Catholic Church. Meanwhile the educational practice of *conscientization* developed by Paulo Freire gave a key tool for exposing cultural ideologies of domination.[8] A Latin American theology of liberation was also appearing in the writing of Gustavo Gutiérrez, part of which I read in 1970 before it had been translated by Orbis into English.[9]

In my circles in Washington, the chief way of expressing anti-imperialism was by protest against the Vietnam War. I joined with fellow opponents of the Vietnam War in protests in downtown Washington and experienced several brief arrests. My children grew up on such protest marches, many of which flowed out of the church we had joined, St. Stephen and the Incarnation. When Martin Luther King Jr. was assassinated on April 4 of 1968,

---

7. Cone, *Black Theology and Black Power* (New York: Seabury, 1969); Cone, *A Black Theology of Liberation* (Philadelphia: Lippencott, 1970).

8. Paulo Freire, *Pedagogy of the Oppressed* (New York: Herder & Herder, 1970).

9. Gustavo Gutierrez, *A Theology of Liberation* (Maryknoll, NY: Orbis, 1973).

Washington became a riot zone. On Palm Sunday, two days after the assassination, our church marched down 14th Street, then lined with soldiers guarding the stores again the rioters. We carried daffodils and placed a flower in the barrel of each soldier's gun as we processed down the street.

Feminism was also exploding as a movement in the mid- to late '60s. Betty Friedan, author of the formative 1963 book *The Feminine Mystique*, helped found NOW, The National Organization for Women, in October 1966 and was its first president. In the Civil Rights Act of 1964 the word *sex* had been included in the ban against discrimination in employment. This word was inserted to try to defeat the Act, but it was defended and became a permanent part of it, thanks to the energetic organizing work of Black feminist lawyer Pauli Murray.[10] NOW was founded in part to try to ensure that federal cases against job discrimination would indeed include discrimination against women.[11]

Feminism also exploded in the New Left at this time as well. New Left men, rejecting racial and class hierarchy, tended to take their male sexual privilege for granted, reinforced by the sexual revolution. New Left women were expected to be politically subservient and sexually accessible. In 1964 several women from the Student Nonviolent Coordinating Committee (SNCC) wrote a paper asking about the position of women in the movement. Stokley Carmichael responded with what he saw as a humorous retort: "The only position of women in the movement is prone." This comment brought to a head the reality of the sexually exploitative presumptions of New Left men.

Women in the Left grew more militant in their critique of sexism in the civil rights movement and in society as a whole. Consciousness-raising groups appeared, gathering women in separate enclaves to articulate their own experiences of sexism. Women's liberation defined itself as a more militant feminism demanding deeper critique of society and acceptance of lesbianism in the women's movement organizations, such as NOW. Feminist reflection was also appearing in the churches and theological schools. Women became aware that they could be ordained in some denominations (Northern Presbyterian and Methodist) and began to appear in seminaries in larger numbers. They demanded to be in the ordination track, not

10. See Sarah Azaransky, *The Dream of Freedom: Pauli Murray and American Democratic Faith* (New York: Oxford University Press, 2011), 64–66.

11. For an account of this history, see Rosemary Radford Ruether, *Christianity and the Making of the Modern Family* (Boston: Beacon, 2000), 142–44.

just tagged as preparing to serve as laywomen in Christian education. They called for the hiring of women professors and for feminist content in the curriculum.

In the late sixties I began to do my own theological reflection on the heritage of the Christian church. My first essay was titled "Male Chauvinist Theology and the Anger of Women." Influenced by the militant Black Power movement, which did not hesitate to speak out of black anger, I found churches and seminaries shocked when the *anger* word was applied to women's rejection of religiously based sexism. Susan Thistlethwaite likes to describe my giving this talk at Duke University when she was a student there. There was palpable nervousness throughout the room at the use of such a term as *anger* for women's experience.

During this period my image of God or the divine went through a decisive shift or perhaps a clarification. I remember sometime in my twenties focusing on whether or not I really believed that God existed, in the sense of a male person outside and ruling over the universe. At some point I had a vivid experience, something like a dream or visual hallucination. I experienced myself as standing in a great hall of a huge fortress. At the end of the hall was a staircase. I began to climb this staircase and found myself going up level after level of stairs, throwing open a door at the top of each level. Finally I reached what I knew was the top level. I sensed that inside was the throne room of God. With great excitement and nervousness I threw open this door and saw inside a great room with a throne, but the throne was empty!

I saw clearly that there was no God sitting on a throne in a throne-room at the top of a world system in the form of a hierarchical palace. Instead, I realized, the divine was quite different and existed elsewhere. God was a great nurturing and empowering energy that existed in and through all things, sustaining and renewing them. Although not in the image of a human person (not anthropomorphic) this true divinity was more maternal that paternal. The Great Mother or Holy Wisdom seemed the right title for Her. This was the divinity that was really there, that I experienced, could pray to, be in tune with and who represented the source of all that is. I realized that I never had really believed in God as an old man ruling from a throne in the skies. This founding divine energy of the Great Mother came to be my operative understanding of the divine. The matrix of mothers who had nurtured and empowered me as I grew up is the experiential base for this vision of the Great Mother.

During this period I began to delve back into my knowledge of church history to uncover the roots of sexism in the church. The patterns of asceticism and dualism in patristic and medieval Catholicism became newly interesting. I looked at the way ascetic dualism of mind and body became identified with male–female dualism, initially liberating women from an exclusive identification with marriage and baby making, but ultimately tending to defeat the liberating potential of women's spiritual journeys and marginalizing women from leadership in the early church.

I realized that patristic times were also the context of increasing alienation of Christianity from Judaism, of the shaping of an ideology that posited the inferiority of Judaism as a religion and of Jews as a people. This ideology grew into an organized system of marginalization of Jews in the Middle Ages, often punctuated by violence. The nineteenth-century dissolution of Christendom appeared at first to free Jews to become equal citizens in European nations. But fear of Jewish equality helped establish a racial anti-Semitism that found its culmination in Nazi genocide. The response of some Jews to anti-Semitism to create a Jewish nationalism or Zionism, establishing the State of Israel, has led to its own contradiction in the ethnic cleansing of Palestinians. This terrible history of anti-Semitism in Western Christianity and the racial contradictions of modern Western nationalism were among the themes of my essays at this time. But it would be the '80s before I would go to Israel-Palestine and begin to realize the extent of the contradiction of Zionism and the oppression of the Palestinians.

Ecology as a justice issue and as a challenge to the ideology of endless growth of industrial society also began to become evident to me when I read an early analysis of the findings of the Club of Rome report *Limits to Growth*, in 1972. Growing human population and limited resources of the planet were shown to be in a basic conflict. Industrial growth could not continue to go on limitlessly, as the capitalist growth ideology seemed to assume. Not only did human population need to be limited, but the way humans used natural resources and organized technology had to be fundamentally reconstructed to allow for sustainable (and regenerative) human existence on the planet. The reading of this report made a deep impression on me. I realized that the anticolonial struggle to create more just distribution of well-being among communities around the world was challenged by the excess wealth by colonial elites. Global justice was unrealizable without a reorganization of how resources were owned and used between rich and poor people around the world.

I wondered how religion had contributed to the pollution of the earth. It struck me that Christianity, also Judaism and Hinduism, cultivated the idea of the polluted nature of women and their sexuality. How was this related to the pollution of the earth? By shunning women's sexuality and becoming phobic toward human waste making, rather than integrating human waste into the regenerating rhythms of nature, has the religious concept of ritual pollution helped generate actual pollution of nature? I remember discussing this dilemma with my students at the Howard School of Religion, almost all of whom were non-White males, and receiving their blank stares. Clearly what I was saying made no sense to them. But I knew I had embarked on another avenue of theological-social critique that would lead me to new dimensions of thought.

In 1972 I published with Paulist Press a collection of twelve essays titled *Liberation Theology: Human Hope Confronts Christian History and American Power* that summed up all this thinking.[12] Many of these essays had been published in earlier form between 1970 and 1972. There were three articles on the dilemma of the development of Christianity, its sellout of its original eschatological vision for a Constantinian church, and its need to transcend this today. Two essays spoke of the alienation of Christianity and Judaism, the modern emergence of radical anti-Semitism, and the dilemma of Zionism. A seventh essay explored the sexism of classical Christianity linked with mind–body dualism, while an eighth essay raised the relation of ecological sustainability and feminism. Chapter 9 contained my thoughts on Black theology and Black power. The remaining three essays explored the relation of the left-wing church tradition and communitarian socialism, the dilemma of the white Left in the US in its search for new model of society, and finally the appearance of Third World liberation theologies and anticolonial struggle in Latin America and Asia.

This collection of essays is striking to me as I reread them in 2012. In effect I laid out in 1972 all of the issues I would continue to explore in greater depth and detail over the next forty years. In 1972–1973 I would spend a year teaching at the Harvard Divinity School. Somewhat to the surprise of my students there, who expected me to be exclusively concerned with emerging feminism, one of my classes was on anti-Semitism in Christian tradition.[13] In this class I explored the roots of the alienation of Christianity

12. Published as Rosemary Radford Ruether, *Liberation Theology: Human Hope Confronts Christian History and American Power.*

13. Published as Rosemary Radford Ruether, *Faith and Fratricide: The Theological*

from Judaism in the New Testament era, the elaboration of anti-Judaism in the *adversus Judaeus* writings of the church fathers, and the incorporation of this hostility into Christian Roman and canon law in the Christian Roman Empire of the fourth to sixth centuries. These laws laid the basis for the persecution of the Jews in medieval and early modern Europe, culminating in the Holocaust. My final concern was the dismantling of anti-Semitism in Christian theology. This became my 1974 book, *Faith and Fratricide: The Theological Roots of Anti-Semitism.*

The publication of my book on anti-Semitism in Christianity led to many invitations to speak in synagogues and in Christian–Jewish dialogues. In these venues I was often asked about how this history related to support for the State of Israel. I had not regarded my book as having anything to do with support for the State of Israel. Rather I assumed that the issue was cleaning up the remainders of anti-Semitism in Western societies and churches. This question suggested to me that guilt for Western Christian anti-Semitism was being used to demand uncritical support for the State of Israel, silencing any concerns about the treatment of Palestinians by this state. I realized I needed to find out about more this reality in order not to have my work misused.

I took the opportunity to go on a delegation to Israel in 1980, set up by some Canadian Jewish women from Montreal, billed as a "dialogue of Jewish, Christian, and Muslim women." Although the purpose of this trip turned out to be much more of an apology for the State of Israel than real dialogue with Muslims, I was able to get my first glimpse of the situation of Palestinians at that time. My concern for this situation was deepened. In 1986 I was able to return to Israel-Palestine, spending some months at the Tantur Ecumenical Center between Bethlehem and Jerusalem. There I met Naim Ateek, Palestinian theologian, and became drawn into the reflection he was pioneering on Palestinian liberation theology.[14]

At Tantur I taught a course on theology and the Israeli–Palestinian conflict, while my husband, Herman Ruether, taught a course on Islam. Our work together on these topics resulted in the book *The Wrath of Jonah: The Crisis of Religious Nationalism in the Israeli-Palestinian Conflict.*[15] With

---

Roots of Anti-Semitism.

14. Naim Ateek, *Justice and Only Justice: A Palestinian Theology of Liberation*: Foreword by Rosemary Radford Ruether (Maryknoll, NY: Orbis, 1989).

15. Published in 1989 by Harper & Row. A second edition in 2002 was published by Fortress Press.

the publication of this book I was no longer favored by the American Jewish establishment and received no more invitations to speak at synagogues on anti-Semitism, even though I had in no way changed my views on this issue. To be concerned about justice for Palestinians was assumed to be hostile to Israel, hence anti-Semitic, and no friend of Jews.

Over the last twenty-five years I have taken many trips to Israel–Palestine, often as leader of delegations of Christian groups from US theological schools, to learn the realities of Palestinian oppression in Israel and the Occupied Territories. I am also a member of the Board of Directors of the US Friends of Sabeel (the Palestinian liberation theology movement founded by Naim Ateek). These are efforts to counteract the overwhelming role of US Christians in buttressing uncritical support for the State of Israel and to make injustice to the Palestinians visible to US Christians.

Fortunately today, in the second decade of the twenty-first century, more and more Israeli, as well as American, Jews are emerging as supporters of a just coexistence of these two peoples. Some, like American Israeli Jew Jeff Halper, are risking personal well-being to rebuild Palestinian houses destroyed by the Israeli army and to oppose Israel's "apartheid" system.[16] Jewish ethicists Marc Ellis and Mark Braverman have written major books critiquing the ideology of Zionism. They have questioned the manipulation of the charge of anti-Semitism to browbeat Western Christians into uncritical support for Israeli domination of Palestinians and the occupation of Palestine.[17] A new coalition of justice-seeking Israeli Jews, Palestinian Muslims and Christians, and Western Christians, Muslims, and Jews is emerging, mobilizing support for a more just solution to this conflict.

These sociopolitical issues in the Middle East and globally remain of vital importance to me. Yet feminism has become the primary line of development of my thought and the one for which I am best known. I had two major opportunities to develop my work in feminism and theology in the early '70s. In 1972–73 Harvey Cox at Harvard Divinity School invited me to teach one year under the Stillman chair of Catholic Studies. Another

16. Jeff Halper, *Obstacles to Peace: A Reframing of the Israeli-Palestinian Conflict* (Jerusalem: ICAHD, 2005). Also Jeff Halper, *An Israeli in Palestine: Resisting Dispossession, Redeeming Israel* (London: Pluto, 2010).

17. Marc H. Ellis, *Beyond Innocence and Redemption: Confronting the Holocaust and Israeli Power; Creating a Moral Future* (San Francisco: Harper & Row, 1990; see also Ellis, *O Jerusalem!: The Contested Future of the Jewish Covenant* (Minneapolis: Fortress, 1999). Mark Braverman, *Fatal Embrace: Christians, Jews and the Search for Peace in the Holy Land* (Austin: Synergy, 2010).

professor at Harvard Divinity School insisted I didn't have the seniority to hold the Stillman chair and should be called a "Visiting Lecturer in Roman Catholic Studies." I was still to be paid by the Stillman chair. I responded by jokingly defining my position as "under the Stillman chair rather than on it." Despite this slight from some of the faculty, I had a wonderful time at Harvard teaching an enthusiastic group of students. What I taught had little to do with Roman Catholic studies. I did one course on the rise of patriarchy and patriarchal religions in the ancient Near East and the Greco-Roman world and the shaping of early Christianity. The second course was on nineteenth-century European misogynist anthropologies and the beginnings of modern feminism. I also did my course on anti-Semitism mentioned before.

In 1973–74 I was invited to do a year-long course in feminist theology at the Yale Divinity School. Unlike during my year at Harvard, I did not move to Yale full time but flew up to New Haven once a week for my class, while continuing to teach at Howard. This course was very helpful in systematizing my theological critique. During my last years at Howard I published several books on feminism. One was a collection of essays by women (and one man) on how women had been viewed by the male Jewish and Christian tradition, from Hebrew Scripture to Barth and Tillich in modern Western Protestant theology. I wrote the chapter on the fathers of the church.[18]

At that time I also put together a book of my own essays on a range of issues from sexism in the origins and early development of religion to questions of persecution of witches, Jews, and Blacks to the views of women in psychoanalysis and socialism. The last chapter reworked the issue of the relation of feminism and ecology. This book has been called an ecofeminist classic, although the term *ecofeminism* was unknown to me at the time.[19] At the request of Presbyterians I also did a little book on Mariology.[20] Mariol-

18. Rosemary Radford Ruether, "Misogynism and Virginal Feminism in the Fathers of the Church," in *Religion and Sexism: Images of Women in the Jewish and Christian Traditions* (New York: Simon & Schuster, 1975), 150–83. This essay was given at a session of the American Academic of Religion in 1974 under the title, "St. Augustine's Penis," a title that is still remembered with humor or horror, though it was not the official title.

19. Rosemary Radford Ruether, *New Woman, New Earth: Sexist Ideologies and Human Liberation* (New York: Seabury, 1975). This book was republished by Beacon Press in 1995 with a new preface. It also appeared in Spanish as *Mujeres Nuevas, Tierra Nueva* (1977).

20. Rosemary Radford Ruether, *Mary: The Feminine Face of the Church* (Philadelphia: Westminster, 1977).

ogy continues to interest me as a resource for feminist theology. Despite her misuse by Catholic patriarchy, I continue to remember that she was our grade-school goddess.

By the mid-1970s I realized my limitations as a white woman to discuss sexism at a Black, mostly male seminary. I took to teaching a course in feminism with a female colleague, Francine Cardman,[21] at the Wesley Seminary in Washington. But in the course I taught at Howard on social justice issues I asked a Black male clergyman to give the lecture on sexism in the Black church. The students listened to him skeptically, but they did listen to him, while they would not have tolerated my discussion of this issue.

In the '70s, younger Black women were beginning to enter the School of Religion of Howard University. Before that, the only women students were older Black women. They were nonordained pastors in city churches without a theological degree who attended a special program designed for them. One of the younger women students in 1974 did an MA thesis in which she discussed sexism in the Black church. My Black colleagues on the faculty ridiculed her to her face. I tried to defend her and was called in to the dean's office where I was told that I was racist for countering the treatment of this student by the faculty and should be fired.

Meanwhile the Garrett-Evangelical Theological Seminary in Evanston, Illinois, had interviewed me for their new Georgia Harkness Chair in Applied Theology, which they wanted to dedicate to feminist theological studies, balancing the work in Black theological studies to which they were already committed. They favored me for this position as one of the few women scholars published in feminist theology, as well as someone who had taught at a Black school and was familiar with the Black church tradition. Meanwhile I was on a committee at Howard to find a new dean and had helped bring Lawrence Jones from Union Theological Seminary for that position. Once he took charge, it was evident that he would be able to deeply transform and expand the faculty and facilities of Howard School of Religion. Jones was sorry that I was leaving and sought to have me stay. But I had become convinced that it was time for me to move on. The school needed to hire some Black women to deal with issues of women in the Black church and society.

21. Francine Cardman is a Catholic scholar of church history particularly in the patristics area. After teaching at Wesley, she went on to teach at the Jesuit School of Theology in Cambridge, Massachusetts, and presently teaches at Boston College.

Garrett-Evangelical Theological Seminary, the Graduate Theological Union, and Claremont: 1976–2013

At the Garrett-Evangelical Theological School I joined some wonderful women colleagues. Rosemary Keller, teaching on women and American history, was eager to have me join her in developing work together. She was then only hired part time, but was soon brought on full time, although in ethics. The history faculty was unwilling to hire her in her own field of history, fearing she would displace them. D. J. (Dorothy Jean) Furnish had been on the faculty for some years in Christian education. The three of us quickly bonded. In one meeting together we discussed how to expand women faculty. D. J. suggested that we should work systematically to recruit women in every field of study, but not publicly announce it, so as not to arouse resistance.

We heard that Union Theological Seminary women had announced a demand for 50 percent women faculty and had created a backlash. D. J.'s caution reflected that concern. Following her approach, we proceeded to work for women in every field, but without ever announcing this as our goal. With the help of sympathetic male colleagues, gradually we were able to help develop a faculty that included excellent women teaching in all fields. The growing women faculty took to meeting together for a meal once a month, to check in with one another. Rosemary Keller became the first woman dean in 1993. Today (2008 to the present) Lallene Rector, professor of pastoral psychology, is the dean of the school. We were not quite a matricentric enclave in our school, but close to it.

I taught many courses on women in American history with Rosemary Keller; together we became closely bonded colleagues. We also edited a number of books together on women and American religion, an area that I had not studied before but learned through my work with her. Three volumes on women and religion in America in the nineteenth, eighteenth, and twentieth centuries were published in 1981, 1983, and 1986 respectively. In 1995 we put together a fourth volume integrating the previous three volumes. Our culminating work together was the three-volume *Encyclopedia of Women and Religion in North America*, published by the Indiana University Press in 2006.[22]

22. *Women and Religion in America*, Vol. 1, *The Nineteenth Century* (San Francisco: Harper & Row, 1981); *Women and Religion in America*, Vol. 2, *The Colonial and Revolutionary Periods* (San Francisco: Harper & Row, 1983); *Women and Religion in America*, Vol. 3, *1900–1968* (San Francisco: Harper & Row, 1986); *In Our Own Voices: Four*

Rosemary Keller and I developed a wonderfully compatible way of working together. On any course or book on which we worked, we easily divided up what part she would do and what I would do. We each did our part, and then we put together our two parts, integrating introductory and editing material. She was much better than I in getting the contracts, including the contract and funding for the *Encyclopedia*. We had an enormously productive working relation. This continued after she left Garrett to become dean at Union Theological Seminary in New York in 1996. It was with great sadness that I followed the course of her decline in health, leading to her death in June 5, 2008. She did live long enough to see our culminating project, the *Encyclopedia*, in print in 2006. I was touched to see photos of her at Garrett at a celebration of the appearance of this work, holding the three large volumes of the *Encyclopedia* weakly but happily in her arms.

In addition to the work on women's history in American religion, which I did mostly with Rosemary Keller, I also continued research in my field of women's history in Christianity from patristic times to the present. I edited a companion volume to *Religion and Sexism* titled *Women of Spirit: Female Leadership in the Jewish and Christian Traditions*.[23] In this volume I also did the chapter on patristics, but this time on "Mothers of the Church: Ascetic Women in the Late Patristic Age." This was my first venture into what we now call matristics, or the recovery of women leaders like Paula and Melania of the fourth century. I also did an overview of how women had been treated in Western theology, titled *Women and Redemption*.[24] A more expanded history of women in Western religion, going back to the ancient East and forward to Wiccan groups in the late twentieth century, is my *Goddesses and the Divine Feminine in Western Religious Thought*.[25]

A second area of my work is feminist theology strictly speaking, where I sought to reconstruct the major symbols of Christian systematic theology

Centuries of Women's Religious Writings (San Francisco: HarperSanFrancisco, 1995); *Encyclopedia of Women and Religion in North America*, 3 vols. (Bloomington: Indiana University Press, 2006).

23. Rosemary Radford Ruether and Eleanor Mclaughlin, eds., *Women of Spirit: Female Leadership in the Jewish and Christian Traditions* (New York: Simon & Schuster, 1979).

24. Rosemary Radford Ruether, *Women and Redemption: A Theological History* (Minneapolis: Fortress, 1998; revised and expanded 2nd ed., 2011).

25. Rosemary Radford Ruether, *Goddesses and the Divine Feminine in Western Religious Thought* (Berkeley: University of California Press, 2005).

in a feminist perspective. The book I did on that, *Sexism and God-Talk: Toward a Feminist Theology,* has become my basic text for teaching feminist theology, while *Womanguides: Readings toward a Feminist Theology* gathers the key texts of the tradition for rethinking these symbols.[26] I also did a book on rethinking Christian liturgy from a feminist perspective: *Women-church: Theology and Practice of Feminist Liturgical Communities.*[27] Much of this book was developed during my months as a Fullbright Scholar in Sweden in 1985 where I had the privilege of working with lively Swedish feminists also involved in doing feminist liturgy. Several of these women remain good friends until today.

As mentioned above, ecology became a major interest and concern for me from the early 1970s. From the beginning I sought to connect ecology and feminism, both in recognition of the way the domination of the earth is metaphorically interconnected with the domination of women in patriarchal ideology, and also to reveal how women's use and abuse in society interfaces with the abuse of nature. In 1992 I published my major effort to show this interconnection of the domination of women and that of nature in Western ideology, and how liberation of women and of nature connect. This is my book titled *Gaia & God: An Ecofeminist Theology of Earth Healing.*[28]

I have continued to speak and teach in the area of ecofeminism and have published many short articles on the topic. I have come to be seen as a major expert and representative of ecofeminism. I have also sought to reach out to Asian, African, and Latin American women to support their own articulation of ecofeminism from their cultures and contexts. This is represented by the collection of their essays I edited: *Women Healing Earth: Third World Women on Feminism, Religion, and Ecology.*[29] I have found great help in the work of Latin American women on ecofeminism. This is represented particularly by the work of leading Brazilian ecofeminist theologian Ivone

26. Rosemary Radford Ruether, *Sexism and God-Talk: Toward a Feminist Theology* (Boston: Beacon, 1983; 2nd ed., 1993); Rosemary Radford Ruether, *Womanguides: Readings toward a Feminist Theology* (Boston: Beacon, 1985; 2nd ed., 1996).

27. Rosemary Radford Ruether, *Women-Church: Theology and Practice of Feminist Liturgical Communities* (San Francisco: Harper & Row, 1986).

28. Rosemary Radford Ruether, *Gaia & God: An Ecofeminist Theology of Earth Healing* (San Francisco: HarperSanFrancisco, 1992).

29. Rosemary Radford Ruether, ed., *Women Healing Earth: Third World Women on Feminism, Religion and Ecology,* Ecology and Justice (Maryknoll, NY: Orbis, 1966).

Gebara.[30] A key source for this thought is the journal *Conspirando: Revista Latinoamericana de Ecofeminismo, Espiritualidad y Teología*, which began publication in Santiago, Chile, in 1992, drawing on a network of feminist contributors across Latin America.

In my own work in ecofeminism I have sought to discuss both world religions and the socioeconomic context of ecological devastation. These concerns are reflected in my 2005 book, *Integrating Ecofeminism, Globalization, and World Religions*,[31] dedicated to my students at the Graduate Theological Union (GTU) in Berkeley, California, Whitney Bauman and Eileen Harrington, teaching assistants for my ecofeminist and globalization courses I taught there between 1999 and 2005. The students and others I have been delighted to get to know at Garrett, the GTU, and now at Claremont remain good friends and colleagues. They have reciprocated this admiration. Three of my students from Garrett, the GTU, and Claremont, Whitney Bauman, Emily Silverman, and Dirk Von der Horst, have put together a Festschrift on my writings, *Voices of Feminist Liberation*, published by Equinox Press. An academic panel and a party at the November 2011 meeting of the American Academy of Religion celebrated the appearance of this volume.

The predominance of feminism in my writing has by no means excluded other areas of thought. I continue to be concerned with many other problem areas. One of these is a long-standing critique of US American imperialism and its ideologies of election and domination. I returned to this topic in my 2007 book, *America, Amerikkka: Elect Nation and Imperial Violence*.[32] The course I taught as a foundational social ethics course at Garrett from the 1980s on the interconnection of race, class, gender, ecology, and colonialism was written up as a book published in 2009: *Christianity and Social Systems*.[33] I continue to return to the dilemma of Roman Catholicism in modern society, represented by my earlier book, *Contemporary Roman*

30. Ivone Gebara, *Longing for Running Water: Ecofeminism and Liberation* (Minneapolis: Fortress, 1999); Gebara, *Out of the Depths: Women's Experience of Evil and Salvation*, translated by Ann Patrick Ware (Minneapolis: Fortress, 2002).

31. Rosemary Radford Ruether,, *Integrating Ecofeminism, Globalization and World Religions*, Nature's Meaning (Lanham, MD: Rowman & Littlefield, 2005).

32. Rosemary Radford Ruether, *America, Amerikkka: Elect Nation and Imperial Violence*, Religion and Violence, (London: Equinox, 2007).

33. Rosemary Radford Ruether, *Christianity and Social Systems: Historical Constructions and Ethical Challenges* (Lanham, MD: Rowman & Littlefield, 2009).

Catholicism: Crises and Challenges, as well as my 2008 book, *Catholic Does Not Equal the Vatican.*[34]

Recently I have turned to writing about what has long been an area of concern for me and my family: mental illness and the inadequacies of the mental health system based on our family's experience of the mental illness of our son, David.[35]

This is a somewhat rapid summary of my intellectual thought and publications from the late 1960s to today. In these writings I have sought to probe a world system of oppression, divided by race, class, gender, ecological abuse, and imperialism. In my writings and social involvements I seek to probe different aspects of this system and its justifying ideologies, and to imagine how to create a liberated world beyond it. It is this concern that ties all my thought and writings together, across what may appear disparate areas of human activity. In the five following chapters of this book I will examine my thinking and social struggles in several of these areas: the relation to Catholicism; the relations of the Abrahamic faiths, Judaism, Christianity, and Islam; the challenges of nonmonotheistic faiths; sanity, mental illness, and the finite self; and finally ecofeminism and the struggle to sustain a livable earth.

34. Rosemary Radford Ruether, *Contemporary Roman Catholicism: Crises and Challenges* (Kansas City, MO: Sheed & Ward, 1987); Rosemary Radford Ruether, *Catholic Does not Equal the Vatican: A Vision for Progressive Catholicism* (New York: New Press, 2008).

35. *Many Forms of Madness: A Family's Struggle with Mental Illness and the Mental Health System* (Minneapolis: Fortress, 2010).

My mother, Rebecca Cresap Ord

My uncle, David Sandow

Myself and my two sisters, Manette, Rosemary, and Bequita
Radford at the piano at Uncle David and Sophie Sandow's house
in Washington DC, c. 1948.

The Ruether family: Rosemary and Herman Ruether, David,
Mimi, and Becky Ruether, c. 1969, Washington DC.

Rosemary Skinner Keller and Rosemary Radford Ruether, Garrett-Evangelical
Theological Seminary, Evanston, Illinois, examining the first volume of their
documentary history, *Women and Religion in America*, c. 1982.

2

Catholicism
Critiquing, Expanding, Staying

Religion and Family

I was raised as a Roman Catholic by my mother in an ecumenical and interfaith family context. My mother's father's family, the Ords, were English Catholics. Her great-grandfather, James Ord, came to the US from England in 1790 with his adopted family when he was four. Sponsored by Archbishop Carroll of Maryland and the Jesuits, with funds from an unknown family in England, Ord became a student in the first class at Georgetown University in 1800. He joined the Jesuit order and taught at Georgetown University as a scholastic.[1] In his midtwenties and not yet ordained, he left the order, married, and produced twelve children, eight of whom lived to adulthood. His wife, Rebecca Cresap, came from a historical American family and was an Episcopalian. They raised the children in Ord's Catholicism, but open-mindedly so, with permeable relations to the Episcopal Church. Ord valued the classical tradition he learned at Georgetown and named some of his children by such monikers as Pacificus, Septimus, Placidus, and James Lycurgus.

My mother's father, James Thompson Ord, inherited the Ord Catholicism. He married Rose Basavi, of Austro-Hungarian descent and a committed Catholic. My mother and her siblings were born in Mexico. Widowed in 1905 when my mother was nine, Rose Basavi brought her children to San Diego, raising them Catholic. Only one left that tradition. The second

---

1. James Ord's archives for his years at Georgetown University are at Georgetown University.

34

daughter, Mary Mercer, married an Episcopalian and raised her children in that church. My mother also married an Episcopalian, my father, Robert Radford, whose faith was firmly rooted in many generations of Anglican tradition going back to Virginia in the seventeenth century and, before that, to England.[2] But my mother was firm in raising the three of us Catholics, but as discriminating and open-minded ones.

My father's family were members of Christ Episcopal Church, a block from the Radford family home in Georgetown, Washington DC. A family story about the Radford church membership always intrigued me. According to this story, my great-grandfather, Admiral William Radford of Civil War fame, used to take his family to St John's Episcopal Church, the first Episcopal Church in Georgetown, founded in 1796 and attended by Thomas Jefferson. One Sunday morning (in the 1870s?) the pastor denounced from the pulpit those who allowed their children to dance into Sunday. My great-grandfather and his family were a part of Washington society and had many parties. His daughters had danced into Sunday at a family party the night before, and he assumed the pastor was talking about him. He rose from his pew, gathered his family around him and marched them out of the church, going over to Christ Church, where the Radfords became members from then on. I remember walking past St. John's as a child and wondering if they still remembered my family's repudiation of them. (I doubt that they did.)

My father was firmly Episcopalian in his social heritage but did not seem to regularly attend. He never went with us to the Catholic Church, which he tolerated as my mother's tradition, but didn't really like. My mother took the three of us to the Jesuit Trinity church in Georgetown every Sunday and on holy days, but was not averse to letting me go to church with my father on one of the few days he went there. Thus I grew up with a clear Catholic identity, although open to Episcopalianism as a family heritage that I thought of more as a social tradition rather than as seriously religious, like my mother's Catholicism.

My favorite uncle, David Sandow, was Jewish, from a Russian Jewish family who lived in New York City. His two brothers were in the medical field, but my uncle was musical and artistic. He had a beautiful voice and trained as an opera singer. Lacking the self-confidence to succeed in this

2. The Radford family history from the seventeenth century to the life of Admiral Radford in the mid-nineteenth century has been written by the Admiral's daughter, Sophie Radford de Meissner, *Old Naval Days: Sketches from the life of Rear Admiral William Radford, U.S.N.* (New York: Holt, 1920).

field, he turned to art. He became an architect by profession and a Sunday painter. My own father was away at war for much of my childhood. So Uncle David, who had no children, became our surrogate father. He trained my sister Bequita as a singer and me as an artist.

Uncle David loved the Jewish tradition in art but never went to synagogue, as far as I knew. He did once consider becoming a Catholic, taking classes from Fulton Sheen. But he decided against it. When my mother told me this, for her a sad event, I felt spontaneously proud of my uncle. *Good for you, Uncle David*, I thought. *Stay who you are.* I was then perhaps fifteen. This response intrigues me, since it makes evident that at an early age I had absorbed the idea that Uncle David's Jewishness was authentic for him, not to be changed for Catholicism. When a nun at my school made a slighting remark about Jews, I felt instantly offended.

Our family had further religious ramifications. My great-aunt Sophia Radford, daughter of the Admiral, married a Russian diplomat. She adopted his Russian Orthodox Church tradition. My sister, Manette, trained in French by great-aunt Sophia, began to attend a Russian Orthodox Church in San Francisco when she moved there in the 1950s. She found a small community there that was intimate and friendly, more to her liking than Roman Catholicism. She liked Russian culture and cultivated relations with Russians in San Francisco. I went with her to this Russian Orthodox church on the occasions when I visited her.

The Society of Friends also became part of our extended family experience when my mother and sisters moved to La Jolla, California, in 1952. My mother's closest friends, Helen Beardsley and Elizabeth Sellon, an artist, went to the La Jolla Quaker meeting. Quakerism appealed to their pacifism, in preference to their family Episcopal tradition. I was a budding artist in my teens. Elizabeth and Helen asked me to give art lessons to the impoverished Mexican American children whose education they cultivated at the Quaker community. I was drawn to the silent Quaker meeting and began to attend, also going to Mass with my mother. I remember thinking that these two forms or worship, seemingly so opposite, were wonderfully complementary. Mass expressed the spiritual relation to God in vivid outer symbols; in the Friends meeting this same reality was there as an inward presence.

My mother's Catholicism was more than Sunday Mass, particularly after she moved back to California. In La Jolla she went to daily Mass. She also cultivated private prayer in the morning and evening, attended lectures by Catholic theologians she thought intelligent, and did reading in Catholic spiritual classics. I remember that she and her women's reading group chose Meister Eckhart for their study on one occasion. My mother did not push these extended practices on her children. The unspoken message that she gave us was that Catholicism was a profound spiritual tradition that nourished her, but rote and dogmatic demands could be ignored. She had little tolerance for what she saw as ignorant superstition or "vulgar Catholicism."

Once in high school in Washington I was asked to do the artistic decorations for a dance. I painted large images of cupids from Renaissance art. A nun was shocked at their nakedness, other than large blue ribbons, and insisted that they be taken down. My mother laughingly dismissed this response as uneducated. Another time I was attending an art class at my sister's university and doing live drawings of naked models, male and female. Walking through my high school with my art portfolio under my arm, I passed the nun principal. She asked me what I was carrying, and I said it was drawings from my art class. I showed them to her, and she was horrified that these were of naked adults. I couldn't wait to tell my mother and sister of the nun's response, and they both laughed heartily at what they saw as cultural provincialism.

This implicit distinction between a serious intellectual Catholic tradition worth cultivating, and ignorant, superstitious fears that could be dismissed gave me a freedom to think for myself that would be invaluable to me as I grew up. I was able to mostly avoid feeling oppressed by the guilt-tripping aspects of Catholicism since I assumed that anything that made no sense to me need not be taken seriously. Going to Mass was the usual way I could encounter God, but an Episcopal or Russian Orthodox liturgy, a synagogue service or a Quaker meeting, were places where the same God could also be found. These different historical traditions were complementary, not competing rivals or evil others to be avoided.

Crises and Challenges

Oddly enough, my first real confrontation with a denigrating anti-Catholicism was at Scripps College. Although my undergraduate education at Scripps College assumed the value of historical European culture, in the 1950s the liberal Protestantism of some of the professors was deeply hostile to Catholicism. They did not include it in the European culture to be valued. In Humanities I on the ancient Mediterranean world we were taught to appreciate the diverse cultures of antiquity, including the validity of ancient paganism (I discuss this in chapter 4). But in Humanities II where we studied the Middle Ages, the Renaissance, and Reformation, the story line was that medieval Catholicism was ridiculous and corrupt, happily put to an end by the Reformation. The fact that a large Catholic Church lived on into the twentieth century was irrelevant. It should disappear, and they believed it would eventually. The source book we were given to read on the Middle Ages trivialized and ridiculed the medieval world. The professor of history for this period was a militant Calvinist who embodied this hostility to everything medieval. I felt (and still feel) that I had been gypped of a fair appreciation of the thousand years of European culture and thought from 500 to 1500. I have since tried to make up for this lack by reading and teaching on this period, particularly on the women writers.

One outspoken Episcopalian professor who led our humanity's discussion group informed me in peremptory fashion that I should realize that it would be impossible for me to become an intelligent student as a Catholic. If I wanted to be an intellectual, I needed to become a Protestant. When I tried to defend the different experiences I had had as a Catholic, I was abruptly dismissed as ignorant. I felt deeply insulted. The result was to confirm me in my own tradition, while continuing to be open to learning about other traditions.

I did have one period in graduate school where I considered joining the Episcopal Church, a tradition which I saw as a part of my family heritage. A liberal Episcopal priest, who had an attractive mass at the college chaplaincy that I sometimes attended, helped arrange our trip to Mississippi. At one point in my studies I thought deeply about the Catholic Church's view of the pope's infallibility. I became clear that I did not believe in the pope's or anyone else's infallibility. The Catholic Church had erred in making this declaration at the First Vatican Council of 1870. I was living by myself at this time, while my husband was in India, and this sense of isolation, without anyone to talk to about this issue, may have contributed to my consternation. I decided to become an Episcopalian.

The Episcopal chaplain arranged for me to go to an Episcopal retreat center in Santa Barbara where he was also going for a weekend retreat. I drove up with him. He dropped me off at an Episcopal nunnery, telling me that, as a woman, I couldn't stay at the male retreat house. I was shocked at the suffocating atmosphere of this nunnery. This was in striking contrast to the Benedictine priory where I had gone on retreats with lively monastic retreat leaders and no discrimination against women retreatants. I soon decided I could not stay at this nunnery. I walked out the door and down the hill, ending up at the Catholic mission church of Santa Barbara. There I encountered a Mexican American family coming out of Mass who agreed to drive me back to Los Angeles. From there I found my way back to Claremont. I felt shaken but also deeply relieved that I had found myself back home. Although infallibility might be a mistake, it was only one of many mistakes the Catholic Church had made in its history. No church was perfect, but this one was mine.

Since that time I have never again seriously considered joining another church denomination. However mistaken this church might become, and these mistakes are many in recent years since Vatican II, as I will detail later in this chapter, this church retains for me a core sense of my historical identity and concern. I have worked closely with people of other denominations, but this is possible only when they respect me as a Catholic. I, in turn, see them as extended family. I don't need to join them and leave my church. We are already in communion. But my own church, like my nuclear family, remains the place where I have a special responsibility.

Sometimes a Protestant church leader with whom I am working takes it in into his or her head to pressure me to join his or her church, as though I have failed to "get it" that this was the better church that I should join. This happened in Washington DC after I and my family had worshiped for several years at St. Stephen and the Incarnation Episcopal Church. This church was operating ecumenically, with many Catholic members, as a leading peace-and-justice church for the city. I did a lot of leadership there in art, liturgy, and social justice. The pastor was emerging as a proponent of women's ordination and risked his own ministry by illegally ordaining some Episcopal women (for which he was put on trial by the Episcopal Church). One day after this conflict, in which I had supported him, he abruptly turned on me and told me that he could "get me" ordained, but I needed to "get with it" and become officially an Episcopalian. He seemed almost angry that I had failed to do so.

This has happened to me on several other occasions. Protestants who appeared to understand ecumenical mutuality have suddenly, often angrily, demanded that I leave my church and join theirs. On one occasion I spent a weekend speaking to a retreat for United Church of Christ women. On the way back in the car from the weekend retreat, the woman leader of this group attacked me angrily, demanding to know why I didn't leave the

Catholic Church. On another occasion I was asked to speak to a Unitarian church. A woman in the audience berated me in an outraged tone for continuing to be a Catholic. Such people seem to have a stereotyped view of Catholicism, which they find incompatible with who I am. When I explain that this is a very complex community of a billion people, much of which is very compatible with who I am, this seems hard for them to understand. Some seem to think of their church and mine competitively; one has to be better than the other.

This kind of attack is deeply disappointing, as if renewal was a sectarian possession, rather than a life process belonging to us all in our particular historical contexts. When this sectarian demand happened with the pastor of St. Stephens, I left immediately and never went back again, except to attend his funeral many years later. Our family joined the Community of Christ, an ecumenical church of Lutherans and Catholics, also working for church and social justice. In this church Catholics and Lutherans were coleaders and members: one group was not the guest of the other.

Birth Control and Abortion

But I also experienced a body blow from the Catholic Church at this time. When I married Herman Ruether, then a graduate student in political science at the Claremont Graduate School, I came in contact with his local Catholic church in Ohio. Although his pastor of many years created a lively liturgical practice at this church, he had fixed opinions about Catholic married couples and how they should practice their sexuality. He told us pointedly that if we did not have a child by the next year, he would know we were living in sin. I was deeply offended. This was the first time I had been confronted by the Catholic anti-birth control dogmatism. We did not accept his assumption that we could not make up our own minds about having children.

In fact we did have a child before the end of the next year and two more in four years, not because we did not believe in family planning but because we were naïve about practicing it. But by the time I was finishing my doctoral degree, it was clear to us that three were enough children, if I was to have any hope to combining scholarship and family life. Meanwhile the birth-control pill had been developed and came on the market. I arranged to use it after my third child was born. But I had not thought of becoming a crusader on this subject.

This changed in February 1963. I was in the Pomona Valley Hospital where my youngest daughter, Mimi, had just been born. In the bed next to me was a Mexican woman named Asunción. She had just given birth to a ninth child who had been born with the umbilical cord wrapped around its neck. Her doctor came in several times, insisting that she had to start practicing birth control. She might die if she had another child. She wept that her husband and her priest would not allow this. She also revealed that she was living in a cold, crowded home and had to turn on the stove to warm it up, threatening the family's health with leaking gas.

Listening to this drama unfold next to me, I became outraged. I realized that birth control was not my private issue. It was a public issue of deep injustice for millions of women, particularly poor, uneducated women. After I departed from the hospital, I penned a brief article defending my choice of birth control as a Catholic. It was published in the *Saturday Evening Post* as "Why I Believe in Birth Control: A Catholic Mother Speaks Out,"[3] and reprinted in the *Reader's Digest*, thus commanding a national audience.

I wrote a number of other articles on birth control and sexuality in the mid-1960s and soon found myself joining many other lay Catholic men and women campaigning to change the Church's teaching on this issue. William Birmingham, editor of the Catholic journal *Cross Currents*, edited one such collection of essays: *What Modern Catholics Think of Birth Control*. Michael Novak, then a liberal, edited another as *The Experience of Marriage*. A third collection edited by Vatican II theologian Gregory Baum, under the title *Contraception and Holiness,* and endorsed by Archbishop Thomas Roberts, SJ, was distributed to the Church Council Fathers.[4] This growing protest inspired Pope Paul VI to remove the issue from the Council and create a separate birth control commission.

A small commission to consider the issue had begun under Pope John XXIII. Pope Paul VI enlarged this commission to fifty-eight members, the majority laypeople, including theologians, demographers, sociologists, economists, and medical doctors. There were representatives from every continent. Five women were included. Three married couples were appointed from France, French Canada, and the United States—all leaders

3. April 4, 1964.

4. Rosemary Radford Ruether, "A Question of Dignity, a Question of Freedom"; Rosemary Radford Ruether, "The Difficult Decision: Contraception," 69–81; Rosemary Radford Ruether, "Birth Control and the Ideals of Marital Sexuality," 72–91.

of the Christian Family Movement (CFM). Pat and Patty Crowley were the US leaders. They solicited letters from CFM members on their experience of so-called natural family planning. The results were striking testimony to the ineffectiveness of this method and its negative effects on sexual and family life. The Crowleys took hundreds of these letters as a report to the Commission. Later they did an organized survey of three thousand CFM respondents from eighteen countries.

The clerical members of the Commission were aghast at this testimony, which told of many unplanned pregnancies, economic and physical hardship, loss of health, and feelings of fear and resentment caused by the effort to restrict sex to the "sterile" period (most of which coincided with the woman's menstrual period). Most clergy had never heard of this negative reality from married people. This was all the more striking since it did not come from marginal Catholics but from those seeking to be most faithful. After much input and discussion which revealed the untenability of the Church's teaching in practice, the Commission drafted a final report in which they approved the use of any medically and psychologically sound method of birth control within a marriage committed to love and child raising. This report, "Responsible Parenthood," was passed by a vote of 52 to 4, including by a majority of the sixteen bishops. This report was given to Pope Paul VI on June 28, 1966, with a pastoral introduction, discussing how the Church's teaching could be understood as developing on this topic.[5]

Pat Crowley recalls one Spanish Jesuit, Marcelino Zalba, wondering how this teaching could change, given its long enforcement in Catholic moral teaching and discipline. He commented, "What then of the millions we have sent to Hell, if these norms were not valid." Crowley was astonished at his query and responded, "Father Zalba, do you really believe that God has carried out all your orders?"[6] This exchange put the finger on the problem with the Commission report for the pope, namely, his fear that it would result in the loss of the Church's teaching authority. The four members of the Commission who dissented from the report, together with the head of the Holy Office, drafted a protest, which they called the "minority report," although the Commission had decided against any minority report, submitting only one report that represented the overwhelming

5. Robert McClory, *Turning Point: The Inside Story of the Papal Birth Control Commission* (New York: Crossroad, 1995), 113–15.

6. Ibid.,1.

majority. This protest statement focused on the threat to Church teaching authority represented by any change and claimed that the traditional teaching was infallible.

After much hesitation, the pope issued the encyclical *Humanae Vitae* two years later, on July 29, 1968, reiterating the traditional rejection of contraception. The pope was persuaded to reject the overwhelming majority report of his own birth control commission by the fears created by the right-wing group. The majority members of the Commission were shocked. Patty Crowley recalls feeling deeply betrayed. The careful work of the commission was counted for nothing. Moral theologian Charles Curran drafted a criticism of the decision, which was signed by six hundred Catholic theologians from all parts of the world. The Vatican sanctioned theologians who dissented, and some bishops came down brutally on critics. Cardinal O'Boyle of Washington DC suspended Curran and twenty-three other signers of the dissent. Thirty parish priests ended by leaving the priesthood. But many other bishops around the world declined to act against critics, speaking vaguely of the rights of conscience of those who disagreed.

The vast majority of lay Catholics have declined to follow the renewed teaching of anticontraception. Surveys show that 80 percent of American Catholics believe they can be "good Catholics" and reject this teaching. Their practice on the use of contraception is about the same as that of Protestants.[7] Few today would confess this as a sin, which Catholics felt they should do in the 1950s; nor is the anticontraception teaching emphasized any more by most moral theologians and pastors. The Catholic bishops moved instead to a crusade against abortion. Catholic tradition from the patristic era taught that an official church declaration had to be received by the faithful in order to be valid. Some modern Catholic theologians have reclaimed this view to describe *Humanae Vitae* as an example of an official declaration that has not been received by the people of the church.[8]

This overwhelming dissent did not deter Vatican hardliners who were determined to reinforce this teaching. Pope VI himself remained anguished about his decision. But he was followed by Pope John Paul II, who had no doubts about its absolute authority. Karol Wojtyla became pope in 1978, following the brief pontificate of John Paul I. Wojtyla had been one of the sixteen bishops named to the birth control commission, but he declined to

7. Ibid., 148.
8. Ibid., 149.

attend.[9] So he did not participate in the sharing of information and discussions between 1964 and 1966 that led to the majority view. There is no way of knowing if he might have been educated to change his views if he had done so.

As pope, he accepted completely the idea that the traditional teaching was not only unchangeable but infallible. In 1993 he issued an encyclical, *Veritatis Splendor*, which claimed that every act of contraception is essentially evil and no dissent or critical discussion is allowed. Addressing the Catholic bishops, he decreed that no institution, school, medical facility, or counseling service can be called Catholic that does not uphold this teaching.[10] Anticontraception teaching has become a litmus test, along with rejection of women's ordination, for advancement to any leadership position in the Church, whether as a bishop, seminary professor, or head of a religious order. The Catholic Church has been returned in part to the closed, Counter-Reformation church of pre-Vatican II, where dissenting opinions cannot be discussed and anyone who does discuss them is repressed.

One Vatican II theologian who has kept speaking out for intellectual freedom in the Catholic Church is Hans Küng. Realizing that the core of the conflict over birth control for the hierarchy was not the needs of families of the laity but rather the assumptions about Church teaching authority, Küng came out with the book *Infallible?: An Inquiry*.[11] After careful examination of the Church's tradition on Church teaching authority over two millennia, Küng demonstrated that there was no such tradition of infallibility in New Testament, patristic, medieval, or early modern Catholic thought. This idea is an aberration arising in the late nineteenth century in the context of a reactionary Church leadership in the face of modernity.

In a later edition of his book, Küng followed Bernhard Hasler in suggesting that Vatican I, which declared the doctrine of Infallibility in 1870, was itself an invalid council, in which a small coterie around the pope was determined to push through this teaching. Most of the delegates to the council departed, including an openly dissenting group who left the Catholic Church over the issue to become the Old Catholic Church. The teaching was passed invalidly by a minority.[12] Küng believes that no human state-

9. Ibid., 97.

10. *Veritatis Splendor*, August 6, 1993.

11. Hans Küng, *Infallible?: An Inquiry*, trans. Edward Quinn (Garden City, NY: Doubleday, 1971).

12. August Bernhard Hasler, *How the Pope Became Infallible: Pius IX and the Politics*

ment can actually be verbally infallible. Human words exist in a historical and cultural context in which they are always finite. The traditional view of Church teaching authority is not one of infallibility, but rather an assurance that God will remain with us and provide us continually with God's grace of forgiveness and renewal, *despite our fallibility and error.*

For me, Küng's book was no surprise. It expressed a view I had long held in general, although his elaboration of it was helpful. The Vatican retaliated against him, decreeing that he could no long teach as a Catholic theologian. Küng responded by securing funding for a new chair in ecumenical theology at the University of Tübingen under which he has continued to teach there. But losing his position as a Catholic theologian was not a mere matter of wording. In the German university system, where Catholic and Protestant churches have official standing and the authority to authorize those who are their official theologians, it means he cannot prepare students to be Catholic priests and teachers. Losing this role, Küng has used his chair in ecumenical theology to become a part of an interfaith discussion for the creation of a global ethic for all humanity.[13] Interestingly, the Vatican has never sought his condemnation as a heretic or sought to remove him as a priest in good standing.

My own work in reproductive rights expanded in the 1970s from birth control to the more volatile issue of abortion. In the late seventies I joined the board of a small group in New York City, Catholics for a Free Choice. This was a poorly organized and underfunded outfit that was struggling to address this issue as Catholics. In 1980 Frances Kissling, who had held years of leadership in the area of abortion provision, joined this board. She became President in 1982 and moved the organization to Washington DC. A very effective organizer and fundraiser, Kissling soon turned Catholics for a Free Choice into a well-funded movement. This includes the publication of an excellent magazine, *Conscience*, and international outreach. She particularly helped build and fund a network of groups working on reproductive rights in Latin America, which took the Spanish name of Católicas por el Derecho a Decidir (Catholic Women for the Right to Decide). Catholics also have a growing presence in Europe and contacts in Africa and Asia. Kissling retired in 2007 after twenty-five years of very successful

---

of Persuasion (Garden City, NY: Doubleday, 1981).

13. Hans Küng and Jürgen Moltmann, *The Ethics of World Religions and Human Rights*, Concilium 1990/2 (London: SCM, 1990).

leadership. The organization, now called Catholics for Choice, continues under Irishman, Jon O'Brien.

I joined Kissling's CFFC board shortly after she re-created it in Washington DC and have been on the board until recently (2010), when I retired; but I continue as an editorial advisor of its magazine, *Conscience*. I have traveled to Mexico, Brazil, Argentina, and Chile for conferences and networking for CFC and, more recently, to El Salvador and Nicaragua. I also attended the UN conference on development in Cairo, Egypt, in 1994 and the UN women's conference in Beijing in 1995 as part of the CFC delegation. A recent commemorative issue of *Conscience* published in 2011 highlights the twenty-three articles that I had published in this journal from 1988 to 2009. These articles address different aspects of issues having to do with sexuality, abortion, women, the church, theology and ethics.[14]

The importance of CFC in the reproductive-rights field is not one of functioning as a provider, but rather as the advocate that does the rethinking of the religious and moral arguments against birth control and abortion and provides the arguments for their moral validity. In societies where the Catholic Church claims to speak with absolute authority against the legitimacy of both birth control and abortion, this ethical advocacy is very important, both in the United States and also in Latin America and other Catholic areas, such as Ireland and Spain. I have functioned and still function for CFC as one of their moral theologians who provide this intellectual work. CFC has also been, over the more than thirty years of my association with them, a delightful community of friends who stimulate each other and nourish our spirits.

For me abortion is not a morally neutral action. Rather it is an unfortunate decision that seeks a lesser of evil in conflictive situations in which the woman has lost her first choice (to have a child or not have one when she wants it and can raise it adequately), or when the child's or mother's health are imperiled. Abortion should be, to use President Clinton's phrase, "legal, safe, and rare." Making abortion legal and safe goes along with trying to make it rare by giving women access and support for birth control and decision making in sexual relations so that women can reduce the incidents of unbearable pregnancies, and so avoid having to face the question of abortion. The Catholic Church, in forbidding contraception and making

---

14. "Rosemary Radford Ruether: A Commemorative Issue," *Conscience*, June 2011.

abortion illegal, actually increases the likelihood of unwanted pregnancies and unsafe abortions. This is not a defense of "life."[15]

Women's Ordination

The second major issue on which the Vatican has taken a position of absolute negation is women's ordination. This issue has a complex history in Christianity. The earliest ministries in the church were charismatic roles of prophets, teachers, traveling evangelists, and leaders in local congregations. Women were included in all these. Paul, in Romans 16, speaks of women as deacons, apostles, and traveling evangelists, while insisting that they cover their heads when speaking in the congregation as prophets (1 Corinthians 11). The Catholic tradition to today has always accepted the role of women as prophets.

As the Church moved from charismatic to institutional ministry, women became excluded from being bishops and elders, while continuing to be included as deacons (1 Timothy 3). The deaconate remained open to women in the Eastern Church until the ninth century and has recently (2004) been restored to women by the Greek Orthodox Church. The deaconate had an ambiguous history in the Western Church but continued to be accorded to women, particularly as abbesses, in the West into the eleventh century. Leading theologian Abelard defended women's ordination as deacons in the twelfth century. But by then all ordination was being tied to Eucharistic ministry, and women rigidly excluded from the possibility of being ordained, even to the deaconate. For Thomas Aquinas priesthood was tied to representing Christ, and women are excluded by their very nature as females. But even he accepted that women could be prophets, although they should witness to ecclesiastical authorities only in private.[16]

The Reformation did little to change this tradition of women's exclusion from ordination. Luther and Calvin even rejected the idea that women could be prophets, claiming that this was a brief exception in apostolic times. Some radical Protestants pursued a different approach. Baptists claimed the New Testament tradition that "your sons and your daughters

---

15. "Pro-Choice is Pro-life," in ibid., 6.

16. See Thomas Aquinas, "On the Production of Women," I:Q. 92," in *Summa Theologica*. For detailed summary of Aquinas's views of women's ordination, see Kari Elizabeth Børresen, *Subordination and Equivalence: The Nature and Role of Women in Augustine and Thomas Aquinas* (Kampen: Kok Pharos, 1995), 235–43.

shall prophesy" (Acts 2:17) to allow women as public prophet-preachers, while Quakers included women as "public friends" (evangelists) and leaders of women's meetings. It would be another two hundred years before another Protestant group, the Congregationalists, ordained their first woman, Antoinette Brown, in 1853.

Other Protestants were slow to pick up on this challenge. The Methodist Protestant church ordained a few women in the 1880s, but women lost full status as ministers in this church when the Methodist Protestants merged with the Methodist Episcopal Church in 1939. This decision was reversed in 1956 when the resultant Methodist Church accepted the ordination for women. The year before, in 1955, Northern Presbyterians also gave women full ordination. The Lutheran Church in America and the American Lutheran church voted to ordain women in 1970, while the Missouri Synod rejected it and continues to do so today.

This movement of Protestants to ordain women had little effect on the views of the Roman Catholic hierarchy, the members of which do not see these churches as having valid ordinations. A bigger challenge came when the American Episcopal Church voted to ordain women in 1976. (The mother church of Anglicanism, the Church of England, accepted women's ordination only in 1992.) Roman Catholicism does not accept the validity of Anglican orders, but they see that tradition as much closer to their own. So this decision was much more threatening.

The Vatican responded to the decision of the American Episcopal Church by an official statement totally repudiating the possibility that women could be ordained. This was the 1976 "Declaration on the Question of the Admission of Women to the Ministerial Priesthood." The Declaration claimed that women are not ordainable by their very natures as females. This ban is claimed to be divinely founded and unchangeable. It is based on three grounds: Jesus intentionally did not include women in the ordained priesthood, the Church's continuous and infallible tradition excludes women from priesthood, and the priest represents Christ, a male. Maleness is intrinsic to the nature of Christ, which women are incapable of representing.[17]

This assertion evoked a storm of criticism among Catholic theologians and biblical scholars. Some biblical scholars rejected it as unbiblical. The

17. For the text and commentary on this Declaration, see Leonard Swidler and Arlene Swidler, eds., *Women Priests: A Catholic Commentary on the Vatican Declaration* (New York: Paulist, 1977).

eminent theologian Karl Rahner even suggested that such literal essential-ism of the priest's maleness as necessary to represent Christ was heretical.[18] Polls showed that the percentage of US Catholics supporting women's or-dination rose to 60 percent after the Declaration. The Women's Ordination Conference (WOC) was founded in 1975 in response to the struggle within the Episcopal Church and began to organize local groups across the US to support the women's ordination movement. As a national organization it held its second conference in 1978.

WOC was clear from the beginning that it did not simply seek the in-clusion of women in the existing clerical hierarchy of the Catholic Church. Rather it called for a reform of the hierarchy to create a more egalitarian leadership integrated into the ministry of the laity. Nevertheless, by the end of the 1970s, Catholic feminists, such as Mary Hunt and Elizabeth Fiorenza, began to question whether women's ordination was a desirable goal. They saw clerical hierarchy itself as the problem. Incorporating a few women into the clerical hierarchy, including the episcopacy, as was happening in some other churches, did not change this problem. Rather women should create alternative women's "base community" groups, where all members participate as equals and liturgical leadership is shared by all, rather than dividing the church between clergy and laity.

This alternative vision of egalitarian worshipping communities is called women-church. By 1983 Catholic feminists, such as Hunt and Fio-renza, helped reorganize the third WOC conference in Chicago to focus on the idea and promotion of women-church as the goal of the church reform movement.[19] Further conferences focusing on the theme of women-church were held in Cincinnati in 1987 and Albuquerque in 1993. Not everyone in the movement supported this change of focus. Some Catholic women already working as chaplains in hospitals, prisons, and schools felt the need for official ordination to function as equals in these roles. Others not mak-ing a living through ministry found it easier to accept the idea of informal egalitarian communities with no official clergy.

Out of these developments there emerged the Women-Church Con-vergence, a network of Catholic feminist liturgical and social-justice or-ganizations across the US. Women-Church Convergence defines itself as

18. See Paul Imhof and Hubert Bigllowons, eds. *Karl Rahner in Dialogue: Conversa-tion and Interviews*, trans. Harvey D. Egan (New York: Crossroad 1986), 35.

19. For Mary Hunt's understanding of Women-Church, see Hunt, "Women-Church: An Introductory Overview," in Mary Hunt and Diane Neu, eds., *Women-Church Source Book* (Silver Spring, MD: WATER, 1993), 2–5.

a "coalition of Catholic-rooted organizations raising a feminist voice and committed to an ekklesia of women which is participatory, egalitarian and self-governing. Women-Church Convergence is church, a discipleship of equals moving from a paradigm of domination to one of mutuality. Women-Church Convergence seeks to eradicate patriarchy, especially sexism and racism, and to transform church and society."[20]

The Vatican and bishops did not respond to the Women-Church movement. In effect it fell outside their institutional self-definition and control. Catholic laypeople are under no restriction in organizing prayer communities or social-justice organizations outside the institutional Church and its definition of clergy. A challenge to their system arose only with a different development, the Roman Catholic Womenpriests (RCWP) movement. In 2002 seven women from Germany, Austria, and the United States were ordained on the Danube River by several male Roman Catholic bishops. Several of these women were subsequently ordained bishops by these bishops. They, in turn, have developed a church system in which they have approved the qualifications of and ordained many more women as deacons, priests, and bishops. This movement is developing quickly, particularly in the United States. According to their website in 2012, they currently have nine bishops, eighty-one priests, and nineteen deacons in the United States, Canada, and Europe.[21]

The RCWP movement in the U.S. is organized into a number of administrative districts where committees oversee the theological education, preparation for ministry, and ordination of women (and men) seeking ordination through their system. These women seeking ordination typically come from many years of work in parishes and other ministries, such as retreat centers, in the Catholic Church, so they are highly experienced. They are women who have decided they can no longer wait while the official church continues to reject the possibility of their ordination. They need to go ahead with ordination, and the RCWP system offers a way to do that. Once ordained, they develop a variety of forms of ministry. They create worshiping communities and retreat centers, do counseling work, or engage in chaplaincy work in prisons, colleges, or hospitals.

The structure of the RCWP movement seeks to avoid a hierarchy of power, even while accepting the distinction of an ordained hierarchy of deacon, priest, and bishop from the laity. Celibacy is rejected, and many of

20. http://www.Women-ChurchConvergence.org/.
21. http://www.RomanCatholicWomenPriests.org/.

the ordained are married. Gay and lesbian candidates are also welcomed. The bishops have a pastoral role but do not hold hierarchical power. Administration is done by elected teams in consultation with each other. There is no promise of obedience to bishops, but all are called to live in prophetic obedience to the Holy Spirit, individually and as a community. There is no idea of "ontological change" through ordination. Priesthood is a function within community, not a higher sacrality than laity. The ordained are worker-priests, usually finding income through working at other jobs, while doing ministry without salary.

The RCWP group does see itself as holding apostolic succession, claiming that their priests were ordained by validly ordained Catholic bishops and thus stand in a line of succession going back to the apostles of the first generation of the church. They regard themselves as reviving the inclusion of women in ministry of the apostolic church. This claim of apostolic succession raises some questions. Many contemporary historians of the early church realize that this concept of apostolic succession was something of a fabrication of the late second century to validate the emerging church order of bishops. The relation of the actual apostles of Jesus, most of whom did not become bishops, to this second-century church order is ambiguous.[22] I have told this to leaders of the RCWP movement. The reply to me has been that they are not really concerned that this concept may be unhistorical. Rather it is a key symbol for Catholicism of the validity of their ordination that they wish to claim.

But this claim carries no weight with the Vatican. The Vatican has vehemently repudiated this movement, declaring in May 2008 that they are all excommunicated, including the bishops who ordained them. In July 2010 the Vatican appalled many Catholics by claiming that they were not only excommunicated, but that the sin of "attempting" to ordain a woman is a "grave crime" comparable to "sexual abuse."[23] Such an equation of women's ordination with sexual abuse not only is offensive and lacking in moral credibility, but seemed to reveal the frenetic rage with which the

22. Among major books that show the diversity of early Christianity and the lack of historicity behind apostolic succession, see Walter Bauer, *Orthodoxy and Heresy in Earliest Christianity*, trans. Philadelphia Seminar on Christian Origins, edited by Robert A. Kraft and Gerhard Krodel (Philadelphia: Fortress, 1971).

23. The statement was released by the Vatican July 15, 2010. For a critique of it, see Richard McBrien, "Linking Sexual Abuse and the Ordination of Women," *National Catholic Reporter*, September 13, 2010. Online: http://ncronline.org/blogs/essays-theology/linking-sexual-abuse-and-ordination-women/.

Vatican views women's quest for ordination. That these women are seeking to spread the gospel and further the ministry of the church seems to escape these prelates entirely.

Such extreme responses have had no effect in preventing Catholic leaders of the RCWP movement from continuing their work. Most notable is the way some RCWP members are founding exemplary worshiping communities. One of these is the Mary Magdalene Apostle Catholic Community in San Diego, California, created by Jane Via, a Christian educator, lawyer and ordained priest in the RomanCatholicWomanPriest movement. The community draws between about seventy-five and 125 worshipers weekly. Via, together with a male Catholic priest and trained liturgist, Rod Stephens, founded the community in 2005. Mary Magdalene Church is governed by a board of directors and a nine-member community council. It hosts an annual retreat and devotes its weekly tithes to addressing social issues, such as helping abused women, children, homeless people, prisoners and immigrants. Sunday Mass is celebrated in a festive way with an excellent choir and community participation in songs and prayers, including the Eucharistic prayer said by the whole community in several languages.

Nancy Corran, a Protestant woman with theological degrees from Oxford and from the Graduate Theological Unoin in Berkeley, worked with this church as teacher and cominister for some years. In the spring of 2010 Corran decided she wanted to join the Catholic Church and be ordained in this community. After some reflection the Mary Magdalene Church decided that, rather than having her ordained through the RCWP system, they would ordain her collectively as a community. This they felt was the original practice of the Christian community. On July 30 and 31, 2010, Nancy Corran was ordained by the whole community, everyone, including the children, laying hands on her head. Nancy then presided over the Eucharist as priest on Sunday, August 1. This was a powerful nurturing experience for the whole community, as well as friends, such as myself, who attended this wonderful experience of "good church" together.

Mary Magdalene Church has clearly taken the question of the validity of women's (or anyone's) ordination a radical new step. They do not seek to claim apostolic succession through a lineage of bishops. Rather they believe that committed Christian communities have the power to ordain, and that this was original practice of the early church. They are correct on this, in my view. For them their practice is fully apostolic, and they see themselves as belonging to the Catholic tradition.

A significant disagreement divides women-church and the Roman Catholic Women Priest movement. Some representatives of women-church remain suspicious of the RCWP movement, with its adoption of distinctions of bishops, priests, and deacons, and their claims of apostolic succession. They question what they see as clericalism. But those who seek ordination see women-church as inadequate to create inclusive worshiping communities of men, women and children. Women-church tends to be only adult women and so doesn't provide a place for men and children. I think that RCWP movement needs to keep themselves from a drifting to clericalism. But women-church has to recognize its limitations.

Rather than seeing them as being in conflict, however, I am inclined to see these two options as complementary, operating in different contexts. A women-church group tends to be small, informal, led by those with educational experiences that make it possible to pass around liturgical leadership to all members. This is the case with the women-church group that I participate in Claremont, which gathers about twelve to twenty-five people monthly. But when we are dealing with a more organized church community that is doing a weekly liturgy for seventy-five to one hundred or more people, as well as educational work, social ministries, and monetary requirements, a more formal structure becomes necessary. Designating selected people as ordained becomes appropriate in this context, together with a high level of community participation and democratic governance. The role of priesthood should be seen as functional, rather than defined as an expression of a sacral hierarchy.

This decision of many Catholic women to simply move on, creating "good church" for themselves, not waiting for the official church to sanction these changes, widens the gap with the official church, which countenances none of this. This gap has been exacerbated by the behavior of many bishops, and particularly the Vatican, which has not only rejected progress on issues such as reproductive rights and women's ordination, but has systematically sought to minimalize the renewed ecclesiology proposed by the Second Vatican Council between 1962 and 1965. A deep internal schism has opened up in the last forty-five years between the Vatican and, not only more radical Catholics, such as feminists, but also with Vatican II reformers.

Vatican II and Aftermath

To understand this internal schism, we need to briefly review Vatican II and the way its vision of church renewal has been largely undone by the Vatican leaders since its closing. Those present at the Council are very aware that Pope John XXIII's announcement of the Council in 1959 was not greeted with enthusiasm by the Curia or Vatican bureaucracy. They sought to confine the Council to being only a "completion of Vatican I," which defined papal infallibility. They were dismayed when the pope defined the Council as Vatican II, whose agenda was church renewal and modernization, reaching out to the world's bishops for ideas of how the church should adapt to new times.

When the over-two-thousand bishops of the world arrived for the Council, it became evident that this gathering would not be a brief process of a month or two, but a many-year event. As it actually unfolded, it took parts of four years, with over 168 assemblies, opening October 11, 1962, and closing December 8, 1965. It sought fundamental rethinking and reform of vast areas of the Church's life: the nature of the Church itself, divine revelation, liturgy, the pastoral office of bishop, the ministry and life of priests, the training of priests, renewal of religious life, the apostolate of laypeople, Christian education, the missionary activity of the church, relations with Eastern churches, ecumenism or relations with other churches, relations with non-Christian religions, religious liberty, and the mass media. In each case the theologians and church fathers sought a rethinking from the Church's biblical and patristic roots, not just a repetition of Counter-reformation patterns. But reproductive rights were removed from Council consideration to a separate Commission, as we have seen, and women were barely mentioned.

The Curia and its conservative faction deeply resisted this renewal and sought to retain their control and view of the church as a top-down hierarchy. This group was accustomed to centralized domination from the Vatican, with little input even from bishops around the world, much less from priests, laity, and theologians. Once the world's bishops arrived, this curial group became a voting minority, but they remained very aggressive and tried to control the process and ecclesiological perspective of the Council at every turn. This was quietly but consistently opposed by Pope John XXIII, who sought to keep the Council open to the "signs of the times" of modern life. When he died, his successor, Paul VI continued to support the Council and its open process but in a weaker, more ambivalent way.[24]

The resulting documents reflect perspectives that are mixed and inconsistent, containing pieces of different ecclesiologies. They are of uneven quality, some deeply informed by a renewed biblical theology of prophetic transformation, and others, such as the document on the mass media, with little innovative insight. The Curial conservatives made sure that the documents and public statements constantly reaffirmed that there was no departure from strict papal primacy over the whole church. The reformers sought to balance this primacy with a new emphasis on the collegiality of bishops with the pope and each other. In the decree on the Church (*Lumen Gentium*) and on the pastoral office of the bishops (*Christus Dominus*) the reformers sought to clarify that the episcopal office as a continuation of the college of the apostles, in which the pope, like Peter, is a central member, not above them. Bishops are not simply delegates of the pope, but share a collegial leadership with each other in the relation of local churches to the universal church.

The document on the church took a further step and sought to ground its ecclesiology in a vision of the people of God. This is reflected in a significant shift that took place as this document was being developed from its original form, prepared by Curial conservatives, to its final form approved by the Council. Originally this document began with a reflection on the "mystery of the Church," followed by the hierarchical constitution of pope and then bishops, then a discussion of the laity. But in the process of deliberation, this order was decisively revised. The topic of the people of God was placed immediately after the opening discussion of the mystery of the Church. This meant that the shared baptism of all Christians (including non-Catholics) became the foundational ground for the reality of the church. The ordained—the pope, bishops, and priests—were situated within the people of God as servants of the common mission and of the call to holiness that all share, rather than outside and above them as their source.[25]

This shift fundamentally reorients ecclesiology. In the curial "trickle-down" view of the church, God the Father and Christ are the ultimate source

24. For a good survey of how the Council unfolded, see Giuseppe Alberigo, *A Brief History of Vatican II*, trans. Matthew Sherry (Maryknoll, NY: Orbis, 2006). Alberigo was an active participant in the whole process of the Council. He and Joseph Komonchak edited *The History of Vatican II*, 5 vols. (Maryknoll, NY: Orbis, 1995–2006).

25. See Alberigo, *A Brief History of Vatican II*, 43–50.

of the church, but they are seen as imparting redemptive power first to the pope, who in turn delegates this to bishops, then they to priests. The laity fall outside this "perfect society" of the clerical hierarchy, ministered to but with no apostolate of their own. The shift in writing the document that puts the people of God immediately after the "mystery of the Church" recasts this hierarchical ecclesiology. The primary reality that flows from the mystery of the Church, founded by God and Christ, is the people of God born in baptism. The hierarchy rises *within* the people of God to articulate their shared apostolate and to serve them. The inconsistencies in Vatican II documents reflect remnants of the top-down ecclesiology remaining side by side with this very different vision.

In the last months of the Council, before its closing in December 1965, there was a rush to complete and confirm no less than twelve documents. This four-year process was an unprecedented effort to chart a vision of a renewed Church, both in its internal structure and in relation to other Christians, non-Christians, and the "world." But it left a fundamental lack of completion. A vision had been laid out of a more conciliar church grounded in the whole people of God, but, except for the decree on the liturgy, no plan of implementation had been defined. Many of the bishops had been partly or deeply transformed in their understanding of who they were as church, both in relation to the whole people of God and as collegial members of the episcopacy. But with the departure of the bishops to their dioceses around the world, it was the Curia, which had resisted this whole process, that was left in charge to implement the decrees of the Council. Their obvious bias was to minimize the new communal vision and to return as much as possible to the top-down view of the church they favored.

As long as Pope Paul VI remained alive, this reversion was partly impeded. But, with his death in 1978, and the quick demise of his successor, John Paul I, the curial conservatives had on their side a new pope, John Paul II, who largely favored their perspective. For the twenty-seven years of his papacy, followed by that of Benedict XVI, who as Joseph Ratzinger had been the head of the Holy Office (formerly the Inquisition), the world Roman Catholic Church has experienced a monarchical leadership dedicated to restoring top-down centralization. This effort has been addressed to all the major areas of the church institution: the control of bishops, colleges, seminaries, religious orders, charitable work, and theological journals. Any liberation, feminist, or democratic tendencies are opposed in favor of a spirituality and practice of domination and repression.

Pope John Paul II and Benedict XVI have been concerned to rein in progressive bishops and replace them with conservatives, as well as asserting exclusive papal control over episcopal appointments. These popes have not been open to local participation from fellow bishops, priests, or laity in choosing bishops. A number of progressive bishops came to power between the 1960s and '80s, and thanks the vision of Vatican II and their experience of the needs of their people, many converted to more democratic and social-justice views after they became bishops. One thinks of Oscar Romero in El Salvador, who became radicalized as a bishop by his experience of the poverty of his people and the violence of the army, but who was assassinated in 1980.[26] There was Hélder Câmera, who evolved as a liberationist through his long years a bishop of Recife in Brazil, retiring in 1985;[27] and Samuel Ruiz, bishop of Chiapas, Mexico, for forty years (from 1959 to 2000), who was radicalized by traveling on a donkey through his diocese of mostly poor indigenous people.[28] One is hard put to find any progressives of this quality as bishops of the Catholic Church today.

The papal policy has been one of appointment of strict conservatives, sometimes after a progressive has retired. In the case of Hélder Câmera, he was replaced by a conservative who dismantled his work, closing the liberation theology–oriented seminary where prospective priests were trained by grassroots work in the community. This new bishop fired all the staff, including feminist Ivone Gebara, and replaced the school with a traditional seminary. In other cases, progressives, such as Samuel Ruiz in Chiapas and Raymond Hunthausen in Seattle, Washington, were reined in while they were bishops by the appointment of a conservative auxiliary bishop who sought to limit their power. After their retirement these progressive bishops were replaced with conservatives, often from Opus Dei, a right-wing Catholic group that Pope John Paul II made a personal prelature under its own independent power in 1982. When moderate Roger Mahony retired from the Archdiocese of Los Angeles in 2011 after a twenty-five-year reign, he was replaced by Opus Dei product José Gomez. Opus Dei bishops have come to dominate in many other countries, such as El Salvador and Peru.

26. See Oscar Ardulfo Romero, *The Church Is All of You: Thoughts of Archbishop Oscar Romero*, comp. and trans. James R. Brockman (Minneapolis: Winston, 1984).

27. See "Hélder Câmera." *Wikipedia*. Online: http://en.wikipedia.org/wiki/H%C3%A9lder_C%C3%A2mara/.

28. See Gary MacEóin, *The People's Church: Bishop Samuel Ruiz of Mexico and Why He Matters* (New York: Crossroad, 1996).

The other areas where John Paul II and Benedict XVI have sought to impose conservative dominance are equally troubling. One of these is theological education. In the United States the principle of academic freedom has ruled out outside control by churches. Thus it was a shock for Catholic academics when the Vatican demanded a policy in which Catholics teaching theology in Catholic colleges must receive a mandate from their bishop. Although this has been negotiated in various ways with different bishops, the clear pattern that has emerged is that contested issues, such as women's reproductive rights and women's ordination, cannot be discussed at Catholic colleges. Those who do discuss them are not allowed to teach at such colleges.

When I was invited by the theological faculty of the University of San Diego (USD) to teach one course in 2008, Catholic conservatives raised a vehement protest that I should not be allowed to teach because I was a board member of Catholics for Choice (even though I was planning to teach ecological theology, not about choice). The administration felt constrained to cancel my invitation. A large percentage of the faculty of USD protested this decision, but to no avail.

Some Catholic colleges, fortunately, seem to remain open to what people like myself have to say. I have received many invitations to speak at Catholic colleges over the years and hold five of my fourteen honorary degrees from Catholic colleges. For more than twenty years I have given lectures through Holy Names College in Oakland, California, first though Matthew Fox's Creation Spirituality Program and more recently through the Sophia Center, run by Father Jim Conlin. This program brings together ecology, spirituality, and justice and reflects a very creative and transformative vision. Catholic women religious remain a major sector of renewed Catholicism and regularly are found as leading participants of Catholic progressive movements and conferences. This is why they are under such suspicion from the Vatican.

In April 2012 the Vatican issued a condemnation of the Leadership Conference of Women Religious, an organization that represents 80 percent of American nuns, claiming that they "did not follow the bishops' thinking." Catholic historian Garry Wills responded acerbically "thank God they don't. Nuns have a different set of priorities than that of bishops. The bishops are interested in power. The nuns are interested in the powerless. Nuns have been preserving Gospel values while the bishops have been perverting them."[29]

Catholic seminaries have also been reined in and those of the type created by Hélder Câmera in Brazil closed down. Women's religious orders, particularly in the United States where such orders have been democratically reformed and are known to be sympathetic to feminism, have been held under suspicion. They have been put continually under "investigation" to return them to more traditional habits and hierarchical control. Recently Caritas, the major Catholic charity organization, has fallen under the papal demand that charity work should go hand in hand with efforts to convert to Catholicism those who receive it. This demand is diametrically opposed to Caritas policy, in which its credibility worldwide has been based on its nonsectarian way of working.[30]

Sexual Abuse and Corruption in High Places

The systematic effort to put all Catholic institutions under papal control and eliminate independent thinking is disturbing enough. Even more questionable is the revelation of sexual abuse of young people by priests and the failure of Pope John Paul II to take this seriously as an issue. Information on sexual abuse among American Catholic priests began to surface in the 1980s. Reverend Thomas Doyle, a canon lawyer at the Vatican embassy in Washington DC, sent a warning memo on this issue to the Vatican in 1984 and co-wrote a ninety-three-page report on the problem in 1985, which he sent to every American bishop. But the pope gave no response. In 1989 the US Conference of Catholic Bishops sent experts in canon law to Rome seeking a streamlined process to remove convicted child molesters from the priesthood, but the pope refused to accept this.

Church bureaucrats tried to claim that this was a distinctly American problem, or that the anti-Catholicism of the media was responsible for exaggerating it, but more and more evidence poured in of its widespread nature, not just in the United States, but in Ireland, Austria, Germany, and many other countries. It soon became evident that the problem was not

---

29. Garry Wills, "Bullying the Nuns," *New York Review of Books*, June 7, 2012, 64. Online: http://www.nybooks.com/blogs/nyrblog/2012/apr/24/bullying-nuns/.

30. See John Allen, "Identity Pressures at Heart of Caritas Ferment," *National Catholic Reporter*, June 10, 2011, 1, 16. Online: http://ncronline.org/news/global/identity-pressures-heart-caritas-ferment/.

only the sexually abusing priests themselves, but the way in which bishops, religious-order superiors, and school principals concealed the issue, sending the offenders to other locations, sometimes after a stay in a pastoral counseling center. But the pope continued to fail to respond seriously to the issue, seeing it as an unwarranted attack on priests. Finally in 2002 the dying pope did refer to sexual abuse as an "appalling sin," but called for the redemption of abusers through repentance, rather than for defrocking them, and blamed therapists, rather than bishops, for recycling abusive priests to other clerical positions.[31]

While Benedict XVI was pope, he spoke out more strongly against abuse as a sin and apologized to victims, but those concerned with the issue continue to see his response as inadequate, particularly in terms of the way Church leaders need to quickly remove abusers from clerical positions and contact with children. A more shocking scandal is the failure of John Paul II, as well as Cardinal Ratzinger as head of the Holy Office under this pope, to deal with a sexually abusing and deeply corrupt church leader, Marcial Maciel Degollado, founder of the religious order the Legion of Christ.

Maciel was born in Mexico in 1920 and founded this order when he was barely twenty-one in 1941. It presently has eight hundred priests and seventy thousand lay members of the affiliated order, Regnum Christi, and runs fifteen universities. Extremely successful in raising huge sums of money, particularly from rich widows, the order owns vast wealth and has had a very close relation to the Vatican, particularly to the late Pope John Paul II. Early in John Paul's papacy Maciel channeled large sums of money to the Polish Solidarity movement, earning the pope's permanent gratitude. Maciel's envoys regularly delivered envelopes with thousands of dollars in cash to key church hierarchs, such Cardinal Angelo Sodano, Vatican secretary of state. Maciel was able to command access to papal visits, charged fees as high as fifty thousand dollars to those seeking them, and channeled these sums to the pope's personal secretary, Monsignor Stanislaw Dziwisz.

Maciel's sexual abuse of boys is now known to have gone back a long way. Sexually abused himself as a boy, Macial was only seventeen and a student in his bishop uncle's seminary when he was discovered to have a habit of locking himself in a boarding house where he was staying with some of the younger students and sexually abusing them. Maciel was expelled from

31. See Jason Berry, "The Shame of John Paul II: How the Sexual Abuse Scandal Stained His Papacy," *The Nation*, May 16, 2011, 11–15. Online: http://www.thenation. com/article/160242/shame-john-paul-ii-how-sex-abuse-scandal-stained-his-papacy/.

the seminary. But this did not prevent him from founding the Legion in 1940. The order claimed to follow the line of strict orthodoxy and professed a vehement anticommunism. Testimony from ex-seminarians of this order has made evident that Macial regularly engaged in sexual abuse of seminarians. He also acquired a drug habit and used his seminarians to secure Dolantin (morphine) for him. This led to Macial's suspension as head of the order in 1956, but he was able to get reinstated two years later. In 1983 Pope John Paul II approved the bylaws of the Legion that made its members take "private vows" in which they pledged to never criticize the founder (Macial) and to report on anyone who did.

Despite Macial's effort to shield himself from scrutiny by inculcating a regime of fear and secrecy in the order, abused ex-seminarians soon began to try to bring reports of their experience to Church authorities. Nine former seminarians came forward to report to Church authorities, claiming that Macial had sexually abused them when they were students in the 1950s and '60s. Receiving no response, they went public with their accusations in a report published in 1997 in the *Hartford Courant*.[32] This report drew outrage against them from Catholic conservatives, such as William Donohue of the Catholic League, Father John Neuhaus, editor of *First Things*, Mary Ann Glendon, Harvard law professor and lecturer at the Legion university in Rome, and George Weigel, biographer of John Paul II. Neuhaus called the accusations "scurrilous" and proclaimed Maciel's innocence "a moral certainty," while Glendon spoke of Maciel as emanating a "radiant holiness."[33]

In 1998 José Barba and another ex-Legionary abused by Macial flew to Rome and filed a canonical grievance against Macial, seeking his excommunication by Ratzinger's Congregation for the Doctrine of the Faith. Cardinal Sodano defended Macial and pressed Ratzinger not to proceed with the case. Macial continued to enjoy complete support and praise from the pope as late as 2004. Only as the pope was dying did Ratzinger order a canon lawyer on his staff, Charles Scicluna, to investigate the case. In New York, Mexico, and Rome thirty aging men testified to how they had been abused as seminarians.

32. Gerald Renner and Jason Berry, "Head of Worldwide Catholic Order Accused of History of Sexual Abuse," *Hartford Courant*, February 23, 1997. Online: http://articles.courant.com/1997-02-23/news/hc-marcial-maciel-02-1997_1_father-maciel-letters-from-two-priests-legionaries/.

33. See Jason Berry, "Whitewashing John Paul's Culpability," *National Catholic Reporter*, January 7, 2011, 6–7.

By then it had also come out that Macial had at least two wives, two sons by one and a daughter by another, and possibly several other offspring by other women. The sons went public to testify that their father had sexually abused them as early as age seven. In 2006 when Ratzinger became Benedict XVI, he ordered Macial out of active ministry for "a life of prayer and penance." Macial went to his birthplace in southern Mexico, where he reunited with his second wife, a former waitress, and his daughter. He died in the United States in 2008. Benedict XVI took control of the Legion. Refusing to abolish the order altogether, he claimed to be "reforming" it, not a simple task given its power and money.[34]

Macial was not the only mass sexual abuser protected by Pope John Paul II. The pope also blocked an investigation into Austrian Cardinal Hans Hermann Groer, who was his personal friend, accused of molesting an estimated two thousand boys, and he protected Polish archbishop Juliusz, accused of abusing priests in training. The pope ignored charges that Father Lawrence Murphy of Wisconsin molested two hundred deaf boys under his "care."[35]

This evidence of Pope John Paul II's systematic efforts to repress the reforming vision of Vatican II, seeking to restore a papally controlled church, his refusal to deal with sexual abuse, his protection of known sexual abusers, and his enthusiastic support for the deeply corrupt Marcial Macial raises deep questions about the moral and intellectual leadership of the Vatican. Far from being infallible, John Paul and his cohorts seem to lack minimal moral credibility. A deep corruption pervades their clerical culture, open to bribery from sexual abusers claiming to promote strict conservativism, while armed with large envelopes of cash. Although Benedict XVI finally deposed Macial and claimed to be reforming the Legion, he collaborated with this culture for twenty-seven years, from 1978 to 2005. His rush to beatify John Paul II bypassed these questions about his reign. Although perhaps not as open to outright corruption as some others at the Vatican, Benedict XVI clearly was committed to a Church dominated from the top. Hopefully this may change with the new papacy of Francis I.

In June 2011, leading Vatican II theologian Hans Küng called for a "peaceful" revolution by world Catholics against the absolutism of papal

---

34. See Alma Guillermoprieto, "The Mission of Father Maciel, " *The New York Review of Books*, June 24, 2010, pp. 28–29. See also Jason Berry, "Benedict's Gamble: The Risks of Saving the Legion," *National Catholic Reporter*, January 7, 2011, pp. 5–8.

35. *London Times*, 4/4/20; *Extra: The Magazine of Fair 24/7* (July 2011), 3.

power. He made this call through a video message played at a conference of the American Catholic Council meeting in Detroit. Küng compared the power of the papacy to that of the French monarchs overthrown by the people of France in 1789. He called for a similar overthrow of papal absolutism, although peacefully, not violently. "Few people realize how powerful the pope is," he said. Küng also reflected on the failure to carry through the reforms of Vatican II. He acknowledged that many documents were ambivalent because of the power of the Curia to stop the process of reform. "What I did not expect," Küng added, "was that we could have such a restoration movement as under the Polish pope and now under the German pope." Küng believes that the church is in deep crisis, and that many Catholic leaders realize the need for a radical reform.[36]

The American Catholic Council is a new assembly of reform-minded US Catholics that drew two-thousand participants for its inaugural convention. The assembly passed a ten-point Catholic Bill of Rights and Responsibilities. This list included the primacy of conscience; the right to Eucharistic community and responsible pastoral care; the right and responsibility of laypeople to participate in the proclamation of the gospel and to engage in ministry; freedom of expression and the right to dissent; the right to a good name and due process; participation in decision making in the Church, including selection of leaders; and social justice, in both the world and the structures of the Church.[37]

What Küng might mean by a "peaceful revolution" to overthrow papal absolutism is unclear. No democratic structures exist on any level of Catholic Church government by which Catholic people can act to curb this papal power. A new Church Council to do this, given the present papacy, seems unlikely. Following the old bromide that the role of the laity is to "pay, pray, and obey," three sources of power lie in the hands of laity: prayer, money, and disobedience to commands. Laypeople are using all of these. They are forming alternative gatherings, such as women-church base communities and Mary Magdalene Apostle Church, to create worshipping communities more in line with their desires. They are shaping reform organizations, such as Call to Action and the American Catholic Council. They are withdrawing their financial contributions from the hierarchical church to fund their

36. See Jerry Filteau, "Hans Küng Urges Peaceful Revolution against Roman Absolutism," *National Catholic Reporter*, June 10, 2011. Online: http://ncronline.org/news/faith-parish/hans-kung-urges-peaceful-revolution-against-roman-absolutism/.

37. Jerry Filteau, "American Catholic Council: 2000 meet to call for reform in Detroit," *National Catholic Reporter*, June 24, 2011, 5–6.

own community projects, and they are withholding their obedience from decrees that lack credibility, such as *Humanae Vitae*.

My own commitment to Roman Catholicism as a historical community and tradition disposes me to be a part of this movement of resistance. In this sense I am in communion as a Catholic with Catholic progressives, not with the pope or hierarchy, who are apostate and seek to destroy reform and renewal. Catholic progressives relate to the hierarchy as part of "us" by calling them to repent and be converted. Yet, on a day-to-day level, this work of resistance and call for renewal is not a matter of beating our heads against closed doors, which I think is mostly unproductive, but mostly creating alternative organizations and communities for living "good church," and a faithful quest for a good society, now. It also includes efforts to lessen oppression and open up liberating life here and there in Catholic institutions where one might find oneself, such as parishes, religious orders, schools, or charitable organizations.

In July of 2012 another step was taken toward this work of alternative Catholic organizing. Twenty Catholic feminists representing different Catholic peace-and-justice movements and ministries, and teachers in theology and ethics in colleges, met in the Baltimore area to respond to the recent attacks by the bishops to women's work in the church. They discussed how they might create a more organized network of Catholic feminists in the US Church. A national think tank and a network of local organizations related to parishes were among their proposals. In this meeting, Catholic feminists across the nation began to formalize their relation to each other as a community, and to imagine how they might create a movement for greater gender justice in the American Church. This is the kind of Catholic community with which I feel in communion.

Some might ask, "Why not join one of the other churches who are doing a better job of being Christian?" For me, this is an irrelevant question. I am happy for whatever good is being done in other churches. I feel we are already in communion, and we work and celebrate together all the time. But something needs to be done to weaken the powers of corruption in the Catholic context and to help Catholics to use their resources to resist these evil powers and create liberating and life-giving communities. This is a huge job, but not necessarily one that should engulf one's whole life. I see myself as devoting a tithe of at least 10 percent of my energy to this effort to create possibilities for more good and less evil in Catholic contexts, while continuing to work on other projects in ecumenical and interfaith settings.

Yet this 10 percent is a serious commitment to which I readily continue to devote a part of my life. This is how I remain a Catholic as an ecumenical and interfaith Christian.

3

The Warring Children of Abraham
Jews, Christians, and Muslims

My sensitivity to issues of Jews and Judaism was originally sparked by my relationship to my uncle David Sandow. Uncle David came from a New York City family of Jews originally from Russia. At the funeral of his wife, my aunt Sophie, I meet his two brothers—one a medical doctor, the other a psychiatrist—and have since met and exchanged letters and visits with his niece, also named Sophie. Although not a practicing Jew, Uncle David had a deep love of his tradition. I remember his fascination with how the Jewish community was depicted in the art of Rembrandt, his favorite artist. Uncle David was a surrogate father for me and my sisters, and he trained me in art. I went many times with him and my aunt to the Mellon Gallery in Washington DC and also absorbed art history from the art books at his home. He also taught me to play golf, and I went golfing with him and Aunt Sophie often. This relationship sensitized me to Jews and aroused my negative feelings toward any expressions of anti-Jewishness.

This sensitivity was sharpened in 1945 when I, as a nine-year-old at Saturday-afternoon movies, saw vivid pictures of the Nazi death camps that had been opened up by the victorious Allied armies. I was horrified by the piles of dead bodies and the skeletal survivors that were revealed there. My uncle never talked about the Holocaust or Israel, so I am not sure how he felt about them. My impression is that he belonged to a kind of Jewish identity of the twenties and thirties that was non-Zionist, secular universalist, vaguely socialist, and concerned about "worker justice"; but in the McCarthy era this was not something one talked about. When my mother took us to California in 1952, Uncle David saw us off in tears. I named my son David for him. When I went to college and read church history, I became aware of the anti-Semitism of the Christian tradition. From my 1972–73 research on this emerged my book *Faith and Fratricide: The Theological Roots of Anti-Semitism*. I dedicated it to David Sandow.

Christian Relationships with Judaism

The Christian diatribe against Judaism goes back to New Testament times, rooted in the rivalry between the Christian affirmation that Jesus was the Messiah expected by the Jewish tradition and the rejection of this belief by the established Jewish leaders. A bitter polemic was directed particularly against the Pharisees, leading rabbinic reformers at the time, who led the resistance to Christian efforts, to impose their *midrash* (scriptural interpretation) in the synagogues. The Pharisees are denounced in the Gospel of Matthew as "blind guides and hypocrites," petty legalists who are strict in superficial matters, and neglect "weightier matters of the law, justice, mercy and faith" (Matt 23:23). They are said to be "sons of those who murdered the prophets," "serpents, a brood of vipers, deserving of hell," (Matt 23:31). In the Gospel of John (8:44) they are called children of the devil.

This polemic against the Jews and their religion hardened into fixed patterns in the writings of the church fathers (from the second through the sixth century CE), found particularly in the *Adversus Judaeus* (*Against the Jews*) writings of Tertullian and John Chrysostom. In these writings the Christian church is claimed as the true heir of God's election of the people of God, while the Jews are the heirs of those who have always be unfaithful to God, who killed the prophets, and whose final perfidy is killing the Messiah (or God: deicide). Because of this apostasy, God has cast off the Jews, condemning them to be homeless wanderers subjugated to others (the Christians), who represent a new godly world empire.

When Christianity became the established religion of the Roman Empire, this polemic was translated into legal disabilities for Jews. Jews were forbidden to proselytize or to own slaves. (This was not based on antislavery teaching of the church. It was okay for Christians to hold slaves.) With this prohibition of owning slaves, Jews were kept from running larger businesses or agricultural estates. Jews could also not hold political office. Popular riots, often led by Christian monks, destroyed synagogues. Leading bishops, such as Saint Ambrose of Milan, rejected any compensation to the Jews for such destruction.[1]

This pattern of polemic and legal disabilities was passed on to medieval and early modern Western Christendom. It was renewed between the twelfth and fifteenth centuries. Jews were segregated into special sections of cities, made to wear identifying garb, and forbidden the normal range of activities such as farming and artisan guild membership. They were pushed to function in areas forbidden to Christians, such as money lending. Stereotypes related to usury were thereby added to negative religious images. During the crusades Christian armies, on their way to fight the Muslims in the Middle East, sometimes stopped to sack and murder Jewish communities. Jews were expelled from many countries: in 1290 from England, in 1390 from France, in 1492 from Spain, and in the 1550s from parts of Germany.

Although the Christian polemic was murderous, it was not formally genocidal. There remained a place for the Jews as a religious community in Christian society. They were the objects of hate against whom the Christians contrasted themselves, but also of hope for their eventual capitulation and conversion to Christianity. This conversion was projected into Christian eschatology, becoming part of the "last things" that signaled the return of the prophet Elijah, to be followed by the second coming of Christ and final redemption. At that time it was believed that converted Jews would become part of the united people of God.

This ambiguity changed in modern Europe as religious anti-Judaism was translated into racial anti-Semitism, starting in Spain in the late fifteenth and sixteenth centuries, as Christians destroyed the remains of Muslim rule there and expelled Jews and Muslims. (Many Jews from Spain found refuge in the Muslim world.) Negative characteristics of what had been seen as Judaism now came to be seen as characteristics of Jews as a race, or as a matter of blood. In nineteenth-century Europe, assimilated Jews, offered citizenship in European nationalisms, were rejected by anti-Semitic nationalists who claimed that as a people Jews could not truly convert or assimilate into Christian nations but must be eliminated altogether.

In the nineteenth and in the first half of the twentieth century, Jews become the scapegoats for modernizing societies, blamed for both secularism and socialism. This trend culminated in Nazism. Once in power, the

1. See Rosemary Radford Ruether, *Faith and Fratricide: The Theological Roots of Anti-Semitism* (1974; reprinted, Eugene, OR: Wipf & Stock, 1996), 193–94.

Nazis passed laws that segregated Jews, confiscated their property, expelled them, and finally sought to physically exterminate them. European Jews, under such assault, sought one of several solutions: fleeing to nations such as the United States, where they could assimilate as citizens while remaining Jews personally; clinging to religious-fundamentalist enclaves; or embracing Zionism and creating a Jewish national state in Palestine.[2]

After the atrocities of Nazism were revealed in 1945, many Christians were horrified. A few realized that Christian theology held some responsibility for these atrocities and began to rethink some Christian ideas, such as the collective guilt of the Jewish people for Christ's death, the supersession of Christianity over Judaism, and the exclusive redemptive role of Christ. The Second Vatican Council addressed the question of the Jews in the context of a document on the relation of the Church to non-Christian people. The document starts by affirming that all humanity is one community descended from one stock created by God and to be ultimately united in God's work of redemption. All humans are in the image of God and seek the meaning of life. All religions have some true insights into authentic relation to God, and the Church affirms whatever is true in every religion. The document then lays out an implicit sequence of Hinduism, Buddhism, Islam, and finally Judaism: each of these is seen as having progressively more of the truth, and Christianity is understood as the final fullness.

Judaism stands at the highest point in this hierarchy of non-Christian religions, representing the ancestors of our (Christian) faith: the patriarchs, prophets, and Moses. The Jews are the chosen people of God. Although most Jews did not accept Christ when he came, any collective guilt of the whole of the Jewish people for Christ's death must be rejected. Some Jewish authorities, not all Jews, were responsible at that time, and there is no ongoing guilt today. The document claims that at some future time at the culmination of history all humans will come together as one in Christ, but there is no call for evangelization of the Jews or those of any other religion here and now.[3]

2. This account of the history of Christian anti-Semitism follows that found in my book *Faith and Fratricide*. The account also follows the short version of this story found in my article "Anti-Semitism," in *The Cambridge Dictionary of Christianity*, ed. Daniel Patte (Cambridge: Cambridge University Press, 2010), 56–57.

3. "Declaration on the Relation of the Church to Non-Christian Religions," (*Nostra Aetate*, 1965), in *Vatican Council II: The Basic Sixteen Documents*, ed. Austin Flannery (Northport, NY: Costello, 1996), 569–74.

Protestant churches, particularly in Germany, struggled with reformulating Christian relation to the Jews, particularly the question of mission to the Jews. In the 1975 statement of the German Evangelical Church both anti-Semitism and anti-Zionism were rejected and must be actively opposed by Christians. The founding of the State of Israel is assumed to be not only integral to Judaism but also a redemptive event in the salvation history of God's people. Yet the statement stops short of rejecting mission to the Jews. Christ is the final salvation of all people, and Jews can't be seen as exempted from this mission.[4]

A small group of post-Holocaust Christian theologians were dissatisfied with the inadequacies of this response to the historic atrocity of Christian anti-Semitism culminating in the Holocaust. They believed that Judaism must be affirmed as fully redemptive in its own right and any supersession of Christianity over Judaism totally rejected. Christianity must not be seen as in any way a new covenant beyond the one covenant of God with Israel, but simply as a dependent extension of that one covenant to the Gentiles.

This comes close to saying that Christianity can't be seen as having any new and different (much less better) ideas than Judaism. Judaism itself is identified with an affirmation of God's election of the Jews as the one unique people of God and God's gift of the land to them and them alone. Christianity should be simply a dependent expansion of the Jewish mission to be a "light to the nations," to convert all people to the One God of Israel, a mission now centered in the State of Israel. This view was developed particularly by Christian theologian Paul Van Buren in the 1980s and has been reaffirmed by subsequent post-Holocaust thinkers, such as Jim Wallis, Kendall Soulen, and James Carroll.[5]

These thinkers not only reduce Christianity to being a dependent tool of Jewish election, but they ignore the complex struggle within Judaism itself over more than two millennia between exclusivism and universalism.

---

4. Rat der Evangelischen Kirche in Deutschland, *Christen und Juden* (Gütersloh: Mohn, 1975). See also Helga Croner, *Stepping Stones to Further Jewish-Christian Relations* (London: Stimulus, 1977).

5. Paul Van Buren, *A Christian Theology of the People Israel* (Theology of the Jewish-Christian Reality 2, New York: Seabury, 1983); Jim H. Wallis, *Post-Holocaust Christianity: Paul Van Buren's Theology of Jewish-Christian Reality* (Lanham, MD: University Press of America, 1997); Kendall R. Soulen, *The God of Israel and Christian Theology* (Minneapolis Fortress, 1996); James Carroll, *Constantine's Sword: The Church and the Jews* (Boston: Houghton Mifflin, 2001).

In this theology of exclusivism as manifest today, any rights of Palestinians to a standing as a people or to a share of the land are denied or ignored. Post-Holocaust Christianity ties itself to an absolutist Judaism, ignoring the new situation in which the State of Israel is in a process of committing crimes against another people—the ethnic cleansing of the Palestinian people from Palestine. Post-Holocaust Christianity seeks to compensate for Christian guilt for its past crimes against the Jews by ignoring, denying, and collaborating with new crimes today. This Christian response to the Holocaust raises as many problems as it solves, yet Christians have been largely unable to question it. Its first major critique has come from a Mark Braverman, a Jew committed to a universal humanity and the rejection of the ethnic cleansing of Palestinians by Jewish triumphalism.[6]

Christian Relations with Islam

Christianity has also had a largely negative relation to Islam since its rise in the seventh century, but the power relations between the two religions and their people have been significantly different from the relation of Christianity and Judaism. Mohammed developed his religious vision from 613 to 632 CE and was quickly successful in dominating the Arab peninsula. For the next hundred years, from Mohammed's death until 740, Islam expanded its rule over a vast empire from India to Spain. Much of this area from the Middle East to North Africa and Spain was predominantly Christian at that time, although the Persian empire had many Zoroastrians, Buddhists, and Hindus.

Contrary to Christian polemic, Islam did not force Christians to convert by the sword. Christians and Jews were accepted as "people of the book." One Quranic text even forbids "compulsion in religious matters" (Qur'an 2:256). Rather Jews and Christians were put in a "protected" but secondary status based on paying a tax to the occupiers. Yet, with the exception of the Coptic Church in Egypt, many of the Christians in the Middle East and North Africa converted within a century, and the churches of these areas greatly diminished.

The reasons are not that they were forced to convert. Indeed some Muslim leaders sought to discourage conversion since thereby they lost the tax paid by these people. There were several reasons for this conversion.

6. Mark Braverman, *Fatal Embrace: Christians, Jews, and the Search for Peace in the Holy Land* (Austin: Synergy, 2010), 105–24.

Many Eastern and North African Christians were alienated from what they perceived as oppressive Byzantine rule and saw Muslims as preferable. Also by conversion they freed themselves from the tax. Many Christians must also have seen Islam, with its ethics, monotheism, and veneration of Jesus as prophet and Messiah as sufficiently similar to Christianity to be acceptable as a religion.

Yet this rapid expansion of Islam into a world empire, and the disappearance of much of Eastern Christianity were very threatening to both Byzantine and Western Christians. For people of that time (and perhaps still today) success political, military, and cultural—particularly large scale success—implied that God was behind it. Thus Byzantine Christians were challenged to explain how Islam could be so successful and yet contrary to God's wishes. Christians had two categories for a movement coming after Christ that deviated from Christian orthodoxy. One was heresy. The other was that the final conflicts leading to the end of the world and Final Judgment were happening, and the devil was unleashing his agent, the antichrist.

John of Damascus (675–750 CE), a leading Christian theologian reared in Damascus, the administrative and military capital of the Umayyad dynasty, employed both these categories. Mohammed was a "false prophet" "who devised his own heresy." He was a hypocritical trickster who "having insinuated himself into the good graces of the people by a show of piety, . . . gave out that a certain book had been sent down to him from heaven. He set down some ridiculous compositions in this book and gave it to them as an object of veneration." John of Damascus also speaks of Islam as "the superstition of the Ishmaelites which . . . keeps people in error, being a forerunner of the Antichrist."[7]

Western Christians were in less immediate contact with Islam than the Byzantines, except in Spain, where Islamic occupation dominated Jews and Christians from 718 CE. But antagonism heightened with the Crusades, in which Western Christians launched a series of attacks from the end of the tenth century (1096 CE) until the sixteenth century, supposedly to recapture the Holy Land from the Muslims. In the context of this conflict between Christian and Muslim territories, Western Christians cultivated highly polemical views of Mohammed and Islam. The Byzantine view of Islam as a heresy and an expression of the antichrist were repeated. In addition Western Christian diatribe promulgated scurrilous misinformation.

---

7. See "St. John of Damacus's Critique of Islam," Orthodox Christian Information Center; online: http://orthodoxinfo.com/general/stjohn_islam.aspx/.

The Prophet's followers were said to worship him as a god, and the Muslim god to consist of three idols. Mohammed as a trickster used various devices to deceive his followers. He was portrayed as extremely sensual and sexually immoral. He was said to have been killed by a swine while urinating.

One twelfth-century medieval church leader who sought better information about Islam was Peter the Venerable (1092–1156), abbot of the Benedictine monastery of Cluny in France. Peter went to Spain to find accurate documents on Islam and commissioned a Latin translation of the Qur'an. Yet his own writings on Islam repeated much of the negative attack. Islam, which he called "the sect of the Saracens," is said to be a heresy approaching paganism and is "detestable and damnable."[8] Other medieval leaders, most notably Francis of Assisi during the Crusades, visited the sultan of Egypt and advised Christians to live in peace with Muslims in Muslim lands.[9] In appreciation the Islamic leaders in the Middle East made the Franciscans the custodians of Christian holy places in Palestine, a relationship that still exists.

The Renaissance bought a brief period of advocacy of interfaith dialogue. Nicolas of Cusa (1401–1464) wrote *De pace fidei*, advocating mutual tolerance and recognition of harmony between the different religions.[10] But in the fifteenth and sixteenth centuries Islamic power again impinged on Western Christendom with the conquest of Constantinople by the Ottomans in 1453 and the expansion of Muslim power into Greece and Eastern Europe to the borders of Austria.

Western Europe felt deeply threatened by expanding Ottoman power. Luther, among other Western leaders, responded to this with violent anti-Islamic polemic. Luther saw Islam as the scourge of God to punish Western Christians for their sins. Islam represents the Beast of Daniel 7, whose mouth is full of blasphemies. For Luther, Islam and the papacy are twin enemies of God, Islam being Gog and the papacy Magog. He sees God calling Charles, the Holy Roman emperor, to wage relentless war against the Muslim enemy.[11]

8. See "Peter the Venerable," *Wikipedia*; online: http://en.wikipedia.org/wiki/Peter_the_Venerable/.

9. Paul Moses, *The Saint and the Sultan: Islam and Francis of Assisi's Mission of Peace* (New York: Doubleday, 2009).

10. Nicholas, of Cusa, *De Pace Fidei* (Lewiston, NY: Mellen, 1990).

11. See Adam S. Francisco, *Martin Luther and Islam: A Study in Sixteenth-Century Polemics and Apologetics*, Studies in Christian-Muslim Relations 8 (Leiden: Brill, 2007).

By the nineteenth century this threat had retreated. The Ottoman Empire was falling apart, and European colonialists, represented especially by Britain and France, were busy dividing its territory between themselves for their expanded empires. In this context of a weak Islamic power and an aggressively expanding European colonialism, Europeans became more benign toward Islam. It was seen as appropriate to learn about Islam and to cultivate a positive appreciation, which (hopefully) could lead to their conversion to Christianity or at least their acceptance of European power.

The Vatican II statement on Islam in the document on non-Christian religions is entirely positive and suggests that it is very close to Christianity in both its theology and ethical way of life.

> The Church also has a high regard for the Muslims. They worship God, who is one, living, subsistent, merciful and almighty, the Creator of heaven and earth, who has also spoken to humanity. They endeavor to submit themselves without reserve to the hidden decrees of God, just as Abraham submitted himself to God's plan, to whose faith Muslims eagerly link their own. Although not acknowledging him as God, they venerate Jesus as a prophet; his virgin Mother they also honor and even at times devoutly invoke. Further they await the Day of Judgment and the reward of God following the resurrection of the dead. For this reason they highly esteem an upright life and worship God, especially by way of prayer, alms-deeds and fasting.[12]

Yet in the late twentieth century, particularly with the rise of militant Islamic groups seeking to counteract Western colonialism, as well as the growing presence of Muslims as immigrants in Europe and the United States, a new Islamophobia has arisen. Islam is seen as dangerous, by nature violent, congenitally opposed to the enlightened values of the West. Western people should be on their guard against it.

Jews and Gentiles: The People of Israel and the Nations

Rabbinic Judaism did not spend much time discussing relations to Christianity. It was thought of as a heresy, and the less attention to it the better. Some discussion on this relationship does develop in nineteenth-century

---

12. "Declaration on the Relation of the Church to Non-Christian Religions," (*Nostra Aetate*, 1965), in *Vatican Council II: The Basic Sixteen Documents*, ed. Austin Flannery (Northport, NY: Costello, 1996), 571.

Europe. Islam is also mostly ignored, although Jews recently have explored this in terms of the relation of the two sons of Abraham: Isaac and Ishmael. But the dominant discourse in Judaism about relation to other religions and peoples frames this as the relation of Jews to Gentiles, or to "the nations."

Judaism arose as a tribal religion within the Canaanite peoples of the Middle East in the second millennium BCE. Originally the Hebrew God, or Yahweh was seen as Israel's particular god but not the only god or the creator of the universe. Passages of Hebrew Scripture still contain remnants of this view. Thus Psalm 82 says, "God has taken his place in the divine council, in the midst of the gods he holds judgment" (Ps 82:1), while Deuteronomy speaks of God dividing the nations according to the number of the gods, while allotting Jacob as his share: "the Most High apportioned the nations / . . . / . . . according to the number of the gods; the Lord's own portion was his people, Jacob his allotted share." (Deut 32:8–9).

Prophetic writers sought to enforce monolatry; that is, that Israel should worship Yahweh alone, and turn away from other gods (Ba'als), although research has shown that Yahweh was seen, as late as the sixth century BCE, as having a consort, Asherah.[13] But these other gods were assumed to exist. Only at the time of the exile, in the sixth century BCE, was there a movement from monolatry to monotheism: that is, an effort to claim that the Hebrew God was the sole god of the universe. Thus Isaiah 45 says, "I am the Lord and there is no other; / beside me there is no god . . . / . . . from the rising of the sun / and from the west there is no one besides me; I am the Lord and there is no other: // I form the light and the darkness, I make weal and create woe" (Isa 45:5–7).

Yet this God of the universe remains particularly the God of Israel, who has chosen this particular people as "his portion" among the nations This God has promised his people a land: a land that is given various boundaries in the biblical texts, but that is regularly called "the land of Canaan" or the land of various other tribes, thus acknowledging that it belonged to other peoples, although Israel is engaged in claiming it with God's mandate. The covenant of God with Abram in which God promises Abram's descendants a land is described thus: "To your descendants I will give this land, from the river of Egypt to the great river, the river Euphrates, the land of the Kenites, the Kenizzites, the Kadmonites, the Hittites, the

13. See Saul M. Olyan, *Asherah and the Cult of Yahweh in Israel*, Society of Biblical Literature Monograph Series 34 (Atlanta: Scholars, 1988).

Perizzites, the Rephaim, the Amorites, the Canaanites, the Girgashites and the Jebusites." (Gen 15:18-20, NRSV).

These roots of Judaism in a tribal God and tribal claims of land *vis á vis* other people in areas of Palestine has created a long struggle within Judaism between particularism and universalism. Biblical texts such as the book of Jonah rebuke the belief that God is concerned only with the welfare of Israel and proclaims God's equal concern with other people, such as the Ninevites, who are also under God's gracious care. In the Hellenistic period Jewish philosophers such as Philo (20 BCE—50 CE) adopted Platonic philosophy to interpret Scripture in terms of universal categories, such as the divine *logos* generating the universe and the human soul in its journey to this cosmic God. Christian universalism has its roots in this development of universal spiritual categories in Hellenistic Judaism, expressed in its quest to be a new people of God in which there is "no longer Jew nor Greek" (Gal 3:28).

Yet rabbinic Judaism clung to the sense of God as the "God of Israel" who elected this people as his particular people and is committed to their particular welfare. As the Jewish people were scattered among other nations, often hostile to them, this sense of being a unique people under God's particular care and concern, capable of higher holiness than the degenerate and polluted Gentile world, was seen as vital to their survival.

In the modern world these ideas of the election of Israel by God and the claim to a promised land were seen as embarrassingly primitive notions. Reform Jews in 1880s in the United States declared that America was their promised land, that they were a religious community and not a nation. They made no claim to land in the Middle East, against Christian Zionist efforts to urge their "return" to Palestine.[14] However after the Holocaust and the horror of the murder of millions of Jews by the Nazis, the idea of God as uniquely concerned for the well-being of the Jews fell into crisis for many Jews. How can one believe in a God who would let his people be almost annihilated? The traditional solution to Jewish suffering in rabbinic Judaism was that God was punishing his people for infidelity, but when they repented, he would redeem them. But this idea was now seen as unbelievable. No crimes on the part of Jews could have warranted the sufferings of the Holocaust.

14. See David A. Rausch, *Zionism within Early American Fundamentalism, 1878–1918: A Convergence of Two Traditions*, Texts and Studies in Religion 4 (New York: Mellen, 1979), 88–95.

Dissident Jewish theologian Richard Rubenstein published his critique of this traditional theology in his 1966 book *After Auschwitz*. In this book Rubenstein urged Jews to discard the idea of themselves as an elect people. Rubenstein sees this as a dangerous idea that has inspired Christians to emulate the idea that they are "elect nations," either as in the line of or as superseding Israel's election. Jews should cut the root out of this idea by rejecting this primitive claim of election for themselves.[15]

Most Jewish thinkers were not willing to reject this central idea of Judaism, but liberals sought to reconcile it with universalism. David Novak, a professor of Jewish Studies at the University of Virginia (now at the University of Toronto), in his book *The Election of Israel: The Idea of a Chosen People*, sees this as essential to Jewish religious identity. But he says that it should be seen as "interior to Israel's understanding of its collective responsibility to God." It should not be appropriated as giving Jews any kind of power or privilege over other people.[16] God did not elect Israel because they are better than any other people, but to call them to special responsibility and service in the world.

However with the growth of Zionism and the founding of the State of Israel in May 1948, the ideas of the election of the people Israel and of the promised land took on a new life. That Jews have a unique right to an expanse of territory in Palestine through God's gift of this land to them became the founding claim of Zionism, even among Jews who were otherwise not particularly religious.

The majority of the founders of Jewish Zionism, and the majority of Israeli Jews today, are not religiously observant. They claim the land through a secular idea of Jewish nationalism. All people have a right to a nation-state. Jews too are historically a nation, and like any nation have a right to a state. But Jews uniquely have a right to a state because they have been threatened with annihilation. The protection of a Jewish state is vital to their survival, should such a threat arise again (which they assume is likely to happen because of the endemic anti-Semitism of the "nations"). They have a right to a state in this particular land because this was their national homeland historically. This is the general argument of secular Zionism.

15. Richard L. Rubenstein, *After Auschwitz: Radical Theology and Contemporary Judaism* (Indianapolis: Bobbs-Merrill, 1966), 47–58.

16. David Novak, *The Election of Israel: The Idea of a Chosen People* (Cambridge: Cambridge University Press, 1995).

However in the 1920 and '30s a Jewish religious Zionism was developed, particularly by Rabbi Abraham Isaac Kook (1865–1935), Ashkenazi Chief rabbi of Palestine from 1919 to 1935. Kook drew on mystical rabbinic traditions to develop a vision of the unique holiness of the land of Israel and of the spiritual superiority of Jewish people, who can only be fulfilled as a people by dwelling in this holy land given them by God. For Kook this land lies at the center of creation and is closer to God and less separated from God than the rest of the earth. The Gentile world is unholy and polluted, and Jewish life there is degraded by living in that degenerate world. Only in the land of Israel can the commandments be fulfilled with full efficacy. As more and more Jews gather back into their land, and finally all of them return, the whole cosmos will be restored to its center, and the creation redeemed through the restoration of the people Israel to the Holy Land.

For Kook the people Israel themselves are inherently superior to the nations:

> We are not only different from the nations, . . . but we are also of a much higher and greater spiritual order . . . Our soul encompasses the entire universe and represents its highest unity. It is therefore whole and complete, entirely free of all the disjointedness and the contradictions that prevail among all other people. We are one people, one as the oneness of the universe. This is the enormous spiritual potential of our innate character and the various processes of our historical road, the road of light that passes between the mountains of darkness and perdition, leading us to realize the hidden essence of our nature . . . Yes, we are stronger than all the cultures of the ages and more enduring than all the permanencies of the world. Our longing is to reawaken to life the amplitude of our ancestors—and to be even greater and more exalted than they.[17]

For Kook, however, this spiritual potential can only be fulfilled by dwelling and being purified by the holiness of the promised land. As Jews are restored to their land the whole universe is restored to its center.

The implicit racism of Kook's view of the Jewish people in relation to the other "nations" was further developed by his son, Rabbi Zvi Kook, who became the teacher of the Jewish fundamentalist settler movement, Gush Emunim. For Zvi Kook, all Gentiles are inherently polluted, and their presence in the Holy Land pollutes the land. This applies particularly to

17. Abraham Isaac Kook, "Lights for Rebirth, " in Arthur Hertzberg, ed., *The Zionist Idea: A Historical Analysis and Reader* (New York: Meridian, 1960), 427.

the Palestinians. By contrast, the presence of Jews in the land redeems it from unholiness. Thus the mission of Jews must be to settle throughout the Holy Land and drive out the polluted people (the Palestinians, who presently degrade it), thereby redeeming the land. In Zvi Kook's teachings, ethnic cleansing of the land of Israel from Palestinians becomes a messianic redemptive calling.[18]

Racism in Israeli Zionism, including that of Jewish religious fundamentalism, has not been without its vehement critics among Israeli Jews. One consistent critic over many years was Israel Shahak (1933–2001). A Holocaust survivor, Shahak emigrated to Palestine after having been liberated from the Bergen-Bergen death camp in 1945. Shahak dedicated his life to opposing racism and oppression from any group without exception. He was a leading member of the Israeli League for Human and Civil Rights. He collected and translated into English articles from the mainstream Israeli media to expose the faults of Zionist thinking, published as the *Shahak Papers*. He wrote extensively against Jewish religious fundamentalism and its racism.[19]

Among American Jews one of the major critics of Jewish post-Holocaust theology who argues against Jewish Zionist empowerment at the expense of Palestinians is Marc Ellis. Ellis sees both Jewish and Christian post-Holocaust theology as morally blind to the abuse of power by the State of Israel and to its oppression of the Palestinian people. A new theology needs to arise that would encompass the Holocaust and Jewish empowerment but transform this into a theology and ethic of solidarity between peoples.

Ellis parallels the crisis of identity for Christians after the Holocaust and the crisis of identity for Jews after the empowerment of the State of Israel and its ongoing ethnic cleansing of Palestinians. Just as Christians can only go forward ethically with integrity through solidarity with the Jewish people, so Jews can only find a renewed ethical basis of life through solidarity with Palestinians. The empowerment of Jews through the alliance

18. See Ian Lustick, *For the Land and the Lord: Jewish Fundamentalism in Israel* (New York: New York Council on Foreign Affairs, 1991); also Michael Feige, "Jewish Fundamentalism," in Cheryl A. Rubenberg, ed., *Encyclopedia of the Israeli-Palestinian Conflict* (London: Lynne Rienner, 2010), 2:757–75.

19. Israël Shahak, *Jewish History, Jewish Religion: The Weight of Three Thousand Years*, Pluto Middle Eastern Studies (London: Pluto, 1994); Israël Shahak and Norton Mezvinsky, *Jewish Fundamentalism in Israel*, Pluto Middle Eastern Studies (London: Pluto, 2004).

between the State of Israel and the United States has created a new "Constantinian Judaism" allied with world imperial power. Jewish ethics today can only be done through confrontation with this new Constantinianism and solidarity with its victims. These are the "Jews of conscience," who risk marginalization from the Jewish establishment by telling the truth about the relation of Jews to the world power system.[20]

The Islamic View of Judaism and Christianity

Islam has a much more positive view of the Jewish and Christian traditions, whereas Christianity has seen Islam as simply false, heretical, and even the expression of the antichrist. Islam sees itself as continuing and renewing the religion of Abrahamic monotheism. For Islam, the true understanding of God was given to Adam by God. This true understanding of the oneness of God was renewed by Abraham, by Moses and the prophets, and by Jesus. Mohammed represents the final renewal of monotheism, the final prophet. He adds nothing new to this faith but restores it to its original purity.

The faith of both "peoples of the book"—Jews and Christians—are redemptive, if they follow their own traditions and laws of righteous behavior faithfully. They do not need to become Muslims to be saved. Thus the Qur'an says: "Those who believe [in the Qur'an] and those who follow the Jewish [Scriptures] and the Christians and the Sabians, and who believe in God and the Last Day, and work righteousness, shall have their reward with their Lord: on them shall be no fear, nor shall they grieve" (Qur'an 2:62; see also Qur'an 5:69 for a similar text).[21]

The Qur'an holds Jesus in high esteem, speaking of him in over ninety-three different verses as a prophet, as a messenger, as a servant of God, as the Word from God, as one inspired by the Spirit of God, and as the Messiah. Muslims also affirm the virginity of Mary in birthing Jesus. What Mohammed and Islam firmly reject is the idea that Jesus is God or divine. This is idolatry. It represents the major wrong that a monotheist can do; namely, adding something to God's oneness. On the same grounds Islam

---

20. See Marc H. Ellis, *Ending Auschwitz: The Future of Jewish and Christian Life* (Louisville: Westminster John Knox, 1994); Ellis, *Unholy Alliance: Religion and Atrocity in Our Time* (Minneapolis: Fortress, 1997).

21. *The Holy Qur'an*, trans. Abdullah Yusuf Ali (Elmhurst, IL: Tahrike Tarsikle Qur'an Inc., 2008), 2:61, p. 6.

rejects the Christian Trinity. This is polytheism. While Mohammed is the final prophet and is seen as very righteous, he too is not divine.

In the words of the Qur'an, "O People of the Book! Commit no excesses in your religion: Do not say of God anything but the truth. Christ Jesus the son of Mary was (no more than) a Messenger of God and His Word, which He bestowed on Mary, and a Spirit proceeding from Him: So believe in God and His Messengers. Do not say 'Trinity': desist: it will better for you: for God is One God: glory be to Him: (far Exalted is He) above having a son."[22] In contrast to the classical Christian view of Islam, which was scurrilous and misinformed, this Islamic critique seeks to make a serious theological point from the perspective of a strict monotheism.

For Islam, Judaism continues the tradition of Abraham and Moses and thus is essentially true. The one point on which Islam disagrees with Judaism, significantly enough, is on the election of the Jews. By making themselves an elect people, Jews separate from the universal people of God. Although Arabs within Islam have sometimes sought to position themselves as specially designated to lead, generally Islam affirms that belief in the one God makes no distinctions between nations.

Once Islam came to rule vast territories from Spain and North Africa through the Middle East to India, with large populations of Christians as well as Jews, these people fell under a protected status. They paid their Islamic rulers a tax but could continue their own religions unimpeded. This also gave them some self-government over their own communities in a *dhimmi* system. This was a secondary status within Islamic societies, but how oppressive it was varied in different periods and contexts. At times these communities of non-Muslims experienced strict limitations, but at other times the Islamic rulers made free use of the skills of Christians and Jews and appointed them to the high leadership positions. This was true also in the parts of Spain under Islamic rule from 711 to 1492. At times Jews and Christians flourished with Muslims as virtual equals and held high leadership positions. In other periods, especially when Muslim rigorists came into Spain from North Africa and sought to "renew" what they saw as the appropriate order, strict subordination was imposed on Jews and Christians for a time.[23]

22. Ibid., 7:144.

23. For an overview of Muslim Spanish history, see Hugh Kennedy, *Muslim Spain and Portugal: A Political History of Al-Andalus* (London: Longman, 1996).

While Islam has not been a religion that forced Jews and Christians to convert, or even Hindus to convert, in the years it ruled India, it has been, from the time of Mohammed into the Ottoman period, a religion of conquest. This means it has regularly created Islamic states. *Sharia*, or Islamic law, ruled Muslims in these states, and also governed the general way of life of all the people under their rule, although those of other faiths, such as Jews and Christians, maintained certain interior laws related to their own religion. For *Sharia* to be established as the law of the land where Muslims prevail has been a part of the Islamic ideal, so it is a challenge for Muslims to live in Western societies that separate religion and state. This has also been the source of a certain paranoia among uninformed right-wing Americans, who have several times claimed that Muslims in the US are trying to establish *Sharia* as law in some area of the US.

Needless to say, when Christianity took over in Spain in the fifteenth century, completing its reconquest, there was no tolerance of Jews or Muslims at all. Jews and Muslims were told to either get out of Spain or to convert to Catholicism. In practice, the Catholic powers did not allow Jews and Muslims to leave but demanded their conversion. Even those who converted were then put under inquisitorial surveillance on the assumption that these *conversos* and *moriscos* were not really converted but were maintaining their Jewish and Muslim faiths under cover.[24]

Jews, Christians, and Muslims: Becoming Equals in the US? In Israel?

Can Jews, Christians, and Muslims, given this often oppressive history on several sides, become sibling people? Can they work together and come to see each other as people who have more similarities than differences, who share a common religious heritage and ethical values? Can those things which have sharply separated them from each other be put aside and come to be seen as unimportant? In this section of this chapter I will explore how this question is being experienced in Claremont, a town in Southern California, where I live and teach.

On September 11, 2001, planes crashed into the World Trade Center in New York City and into the Pentagon in northern Virginia. A fourth plane, allegedly headed for Washington DC, was diverted and crashed in

24. For a classical study of the Moriscos, see Henry Charles Lea, *The Moriscos of Spain: Their Conversion and Expulsion* (Westport CT: Greenwood, 1901).

Pennsylvania. About three thousand people were killed. Although this is disputed by some,[25] the official American view is that this attack was carried out by militant Muslims from the Al-Queda movement. This attack unleashed a wave of Islamophobia in the United States, causing random attacks on Muslims or people assumed to be Muslims.

In Claremont the Muslim community was afraid that there would be some hostile gestures toward their children going to and coming from a local Muslim school. People from several Christian churches organized themselves to come out and for two weeks formed a protective line around these children as they went to and came from school. No hostile gestures actually happened, but this Christian response helped establish a new sense of relationship between the Christian and Muslim communities in Claremont.

New forms of relationship between Christians, Jews, and Muslims began to develop in this area. Claremont is an academic town and has five undergraduate colleges: Pomona College, Scripps College, Harvey Mudd College, Claremont McKenna College, and Pitzer College; two graduate schools: Claremont Graduate University and Keck Graduate Institute of Applied Life Sciences; and a theological seminary: Claremont School of Theology. At many colleges and universities in the United States at this time, there was a strong insistence on having a Muslim presence on the teaching faculty, particularly in the field of religion. Institutions in Claremont were no different. A Muslim woman was hired to teach at Pomona College in the field of religion, and a Muslim scholar joined the faculty of the School of Religion in Claremont Graduate University.

At the same time, the Claremont School of Theology began to make plans to become an interfaith seminary. This meant more than simply adding some world religion courses to a Christian curriculum and encouraging Christian students to take one or more classes on other religions. It is seen as developing additional schools, with faculty and students of other religions, that would join with the School of Theology to offer a full curriculum to prepare students of the other faiths to become leaders in their own religions. The Academy for Jewish Religion, California, a transdenominational Jewish institution to educate rabbis, cantors, chaplains, and counselors, and the Islamic Center of Southern California to train imams

25. A small group of dissidents believe that this attack was actually carried out by the Bush administration of the American government to facilitate an invasion of Iraq: see David Ray Griffin, *The New Pearl Harbor: Disturbing Questions about the Bush Administration and 9/11* (Northampton, MA: Olive Branch, 2004).

and other Muslim leaders, have joined in this coalition. In the fall of 2011, the Federation of Jain Associations of North America and the International School for Jain Studies also were finalizing their relation to this coalition as well.

In the summer of 2011 a new university was announced: the Claremont Lincoln University, to provide the umbrella institution for these additional schools. The School of Theology will continue as a Christian seminary, but it has also added to its faculty a Muslim woman from Kashmir in religious education and a Jewish man from Argentina in global ethics. This is an unprecedented development in Western theological education. Educating together men and women of these many faiths is a radically new experiment. It is as yet unknown how these students and faculty will come to experience working, teaching, learning, and living together in this way. But at the very least it means that the Christians put aside Christian theological exclusivism.

At the same time in Claremont additional interfaith activities were developing. The traditionally Christian Pomona Valley organization on Peace and Justice came to be headed by a Muslim, so people became used to public observances (such as Hiroshima Day, mourning the dropping of the atom bomb on Japan in 1945) being led by an imam. Peace marches became interfaith, with the witnesses moving from a synagogue to churches to a mosque, stopping for prayer and song at each place and hearing speakers from the three traditions.

The high point of this joint religious social justice sharing in 2011 was an interfaith Seder, called From Slavery to Freedom. Sponsored by the Claremont Working Group on Mid-East Peace and prepared by Jewish, Christian, and Muslim leaders, it was held at a mosque on Sunday, April 17, 2011. A similar interfaith Seder was celebrated again in April of 2012. A few quotes from the 2011 liturgy give a very slight sense of the richness of this moving yet festive celebration.

The introduction read,

> All of our religious traditions share the basic values necessary to create a world where tolerance and peace prevail. We have an opportunity and also the challenge to build bridges between our faiths. Those who attempt to repeat history by dividing humanity along religious and ethnic lines must not be allowed to succeed. We must find a way out of the deadlock, despair and desperation, reaching out to one another, not with the wrong kind of farsightedness, but with confidence, courage and reconciliation. This

is why we join as one this afternoon to celebrate all of our journeys from slavery to redemption, as viewed through the window of the age-old ritual of the Passover Seder. We come to celebrate the message of freedom—through which must come truth and reconciliation.[26]

The opening lighting of the candles evoked the common lineage from Abraham, our ancestor. Texts about deliverance from many successive slaveries through Jewish history were paralleled with a Islamic perspective, which concluded with the following affirmation: "Negation of all forms oppression—the basic message of all the prophets, through sustained peaceful struggle is real Faith (or *Iman* in Arabic) and a passionate commitment to justice and peace is real submission to God."[27]

The first cup of the Seder, calling people together, included the famous inclusive blessing from Isaiah 19:25: "Blessed be Egypt my people, and Assyria the work of my hands and Israel my inheritance." The Seder then went on to reflect on the parallel stories of the two children of Abraham: of Ishmael, child of Hagar, and Yitzchak, child of Sarah. The separation and sufferings of each must be overcome by a new coming together, as these two sons came together to bury their father Abraham. These two children are then identified with the two people, Israelis and Palestinians, and they are called to share the land together, even as we share the same bread of the Seder.

Jesus is quoted in summoning us to the difficult task to "love your enemy." This is followed by a reading from the prophet Mohammed's last sermon: "All mankind is from Adam and Eve, an Arab has no superiority over a non-Arab, nor a non-Arab over an Arab; a white has no superiority over a black, nor a black any superiority over a white except by piety and good action. Learn that every Muslim is a brother to every other Muslim and that Muslims constitute one brotherhood. Nothing shall be legitimate to a Muslim which belongs to a fellow Muslim unless it is given freely and willingly. Do not therefore do injustice to yourselves."[28]

At the interfaith Seder, various Passover foods were interpreted in the light of this quest for reconciliation. This included the egg as a symbol of fertility and birth. It was said that today Hagar and Sarah must give birth to

26. "From Slavery to Freedom: An Interfaith Seder," March 24, 2013, p. 2 (unpublished).

27. Ibid., 3.

28. Ibid., 4.

two new people, Hagar to the children of Israel and Sarah to the children of Ishmael. The Seder culminated with each group around each of the different tables telling each other the stories of their own struggles for freedom and what liberation from oppression has meant to each of them. The final blessing says, "We all dream of a world not threatened by the destructiveness of war, of bigotry, of pollution. We dream of a time of brotherhood and sisterhood. We dream of a time when all people are free to be themselves and live with dignity. We dream of a world at peace."

The theology of this Seder liturgy suggests ways in which Jews, Christians, and Muslims, when they worship together, begin to recognize their mutual enrichment from one another's tradition. Although each retains its distinctiveness and no one is called to disappear into the other, yet each begins to see the others as the religious cousins that they are. For Jews, Jesus ceases to be the threat that calls them to disappear into a new covenant and rather is revealed as a Jewish prophet. Not God's "only son," but one Jewish prophet among others—perhaps a minor one, but one whose language can be very much recognized as belonging to Jewish prophetic self-critique and liberating hope.

So too for Christians and Jews, Mohammed can cease to be the alien fanatic speaking an unknown tongue. Many of his sayings can be recognized as helpful prophetic admonitions and calls to justice. For Muslims he is the final prophet. For Jews and Christians he might not be the final prophet but a recognizable latter-day prophet. For Muslims, Moses and Jesus are already prophets, but actual study of the Scriptures of these earlier faiths makes it less necessary for Muslims to dogmatize their "distortion," even as the Qur'an remains as their touchstone. In these ways Judaism, Christianity, and Islam cease to threaten one another and become assets for one another.

This Seder was a brief moment of exhilarating togetherness, but deep separations continue to exist in the larger world between people of the three faiths. Jewish exceptionalism, particularly as institutionalized in Israel as a Jewish state, oppresses Palestinian Christians and Muslims, even preventing them from getting to church and mosque in Jerusalem. Christian exclusivism, claiming that Christ alone is God's son and humanity's savior, is the rhetoric of most Christian worship services. There are still states where Catholicism is the established religion, making Protestants, as well as other religions, second class. Islamic states make Christianity second class in many areas, and in some areas this erupts in violence against churches. Thus we are far from a world of peaceful coexistence of religions.

The establishment of religious states where one faith is the favored religion of the state, and all others are second class, repressed or excluded, has been the historical context of religious exclusivism. Catholic or Orthodox Christianity was the established church of Christendom after the reign of Constantine in the fourth century, and this lasted into the nineteenth century. Separation of church and state and the offer of citizenship to the Jews in Europe created an anti-Semitic backlash, leading to Nazism and the Holocaust. Today Europe, the US, and Canada take for granted separation of church and state, privatizing religion and making all religions supposedly equal before the law, although this is questionable in France, where Muslim women are not allowed to wear the *nigab* (face veil) in public. But the continued existence of Islamic states and the creation of the Jewish state in Israel create disabilities for people of different religious-ethnic communities.

In the United States privatization of religion and secularization of the state were foundational principles. Thomas Jefferson inscribed into the 1791 Bill of Rights the basic rule: "Congress shall make no law respecting the establishment of religion or prohibiting the free exercise thereof." But most Americans assumed that meant the equality of all Protestant Christians. Catholics and Jews were looked on with suspicion, and anti-Catholic movements insisted that Catholics could not be "real Americans." The election of John F. Kennedy in 1960 served to dissipate this prejudice. In 2011 the nine justices of the United States Supreme Court were six Catholics, three Jews, and no Protestants, a surprising change given that this body historically has been made up mostly of male Protestants.

Into the second decade of the twenty-first century Muslims are subject to a similar suspicion, with many Americans claiming that Muslims can't be "good Americans." Islamophobia is rife among some groups of congressional leaders. Congressmen Peter King, in hearings before the House Homeland Security Committee claimed that 85 percent of American mosques were led by Islamic radicals.[29] A June 2011 report by the Center of Race and

---

29. WND-TV reported that in a 2004 interview with talk-show host Sean Hannity, King said that "80–85 percent of mosques in this country are controlled by Islamic fundamentalists," and that he could "stand by the number of 85 percent" (online: http://www.wnd.com/2004/02/23257/). This number appeared on the Politico blog in September of 2007. See the transcript of the hearing online: http://www.gpo.gov/fdsys/pkg/CHRG-112hhrg72541/pdf/CHRG-112hhrg72541.pdf/.

Gender at University of California, Berkeley, reported that Islamophobia is on the rise in the US. Plans of Muslim communities to build a mosque in particular areas sometimes bring vehement protests from Christians in the neighborhood. Muslims are put on the spot to prove that they are democratic, even though all evidence has shown that Muslims in the US are generally upper middle class, educated, and well integrated into American society. In 2007 Minnesota elected the first Muslim in Congress, a Black American convert who took his oath of office on a Qur'an that had been owned by Thomas Jefferson.

The development of the inferfaith theological seminary in Claremont is an opportunity for a sector of American Muslims to develop what they can see as a distinctively American understanding of Islam. Heretofore many mosques have been dependent on imams trained in the Middle East, with Saudi Arabia playing a major role in sending religious leaders to the United States and other nations around the world. What does it mean for Muslims to accept separation of religion and state as normative for society, in contrast to the historical Islamic tradition?

This is a topic of considerable interest to a new generation of Muslim thinkers, including to Tariq Ramadan, Swiss-born Muslim philosopher and professor at Oxford University. Ramadan was barred from teaching at the University of Notre Dame in 2004 and from speaking at US conferences on the grounds that he is a radical. This ban was finally lifted by Hilary Clinton in 2010. Ramadan argues that Islam is diverse and is undergoing new development in the West. Among his works exploring these themes is his *Western Muslims and the Future of Islam* and *Radical Reform, Islamic Ethics, and Liberation*.[30] These are topics that will be undoubtedly of interest in the new interfaith university in Claremont.

Despite the current waves of Islamophobia, Muslims are clearly on their way to becoming a part of American society, and Islam accepted as an American religion. Muslims, on the basis of American separation of religion and state, have the legal basis for equality. They are integrating into American society while maintaining their own distinctive traditions. This integration makes it possible for them to reach out to interrelate with Jews and Christians, as well as with other religious groups. Yet simply becoming American is not a sufficient goal. Islam, Judaism, and Christianity are

30. Tariq Ramadan, *Western Muslims and the Future of Islam* (Oxford: Oxford University Press, 2004); Ramadan, *Radical Reform, Islamic Ethics, and Liberation* (Oxford: Oxford University Press, 2009).

prophetic religions. Once freed from fusion into religious states and their power agendas, they can reclaim their prophetic visions of peace and justice. As in the vision of the Freedom Seder, the three faith communities of the Abrahamic tradition are coming together as prophetic communities that can call America and all human societies to better justice and peace.

Can this call be heard in relation to US policies in the Middle East? Can the wall that separates Jews from Palestinians in Israel be torn down? Can democracy begin to flourish in Libya, Egypt, Syria, Iraq, Iran, even Saudi Arabia? Can Israel take its place as a people of the Middle East rather than as a hostile presence? Can Muslims, Jews, and Christians enrich one another with their skills and intelligence, rather than being set up to tear one another down? It remains to be seen how interfaith friendships in some small corners in the United States, such as in Claremont schools and churches, can make spaces in which the imperial role that the US plays (and that American Christians play) in keeping these unjust power relations in place in the Middle East and globally are honestly discussed. Can this new dialogue and interrelationship become a base for this broader transformation? This is our hope.

4

Explorations in Religion and Atheism
Beyond Monotheism

When I arrived in Claremont in 1954 to start college, I was disposed to an interest in the study of religion. My work with Quakers in La Jolla and participation in protest marches with Helen Beardsley gave me the sense that religion was or should be on the side of social justice and peace. I wrote some editorials on religion and justice for the school paper I edited and was asked to give the address on "A Time for Religion" at my high school graduation.

This interest was confirmed by an experience I had soon after arriving at Scripps College. Some information I was given promoting the study of science at the Claremont Colleges hit me in a very negative way. Science was described as giving access to factual truth in a way that seemed to disparage moral, mystical, or aesthetic knowledge as unscientific. I don't remember where this information came from and have no reason to think it represented the view of scientists at the Claremont Colleges. But the viewpoint chilled me, as if I had confronted a negation of the forms of meaning dear to me. My interest in the study of religion was thereby shaped by a quest for hope and meaning that included the forms of knowing that were being negated by this reductionist view of science. Religion, for me, did not necessarily mean Christianity.

Studies in Greek and Ancient Near Eastern Paganism

Although I had come to Scripps College to study painting, I was soon drawn into the circle of students who did classics under the tutelage of Robert

90

Palmer (as mentioned in chapter 1). Palmer had a significant effect on my studies in religion in my first years in college. Palmer was negative toward Christianity and felt it was too bad that it had won at the end of antiquity, rather than some other more humanistic form of cosmological thought on offer at the time. But he was deeply interested in the religions of the ancient Greeks. For him the cultures of the Greeks—from Homer's *Iliad* and *Odyssey* through the poets and tragedians, as well as the plastic arts—were more than aesthetic and literary. They were profoundly rooted in a religious vision. This vision he sought to communicate through his teaching.

I remember vividly a lecture in which Palmer introduced us to this perspective on Greek religion with the phrase, "first the god, then the dance and then the story." Religion begins in theophany, in the appearance of the god in human experience. The god does not begin as a theory or an intellectual construction. The god is really there, even if not seen by everyone. One experiences her awesome presence. This compelling experience is then re-created in liturgy, dance, song, and ecstatic mime. Cult is the expression of these experiences of the deity. From cult then comes the story or the myth, as the third-hand derivative of theophany and its cultic re-creation. Dogma, or intellectual theory and rationalization, is even further removed from the actual experience of the appearance of the god, a much later speculation on story or myth when the actual experience has grown cold and is being lost.

In this view of Greek religion, Palmer was deeply influenced by the German classicist Walter Friedrich Otto, author of *The Homeric Gods* (1929) and *Dionysus: Myth and Cult* (1933). Palmer was the translator of Otto's second book on Dionysus.[1] For Otto, Christians have failed to recognize the Homeric gods as religious. They have assumed that they were trivial and even immoral, entirely missing the spiritual vision expressed by these gods. This spirituality is the polar opposite of the Christian view, but nevertheless deeply pious. Far from being antinatural and a negation of this world, as is the classical Christian view, the Homeric gods reveal the depths of distinct realms of the natural itself.

For Otto the Olympian gods that shape the spirituality of the Homeric epics were themselves built on the transcendence of an earlier world of gods: the "dark" earth mother and her manifestations, the *Moirai* or fates who decree the limits of human life, and the *Erinyes* or "furies," who protect

---

1. Walter F. Otto, *The Homeric Gods: The Spiritual Significance of Greek Religion* (New York: Octagon, 1978); Otto, *Dionysus: Myth and Cult*, trans. and with an introduction by Robert B. Palmer (Bloomington: Indiana University Press, 1965).

the blood claims of the clan and especially of the mother. These earth powers are left behind by the Olympians, who represent the triumph of the "masculine over the feminine"—clarity and rationality over "blood." Even though leading Olympians, such as Athena, Artemis, and Aphrodite, are female, at their center is the Father God Zeus. All dwell, not in or on earth, but in the heavens, beyond the literal mountain of Olympus.

Yet the Olympians are not antinature but manifestations of distinct essences of the natural world. The earth powers, while transcended by the Olympians, are not abolished but rather limited to a restricted sphere. Thus in the classical tragedy of Aeschylus's *Oresteia*, the rights of the mother are represented by the earth dieties, the Erinyes; and the rights of the father are represented by the Olympians Apollo and Athena. Athena casts the deciding vote in favor of father-right, as a father's daughter born from Zeus's head: "For me no mother bore within her womb, and save for wedlock evermore eschewed I vouch myself the champion of the man, not of the woman. Yea, with all my soul, in heart, as birth, a father's child alone. Thus I will not too heinously regard a woman's death who did her husband slay, the guardian of her home, and if the votes do equal fall, Orestes shall prevail" (*The Eumenides*, 734–44).[2] But the Erinyes are not destroyed, but only contained, their furious power reconciled to the new society as the "kindly ones," or the Eumenides.

Walter Otto delights in illuminating the distinct human/natural sphere in which each of the key Olympians appears in Homeric literature. Athena is an armed goddess, devoid of maternal feelings and wholly on the side of male heroes. She makes her appearance to a favorite hero (seen only by him) in crucial moments when she always stands on the side of the effective decision in the midst of action, against rash impulse that can lead to destruction. Apollo, by contrast, represents distance, cool self-knowledge, a purity of mental-bodily harmony, represented by the music of the lyre. The "far-darter," he strikes with his arrows but also heals. Artemis, Apollo's sister, is also distant, but the distance of the untamed wilderness that no man can conquer. She nurtures wild animal cubs but also strikes animals down with her arrows. She is the huntress.

Aphrodite, by contrast, is all erotic attraction, feminine nature in bloom, born from the sea, but not confined to marriage and conjugal

2. Aeschylus's *The Eumenides*, in Whitney J. Oates and Eugene O'Neill, eds., *The Complete Greek Drama* (New York: Random House, 1938), 1:297.

duties. She lures men and women to transgress the social bonds of family and marriage, drawn by the promise of sexual delight in the love embrace. Hermes, the messenger of the gods, is not fully an Olympian but bridges between earth and heaven. He is a trickster, kind to robbers, giver of windfall luck and patron of the quick draw of the successful merchant. He is the psychopomp who accompanies the souls of the dead to their underworld resting place, but also occasionally leads a soul upward back to the living world. For modern interpreters of texts he is the genius of "hermeneutics." Each of these gods represents, not just an idea or a particular physical force, but a realm of human experience in the context of living activity.

Otto saved a separate book for his disclosure of the being of Dionysus, a god whose presence also fascinated Palmer, the translator of Otto's book. Dionysus also is not quite an Olympian. He stands between the dark world of earth goddesses and Greek lyric culture. He is the spirit of ecstatic joy and madness; the power of the vine. He is surrounded by women, but women who have transgressed their domestic sphere and rushed out into wild nature in violent pandemonium, tearing apart representatives of male social authority and devouring children. Horror, tragedy, and finally death appear in the wake of Dionysus and his maenads, realms alien to the Olympians in their heavenly sphere. He is phallic power, fullness of life, but also sudden death, yet death from which new life arises. Again, for Otto (and Palmer) Dionysus is not mere idea or physical force, but a whole realm of being, a god.

For me, reading this literature, as a part of reading Greek classics, was fascinating. But it also raised questions. Along with a Jewish friend who also studied classics with Palmer, I took a course on the Hebrew prophets and was introduced to a very different deity. He too was violent and warlike but also demanded justice in human affairs, an idea foreign to the Olympian gods. I remember reflecting on which of these gods really existed and deciding that they both existed. The demand for justice was something important to me, something I wanted to make integral to my understanding of truth; but the Greek gods, disclosed in realms of nature, were also real. One did not trump the other, but stood each in their distinct worldviews.

In my doctoral thesis on the fourth-century Cappadocian church father Gregory Nazianzus, I became aware of the ambiguity of patristic Christianity toward the Greek classics and their gods. In treatises "against the nations" (i.e., against Greek paganism) of the second to fourth centuries, written by such church fathers as Tatian, Tertullian, and Clement of

Alexandria, the pagan gods are dismissed as utterly debased and immoral.[3] Much is made of the sexual dalliance of gods, such as Zeus, to show the complete unworthiness of paganism as religion. In this the church fathers were not original but largely followed the line that had already been laid out by Greek philosophers who decried the immortality of the gods, but in the service of turning paganism into philosophical allegory.

The emperor Julian the apostate, who wished to revive paganism as the religious basis of Hellenistic culture, tried to trap the Christian leaders at their own game. Since many of them, such as Gregory Nazianzus and Basil the Great, had been trained in Greek rhetoric, based on Greek literature that celebrated the gods, he sought to ban Christians from teaching rhetoric (that is, teaching higher culture at all) by decreeing that those who did not believe in the Greek gods should not be allowed to teach the literature that celebrated them.[4]

Gregory and Basil were outraged, but Julian soon died and the threat was removed. Christians who cultivated rhetoric realized that they needed to defend their use of Greek culture for literary style while denying the gods. Basil the Great wrote the key treatise on this: "Admonition to Young Men on the Profitable Use of Pagan Literature." Basil argues that this literature is very profitable to learn elegant linguistic style, but one needs to ignore the content having to do with the affairs of the gods: "separate the honey from the thorns" is his advice.[5]

By this strategy the church fathers helped preserve Greek literature as culture, by making it purely aesthetic. The gods lived on in Western Christian art and literature, the literary basis of Western education into the twentieth century, by teaching Christian students to delight in the outward form while firmly disbelieving in its content. Walter Otto, trained in this same literature in the late nineteenth-century German university, transgressed these rules by reading this literature more deeply and rediscovering the experience of the Greek gods as religious.

The interpretations of the classics that I read in the 1950s contained not only a belief about the religious validity of the Greek gods but also a theory about the evolution of gender in Greek society. Walter Otto, as well as his disciple and our teacher, Robert Palmer, assumed a two-stage

---

3. Tatian, "Oration to the Greeks"; Tertullian, "Ad nationes"; and Clement of Alexandria, *Protrepticus* or "The Exhortation to the Gentiles."

4. Julian was emperor from 355 to 362. See his *Against the Galileans*, c. 362.

5. See Basil the Great, "Admonitions to Young Men on the Profitable Use of Literature."

theory of the development of society and the gods. There was the old world, presumably going back to the Minoan period of the second millennium BCE, of the earth goddess and her "dark, feminine" powers, which was superseded by the Olympians sometime in the eighth century BCE as the triumph of "masculine" heavenly spirituality over "feminine" "tellerism." This dualism of feminine and masculine as earthy and heavenly was assumed to have something to do, not only with the nature of the gods of each stage, but also with the nature of women and men. Women as a group were presumed to be tied to irrational earth power, while males have a capacity for transcendent rationality.

This view of female earthiness versus masculine spirit is reflected in a typical passage in Otto: The earth goddesses "are bound up with the stuff of the earth and partake of its grimness and constraint. Their favors are that of the maternal element, and their law has the sternness of all ties of blood . . . the female sex is predominant among the divinities of this world. In the heavenly group of the Homeric religion, on the other hand, the female sex recedes in a manner that cannot be accidental. There the gods who are dominant are not only of the masculine sex, but most decidedly represent the masculine spirit. Though Athena is associated with Zeus and Apollo in the supreme triad, she expressly denies her feminine aspect and makes herself a genius of masculinity."[6]

In this hierarchical sequence of masculine over feminine, heavenly over earthly, Otto and other classists of that period reflected the dominant anthropology of the late nineteenth century, shaped by Johann Jakob Bachofen. This anthropological theory was not based on empirical research into existing "primitive" societies, but was itself an extrapolation from the Greek classics. Not surprisingly, classicists like Otto found it congenial. For Bachofen, human society evolved through three stages. The oldest and most primitive was unlimited male promiscuity. This was followed by a matriarchal stage in which women as mothers dominated, and descent was traced through the mother. The third and highest stage comes about through the overthrow of matriarchy, the suppression of its earth-bound patterns, the imposition of patriarchy, father rule and the tracing of descent through the father. This patriarchal revolution is represented by the Olympian gods and, at its fullest, in the creation of Roman law.[7]

6. Otto, *The Homeric Gods*, 154.

7. J. J. Bachofen, *Myth, Religion and Mother Right: Selected Writings of J. J. Bachofen*, Bollingen Series 84 (Princeton: Princeton University Press, 1967).

In addition to Otto, one of Palmer's favorite scholars of the evolution of classical culture was Jane Ellen Harrison (1850–1928), whose writings we also read assiduously. Harrison assumed a similar view of the evolution of female earth religion superseded by patriarchal sky religion of the Olympian gods in the emergence of Greek society. In her 1903 *Prolegomena to the Study of Greek Religion*, Harrison delineates a matriarchal stage where women as mothers and agriculturalist dominate.[8]

But this female dominance was based on a mistaken belief that women alone possessed the power of fecundity in humans, animals and the earth. Once men realized their own possession of male inseminating power, it was a short step to subjugating women's fertility and, with it, women themselves as weak and dependent. Although Harrison sees this as a regression, she nevertheless regards it as a necessary stage leading to a third possibility in which women along with men can free themselves from subjugation to reproductive power and become celibate spiritual beings, a stage she finds in gnosticism, Christian asceticism, and in her own life in the early twentieth-century university.[9]

By the end of the 1950s I began to question this anthropological narrative. The theories of the transcendence of patriarchy over matriarchy as universal stages in human evolution began to appear increasingly questionable in mid-twentieth century anthropology as empirically based research into many particular societies gained over nonempirical theory based on classical literature. Female anthropologists began to emerge and to demonstrate the variety of ways in which gender, as well as class and age, are organized in different societies.

It thus came as something of a shock to me when there emerged in feminist theory in the late 1970s a new version of the narrative of "original matriarchy" seen as a universal stage of female dominance, represented by the worship of a single Great Goddess. Far from being identified with an inferior earth-bound irrationality, women and goddess rule were hailed as the garden of Eden, humans in harmony with the earth and one another. This mother rule was seen as governing all societies from earliest Paleolithic times until about the fifth millennium BCE.

8. See Jane Harrison, *Epilegomena to the Study of Greek Religion* (1921; reprinted, New York: University Books, 1962). See also Harrison, *Themis: A Study of the Social Origins of Greek Religion* (New York: University Books, 1962).

9. See my analysis of Harrison in Rosemary Radford Ruether, *Goddesses and the Divine Feminine* (Berkeley: University of California Press, 2005), 260–63.

The overthrow of original matriarchy by patriarchy was now seen as a fall rather than as progress, as it was in the system espoused by Bachofen and Otto. This fall was seen as coming from the invasion of violent, horse-riding, militaristic males subjugating the earlier harmonious society, leading to increasingly oppressive social systems and ecodestruction, ending in a final crisis threatening the survival of humanity and the earth today. Feminists, women and men, were called to overthrow this violent and oppressive world system and recover that ecologically harmonious goddess-worshiping society of prefallen humanity. Male monotheisms of Judaism, Christianity, and Islam were assumed to be the expressions of the religion of patriarchy, while all paganism partook of prowoman goddess worship.

This worldview, as it was being announced by a some thinkers in the late 1970s, struck me as an mistaken ideology that reduced to a simplistic dualism the complex ways human cultures had developed, not only worldwide, but also in those sites of the emergence of Western religion in the ancient Near East and Greece. Having struggled to sort out this history and its theoretical interpretation for more than twenty years, I was astonished to see how the rediscovery of several texts of nineteenth-century matriarchal theory, themselves questionable, were being misread in a new way.

I tried to raise some questions about this in a couple of articles,[10] only to receive a vehement counterattack that assumed that I spoke simply as a Christian averse to taking paganism seriously as a religion. Since I had been taking paganism seriously as a religion since the mid-1950s, this had little to do with the background of my questions. I realized that much of this vehemence had little to do with me, but rather expressed the woundedness of women freeing themselves from patriarchal religions that had injured them and feeling hurt that a leading feminist from the previous generation would seemingly question their newfound liberation. I realized that I needed to withdraw from the immediacy of this fray and put these questions of gender status, human and divine, in a larger context. The result twenty-five years later was my 2005 book, *Goddesses and the Divine Feminine: A Western Religious History*.

This book begins with an exploration of the theory of prehistory of Marija Gimbutas, author of such books as *Gods and Goddess in Old*

---

10. See Rosemary Radford Ruether, "A Religion for Women: Resources and Strategies," *Christianity and Crisis* (December 10, 1979) 307–11; and Ruether, "Goddesses and Witches: Liberation and Counter-cultural Feminism," *Christianity and Crisis* (September 10–17, 1980) 842–47.

Europe.[11] Gimbutas's views formed the historical basis for the thought of those feminists arguing for a long, universal stage of Eden-like matriarchy. Gimbutas's views have been vehemently contested by paleoanthropologists such as Margaret Conkey and Ruth Tringham.[12] They also disagreed with the dominant-male anthropologists, who claimed universal patriarchy. Rather Conkey and Tringham see various ways in which gender was negotiated in prehistory, but generally in ways that give women active roles.

In my book I then move on to discuss early Babylonian, Canaanite, Egyptian, and Greek societies where patriarchal patterns were being established. I discuss particularly four major goddess figures of these societies, Inanna/Ishtar, Anat, Isis, and Demeter. There is no evidence that these goddesses descend from some earlier stage of matriarchal societies. As they exist in their particular societies, they express a construction of female divinity that sacralizes royal or aristocratic dominance in which women have power with men in this ruling class. The only goddess tradition where there is evidence of some resistance to male dominance is that of Demeter, but there too males predominate, even in the leadership of Demeter's cult.

A third chapter discusses the polytheism and existence of a female consort of Yahweh in early Hebrew religion. Although these elements are gradually eliminated for monotheism by the sixth century BCE, the female companion or agent of God takes a new form in the figure of Sophia or Wisdom from the fifth to first century BCE. Jewish mysticism continues to cultivate into modern times a female personification of God, often seen as God's wife, in the figure of the Shekinah. The figure of Wisdom is also key for the presence of female expressions of God in Christianity, playing a role in the development of Christology and reappearing in medieval and early modern Christian mysticism. Thus while male imagery for the divine predominates in Judaism and Christianity, neither religion is devoid of images of female divinity.

---

11. Marija Gimbutas, *Goddesses and Gods of Old Europe, 6500–3500 B.C.* (Berkeley: University of California Press, 1982).

12. See Lynn Meskell, "Goddesses, Gimbutas and New Age Archaeology," and Margaret W. Conkey and Ruth Tringham, "Archaeology and the Goddess," in Donna C. Stanton and Abigail J. Stewart, eds., *Feminisms in the Academy*, Women and Culture Series (Ann Arbor: University of Michigan Press, 1995), 199–247; also Margaret Conkey and Ruth Tringham, "Rethinking Figurines: A Critical View from Archaeology to Gimbutas, the 'Goddess' and Popular Culture," in Lucy Goodison and Christine Morris, eds., *Ancient Goddesses: The Myths and the Evidence* (London: British Museum Press, 1998), 22–45.

The most exclusively male expression of Christianity is actually mainline Protestantism, developed in the sixteenth century, which eliminates Mariology and the role of saints. But even in Lutheranism there is the deviant mystic, Jacob Boehme, with a powerful imagery of the reciprocity of the male and female, or the Wisdom dimensions of God in the redemption of the soul. From Boehme's tradition flows a whole line of Protestant mystical-millennialism, culminating in the nineteenth-century Shakers, who entertain a dual, male–female idea of the divine.

Nineteenth-century Europe saw the beginning of a feminist challenge to patriarchal rule. In response, patriarchal theorists sought to reassert women's natural inferiority and the perennial dominance of males in all societies, or else an idealized complementarity of women's roles in the privatized family in relation to males as rulers in the public sphere. It is in this context that male historians and archaeologists reread the development of ancient Mediterranean society as the rise of spiritual patriarchy from earlier earth-bound matriarchy, theories reflected in the thought of anthropologists such as Bachofen and classicists such as Walter Otto.

The concluding chapter of my book traces how renewed feminism found one expression in the 1970s in a vision of an original, ideal matriarchy and the development of the religious practices of a goddess movement. This movement sought a comprehensive transformation of cultures from male dominance to the empowerment of women and the restoration of a just and harmonious ordering of society. Although I question the theories of prehistory in this movement, I agree with many of their ideas about the crisis of male-dominant society and see the need for a transformative alternative. Today Wiccan or goddess-worshipping groups have become an organized religion in the American religious spectrum, even winning a place as chaplaincies in the army and in the prison system.

As these groups have developed, there is less dogmatism about what must have existed in prehistory. More important is what kind of society and spirituality needs to exist today. Ecofeminists among Christians and in other established religions share many of the same values as Wiccans, both in terms of human rights for women and the need for harmonious relations with the environment. An alliance across these groups, I think, is appropriate. In my own teaching in feminist theologies in North America, I regularly include speakers and readings from Jewish, Muslim, and Buddhist feminism and from Wicca.

The Challenge of Buddhism

Having discussed the role that studies in pre-Christian paganism have had in my intellectual development from 1954 to today, I turn to the importance of another non-Christian religion in my thought, namely, Buddhism. In the early 1980s I was invited by John Cobb, professor of process theology at the Claremont School of Theology, to participate in the International Buddhist–Christian Theological Encounter, which he was founding with the Japanese Buddhist thinker Maseo Abe. Initially I turned down the invitation on the grounds that I knew nothing about Buddhism, and I felt my plate was already overloaded with the interreligious dialogues in which I was already involved.

A couple years later Cobb got back in touch with me, urging me to become a part of this dialogue. I repeated my reluctance to join this group, but conceded that I would be willing to do so if my husband, Herman Ruether, could also attend, since he was the scholar of Asian religions and society rather than I. This was accepted, and we began to attend this dialogue. Later I learned that this urgent renewal of the invitation was due to the fact that the dialogue had been faulted for a lack of female members! Despite my initial reluctance, I am very happy that I became a part of this experience. Buddhism has greatly enriched my sense of the range of religious options in human cultures.

The Buddhist–Christian Theological Encounter met approximately every eighteen months to two years for about three days at a time. For the first eight years or so the dialogue concentrated on what might be called "doctrinal" issues, comparing themes in the two religions that were seen as parallel, but that also represented different views of these themes. Thus there was one dialogue on the theme of "Ultimate Reality: God or Nirvana?" Another time it was, "Material Existence: Creation or Maya?" A third time it was, "The Founder: Christ or Buddha?" The fourth time, the topic was, "The Path of Transformation: Conversion or Enlightenment?" The final topic was, "Religious Community: Church or Sangha?"

The dialogue had about thirty members, divided equally between Buddhists and Christians. This included Western and Asian Buddhists, and also Western and Asian Christians. At each meeting two primary papers on the theme were written by Christians and two by Buddhists, as well as two papers by Buddhists in response to the Christian papers, and two by Christians in response to the Buddhist papers. Thus one got a range of perspectives from both religious traditions on the theme of the discussion.

The basis of the dialogue was not one that assumed that the Christians were experts on Buddhism or vice versa, but that each side was open to understanding and appreciating the other tradition. We were not there to convert the others to our religion. Each was expected to be knowledgeable about his or her own tradition and to speak as a believer and practitioner of that religion, not simply as a scholar.[13]

After several dialogue meetings based on this process, I became deeply intrigued with the parallels yet differences between the two religious traditions. In no case could the parallel themes be reduced to being simply two different ways of saying the same thing. God and Nirvana both had to do with ultimate reality, but with very different views of ultimate reality. Likewise creation and maya are different ways of understanding material existence. Christ and Buddha are very different understandings of the founding figures of the two religions. Church and sangha are very different kinds of religious community. These differences adhered to the two different systems of belief, worldview, and practice of each religion. Each system represented a coherent whole, but a different whole. This learning to see each religion as complete, functioning worldviews in themselves represented a very different understanding of truth from the idea that different religions can be reduced to different ways of saying the same thing, or that one is right and the other wrong.

By the end of these five discussions I also became aware of the limitations of this method of dialogue. Basically it was very intellectual and abstract, which I suspected represented more the style of Western academic theology than the Buddhist tradition. While Buddhism can be translated into ideas, its truths are realized more through the practice of meditation. Christianity also has been a tradition of concrete practice: conversion, baptism, Eucharistic experience, and contemplative prayer. But in our dialogue there was never any suggestion that we might sample each other's ways of prayer or meditation. I think this method of simply comparing abstract ideas or theories significantly flattened the complexity of what the two religions are all about, how their truths are actually experienced.

13. The papers and responses from the Theological Encounter were published in successive issues of the journal *Buddhist–Christian Studies* from 1981 to 2005. The perspective on dialogue presumed in the encounter is found in the conversation of John B. Cobb and Maseo Abe, "Buddhist–Christian Dialogue: Past, Present and Future" *Buddhist–Christian Studies* 1 (1981) 13–19. A summary of the Encounter with papers by various participants about their understandings of religious identity, including one by Rosemary Radford Ruether, is found in *Buddhist–Christian Studies* 25 (2005) 1–46.

After finishing this round of discussion of comparative theological themes, the Buddhist–Christian Theological Encounter decided to continue with a second stage of dialogue, this time around social justice issues. Here we were not discussing parallel theories but rather how each tradition approached the same social justice challenges. We also did not have an overall agenda of what we would discuss, as was the case in the first round, but, after each dialogue, decided on the topic for the next discussion. Again there were eight papers, four primary papers, two from each tradition, and four response papers, two from each tradition, responding to the papers from the other tradition.

Our first topic was ecology, a topic suggested by the Buddhist side. It is significant that this was the first concern of the Buddhists, while nature tends to be the last on the list for Christians. We discussed how each tradition has responded to the environment, and how these traditions have resources and also create problems for coping with the ecological crisis.

This discussion was being greatly helped by the dialogues on world religions and ecology that were being held at Harvard in the mid-1990s. During this time the Forum on Religion and Ecology held ten major conferences on ten world religions and their resources for ecological thinking. These conferences dealt with Hinduism; Jainism; Buddhism; Confucianism; Daoism; Judaism, Christianity, and Islam; indigenous religions; and Shinto. The papers from each of these conferences, except the one on Shinto, were published as volumes by Harvard University Press.[14] I edited the volume on Christianity and ecology with Dieter Hessel.

Our next theme in the Buddhist–Christian dialogue was war and peace. The two Christian papers, one written by myself, were on the just war tradition, criticizing the tendency of justification of war to turn into holy war. Unfortunately there was no Christian member from the peace churches, such as a Quaker. Our discussion would have been helped by the presence of that tradition in Christianity. I remember being stuck by the aggressive tone of the Christian side in their denunciation of war-like tendencies in Christianity. This contrasted with the Buddhist side, which tended to start by emphasizing the need to become peaceful within oneself as the beginning point for making peaceful relations in society. I remember

14. See a summary of these conferences and their bibliography in Rosemary Radford Ruether, *Integrating Ecofeminism, Globalization, and World Religions*, Nature's Meaning (Lanham, MD: Rowman & Littlefield, 2005), 45–81 and notes 7, 81, and 82.

the surprised looks on the faces of the Buddhists at the lack of interest in inner peacefulness among the Christians.

Our third discussion, which took place in August of 2000, was on poverty and economic justice. Both religions have monastic traditions that have emphasized renunciation of wealth and the cultivation of simple living, but in both cases monastic institutions have grown wealthy and have been allied with the rich and powerful in society in practice. How do we enter into solidarity with the poor in global society? In Christianity this has been addressed by liberation theologies, while Buddhists have cultivated a somewhat similar tradition of socially engaged Buddhism. In this tradition the spiritual disciplines of renunciation of greed, hatred, and delusion are applied to the social structures of capitalist consumerism, global violence, and advertising propaganda.[15]

My own acquaintance with this tradition in Buddhism was deepened by attending the international conference on "Alternatives to Consumerism," organized by the leader of socially engaged Buddhism, Sulak Sivaraska, in Bangkok in December of 1997. The event brought together 250 people from twenty-six nations, most of them non-Christians—Buddhists or Hindus—from Asia. For someone used to going to primarily Western Christian gatherings on social justice, this conference was very enlightening.

In this conference, from the beginning, there was an integration of spirituality and social organizing. Buddhist monks opened each session with chanted prayers. We also attended an additional conference in which leaders of social movements from different Asian countries discussed practical ways of resisting the global system of consumerism, combined with the developing alternative communities and ways of living. For example, several communities used local fruits to create popular drinks that were inexpensive and nourishing, and taught their communities to resist buying bottled drinks, such as Coca Cola, from Western companies. This practice helped alleviate poverty and also promoted peaceful living and care for the environment.

Our last gathering of the Buddhist-Christian Theological Encounter focused on sexuality. This was a surprising session for the Christians. We were all painfully aware of the revelations of sexual abuse of the young by clergy and expected severe questioning of the roots of this abuse in Christian traditions of sexual repression. What we did not expect was candid

15. See the writings of Sulak Sivaraska, such as his *Seeds of Peace: A Buddhist Vision for Renewing Society* (Berkeley, CA: Parallax, 1992).

discussion by Buddhists of similar sexual abuses of child monks by older monks in Buddhist monasteries. Our dialogue over its twenty-year span had started with very abstract discussion of theories, but it ended in this final dialogue in very practical confrontation with concrete realities!

One of the Buddhist members of the dialogue, who had spent many years in a Tibetan monastery, identified as homosexual. At the time of our final dialogue he was in the process of organizing a delegation to meet with the Dalai Lama to ask him to acknowledge the legitimacy of homosexual relations. I later heard that they were received cordially by the Dalai Lama, who was sympathetic to their concerns but also reluctant to make such a statement in public. The Catholics in our groups could only sadly contrast the accessibility of the Dalai Lama to these Buddhists with the imperial hauteur of the papacy.

One of the members of the Buddhist–Christian Theological Encounter with whom I have developed a strong friendship over the years is Rita Gross. From a Wisconsin Synod Lutheran farming background, Rita Gross did her graduate education in religion at the University of Chicago. There she became a practicing Jew and wrote some of her first essays on feminism and religion as a Jew. She later moved on to Buddhism and has become an active Dharma teacher in Buddhist circles, while also teaching comparative religious studies at the University of Wisconsin at Eau Claire. Rita Gross is the author of the major book on rereading Buddhism from a feminist perspective: *Buddhism after Patriarchy*.[16]

Gross's argument is that Buddhism has good potential for feminist reading. It lacks a male patriarchal concept of God or ultimate reality and patriarchal legal codes, but it has been shaped institutionally by patriarchal social patterns in Asia. There are also specific teachings that have been misogynist and have subordinated women. One of these is the tradition that the Buddha originally refused to institute female monastic life. He was eventually persuaded to do so, but this was seen as a defect that resulted in an earlier demise of Buddhism. Buddhist nuns have had to pay for their establishment in monastic life by accepting eight rules of subordination to male monks. Among these are the rules that every nun, no matter how old, is subordinate to every monk, even the youngest. A nun's ordination has to be accepted by monks. Nuns cannot criticize monks.

---

16. Rita M. Gross, *Buddhism after Patriarchy: A Feminist History, Analysis, and Reconstruction of Buddhism* (Albany: State University of New York Press, 1993).

Another theoretical problem for women is the idea of *Karma*, which Buddhism took over from Hinduism. Here it is taught that being born a woman, like being born poor and low caste, is an inferior social position that comes about as punishment for bad behavior in a previous life. Abuse and discrimination against women are thus justified as a reflection of this culpable low status. Gross feels that these negative traditions and organization of Buddhism have a chance to be changed in Western Buddhism, which is being developed in Western liberal societies. Here these rules are being dropped, and women can become equal practitioners and teachers.

Interestingly enough, however, some of the most progressive Buddhist female monasticism is being developed in Asia, particularly in South Korea, Japan, and Taiwan. In June of 2010 I had the opportunity to give lectures in Taiwan and was amazed to discover that 90 percent of the Buddhist monastics in that country are women. Buddhist nuns there are getting an excellent education (including PhDs), founding universities, and engaging in a variety of social ministries.[17] The rules of subordination of nuns to monks are being officially or quietly dropped. One of our Buddhist-Christian dialogue members, the Venerable Yifa, is a member of a major Buddhist monastery in Taiwan and is herself a teacher with a PhD from Yale University. Although she was in China escorting a group of her students there when I was in Taiwan, we visited her institution and were well received. This same group of Buddhist nuns also runs a major temple center and a university in Los Angeles.[18] Thus Buddhist nuns are forging ahead and running global institutions today.

Rita Gross and I have given several talks together on Buddhist and Christian feminist theologies. I also was delighted to participate in the celebration of Rita's life work, which was put on by the Buddhist section of the American Academy of Religion at their November 2010 meeting in Atlanta, Georgia. Rita's and my major project together was a dialogue we did together for the Catholic community called The Grail, at Grailville in Loveland, Ohio, in October of 1999. This dialogue was subsequently written up and published as a book, *Religious Feminism and the Future of the*

17. See Elise Anne DeVido, *Taiwan's Buddhist Nuns* (Albany: State University of New York Press, 2010).

18. The Venerable Yifa has been a nun in the Fo Guang Monastery in Taiwan since 1979. She has a PhD in religious studies from Yale University (1996). She has been provost at the Fo Guang Shan Buddhist College and dean of Hai Lai University in Los Angeles and Taiwan. She is the author of *Safeguarding the Heart: A Buddhist Response to Suffering and September 11* (New York: Lantern Books, 2002).

Planet.[19] This dialogue consisted of five major sections, each one with an essay by one of us from her perspective and a response by the other.

The first section contained two essays—one on each of our life journeys, telling how we have each developed our intellectual perspectives. Rita Gross's story is particularly dramatic. As the only child in a farming family, she had to do major work on the farm and was not expected to go to college, much less become an intellectual. She had to fight each step of the way to become educated, starting with the struggle to get a library card from the closest library. Her conservative Lutheran church was offended when she began to sing in the choir of a more liberal Lutheran denomination and, even more, when she became a Jew. Her pastor came to her house to rebuke her and ended by excommunicating her. She also had to struggle with her professors at the University of Chicago who accepted her as an intellectual but thought feminism was unnecessary. Her critique of androcentrism in academic religion (and in other academic fields) was very much shaped by her struggles in this university setting.

Rita and I then wrote parallel essays on what we have found most problematic in each of our traditions. Rita wrote on Buddhism rather than on her earlier experiences in Wisconsin Synod Lutheranism and in Judaism. I wrote on issues of sexism in Christianity. This was followed by two parallel essays on what we have found most liberating in each of our traditions. Then there are essays on what we have found most inspiring in the other tradition. And finally there are two parallel essays on ecological concerns and how each of us is drawing on our religious traditions to promote a sustainable future for the planet.

I will discuss here some of what I said in section 4 of this book, where I elaborated on what I have found most helpful in Buddhism for my own theological perspective. This falls into four major topics: the Buddhist understanding of the self, the Buddhist understanding of reality, the meditational practice of mindfulness, and the development of socially engaged Buddhism. My acquaintance with this last development helped correct my initial impression that Buddhism was a rather individualistic and inward tradition of negation of society and escape into an "other" world.

The Buddhist spiritual disciplines put major emphasis on letting go of the ego. But this means something different from Christian asceticism where the interest is in repression of the appetites, in order to unify the

19. Rita M. Gross and Rosemary Radford Ruether, *Religious Feminism and the Future of the Planet: A Buddhist-Christian Conversation* (New York: Continuum, 2001).

immortal soul with God. In Buddhism there is no immortal self or God. Rather the ego is a delusory belief that the self is immortal and the false effort to cling to this illusion of permanence. Egoism takes the form of various kinds of grasping for power and possessions. Liberation from this ego grasping happens through meditation. Through meditation one gets in touch with one's impermanence and learns to let go of this grasping. One becomes aware that the self is a temporary concatenation of experiences in interrelation with others that are part of a process of coming to be and passing away.

This Buddhist view of the self corresponds well to the sense of the self that makes sense to me. This does not mean that the self is valueless, but simply that it is part of a network of relationships, not an autonomous entity. We are called to live ethically and responsibly in these relationships within our lifespan without imagining that we have a transcendent, ontologically permanent soul unrelated to this context. For Buddhism also the recognition and acceptance of our impermanence and the letting go of ego grasping is expressed ethically in compassion for all sentient beings. This concern for the other is not limited to other human beings, much less to human beings only of your ethnicity, gender, or economic group, but extends to all beings that can feel and have experiences, such as sentient animals.

The Buddhist sense of ultimate reality parallels these understanding of the impermanent self. For Buddhism there is no ontological God as an immortal, immutable Supreme Being to whom you can go in a heavenly world outside this world. Buddhism speaks of the understanding of reality as codependent arising. Visible things arise as a process of coming to be from an ultimate void or Nirvana, in interrelation with all other things are that arising, and returning to this void, only to arise again in new forms.

This view also corresponds very much to my own sense of reality. As I explain in chapter 1, what I have come to call the divine, the great Mother, or holy Wisdom, is this source or ground of creativity out of which all interdependent phenomena of contingently existing reality burgeon forth and coexist in relation to one another, only to dissolve into nonexistence and arise again in new forms. This process promotes fruitfulness as well as making for limitations. It calls us to seek loving and just relations to best flourish in these temporary relationships. There is no immortal life for separated souls outside this process, but there is the ongoing legacy of good or bad relationality that is passed on from one generation to the next.

Whether we create abusive relations or loving relations affects those shaped by that context. This does not mean total determination. There is freedom to change that is integral to flux itself, but this freedom is enabled or debilitated by the good or bad context of relations from which these beings come. My hope lies in the continually renewed impetus for loving and flourishing relationships, but without denying their limits and contingency. To create the once-and-for-all kingdom of heaven in history is not an option. For me these two key understandings of the self and reality are the major challenges that Buddhism offers to Christianity and to its philosophical basis in Greek Platonism. For many, Christianity could not exist without the basic beliefs in the immortal soul separable from the body and God as the Supreme Being existent outside the world. For me, both of these ideas do not correspond to my own sense of reality, which is better expressed in the Buddhist view.

Another very useful theme in Buddhism is the meditational practice of mindfulness. Mindfulness, as I understand it, is a constant reminder to slow down and to become aware of where you are, here and now. Western culture is imbued with a demand to endlessly rush ahead to a desired future, negating as inadequate where you are now. This is an integral part of its flight from finitude and its quest for the final better life as the ultimate resting place of the immortal soul. To let go this ego drive is a step toward becoming more fully alive and present to where you are, here and now.

I find the practice of mindfulness particularly helpful when driving on Los Angeles freeways. While still moving at the necessary speed to keep up with the flow of traffic, I try to practice an awareness of where I am in each moment, of my body and breathing, of the people in cars around me, of the sky and trees above me. I relax and cultivate a calm center, letting go of the frenetic urgency to get somewhere else, while frustrated and annoyed at others who are "in my way," rather than being where I am in each moment. This is doubtless a superficial understanding of the profundity of the practice of mindfulness, but it is very helpful to me in my daily life.

Finally, I deeply appreciate the tradition of socially engaged Buddhism. This I think complements very well the Christian, Jewish, and Muslim developments of liberation theology, with their prophetic critique of oppressive social structures and false ideology. But the Buddhist view helps correct the millennialism that tends to be a part of Western monotheist theologies. Socially engaged Buddhism provides a penetrating analysis of the impulses of greed, hatred, and delusion writ large in social structures, but it doesn't imagine it can create the kingdom of heaven on earth. Rather it seeks modest challenges to these oppressive structures and modest alternatives, knowing the partiality and impermanence of our efforts. To make situations better here and now or even to make the effort to do so, without great success, is a good enough goal. This helps Westerners get over their assumption that something isn't worth doing unless it is going to be totally successful permanently.

Religious Thought and Scientific Atheism

In the first decade of the twenty-first century a series of books were published by writers from the perspective of a certain concept of scientific truth based on empirical evidence, arguing that belief in God is a delusion, and that religion based on this delusion is causing great harm to society.[20] These books were doubtless inspired by the new prevalence of religious perspectives in political cultures worldwide, particularly among the political Right in the United States. The new emphasis on strident, politicized religion appeared to be a major aspect of terrorist movements and of a general hostility to scientific reason. I am generally sympathetic to this critique of religion when it acts as an ally of right-wing violence and antisocial intolerance. Consequently, I set about to read a sample of this literature to see what insights I could get from it. Generally, I was very disappointed in these books as a helpful expression of a possible dialogue with progressive religion.

First of all, these books do not seem to recognize that there is such a thing as progressive religion. They appear to be quite unacquainted with the way religious teachers in theological schools talk about theological meaning. They assume that anyone who defines him- or herself as a believer is a literalist about the existence of God as a supreme ontological entity outside of the world who creates and runs the whole world. Several of the writers respond with annoyance at the proposal of scientist Stephen J. Gould that religion and science should be seen as "non-overlapping magisteria," with science having to do with facts and religion with values.[21] This

20. Among these books are Richard Dawkins, *The God Delusion* (Boston: Houghton Mifflin, 2006); Sam Harris, *The End of Faith: Religion, Terror and the Future of Reason* (New York: Norton, 2004); Christopher Hitchens, *God Is Not Great: How Religion Poisons Everything* (New York: Twelve, 2007); Victor J. Stenger, *God: The Failed Hypothesis; How Science Shows that God Does Not Exist* (Amherst, NY: Prometheus, 2007); and Daniel C. Dennett, *Breaking the Spell: Religion as a Natural Phenomenon* (New York: Viking, 2006).

21. Stephen J. Gould, *Rocks of Ages: Science and Religion in the Fullness of Life* (New

proposal is dismissed as avoiding the issue of religion's factual claims about the existence of God and having nothing to do with the way believers actually think.[22]

The writers of the "new atheism" are unaware that this distinction of science and religion as separate realms of fact and value is not a new theory invented by Stephen Gould in the 1990s. It is a view that goes back to the writings of German Protestant theologian Albrecht Ritschl in the 1850s to '80s. Ritschl argued in his writings that religious beliefs should not be seen as similar to scientific facts to be proven by empirical demonstration. Rather faith statements are value judgments having to do with the meaning of life.

A large percentage of Christian theologians, and probably many Jews as well, who teach in theological schools, would affirm some similar distinction. Faith statements are about meaning and value, not about facts to be proven or disproven by the scientific method of empirical research. This means that much of what is argued in these five books of the so-called new atheism is irrelevant to progressive theology, in the sense that they are arguing against something that most educated religious thinkers are not claiming.

But these writers also make tendentious claims about the evil and irrational nature of religion that are exaggerated and don't stand up to the complexities of cultural realities. Professor of physics Victor Stenger, for example, begins his book *God: The Failed Hypothesis: How Science Shows That God Does Not Exist*, with the following statement: "Throughout history, arguments for and against the existence of God have been largely confined to philosophy and theology. In the meantime science has sat on the sidelines and quietly watched this game of words march up and down the field."[23] For Stenger, it is time that science actively intervenes to show that belief in "a supreme being that much of humanity worships as the source of all reality" does not exist.

One wonders where Stenger got his history of science. The image of science as a secular discipline sitting on the sidelines "throughout history," apart from philosophy and theology, who are busy debating for and against the existence of God, has little to do with the historical reality of any of these areas of thought. Science did not exist as a separate, secular

---

York: Ballantine, 1999).

22. See Dawkins, *The God Delusion*, 54–61.

23. Stenger, *God: the Failed Hypothesis*, 9.

discipline until nineteenth-century Europe. Greek science appears in writings such as Plato's *Timaeus* in fourth-century-BCE Athens, as an integral part of Plato's philosophy, which assumed the existence of a Creator who shapes the universe from a combination of preexistent matter and ideas. Medieval science was done as an integral part of Scholastic philosophy and theology. Even early modern scientists such as Isaac Newton claimed to be Deist theologians. That scientists have not spent a lot of time arguing for the unscientific nature of the existence of God in the last hundred years may have something to do with the "separation of spheres" of science and religion that came to be accepted in nineteenth-century Europe, aided by theologians such as Albrecht Ritschl.

An argument that runs through several of these authors is that religion is the source of all intolerance that is the cause of violence and terrorism. Thus we need to get rid of religion in order to affirm a culture of rationality and tolerance. This is particularly the view of Sam Harris, author of *The End of Faith: Religion: Terror and the Future of Reason*, who sees the monotheist religions, particularly Islam, as the prime sources of terror. Harris opens his book with the story of a young man boarding a bus wearing an overcoat under which he has a bomb, nails, ball bearings and rat poison. The young man sets off the bomb, killing himself and twenty-two others. Harris then asks: "Why is it so easy, then, so trivially easy—you-could-bet-your-life-on-it easy—to guess the young man's religion?"[24]

Harris answers that, of course, we all immediately know that this young man is a Muslim and that Islam is the source of his violent inclinations. Neither of these assumptions is in fact obvious, except in a context of Western Islamophobia. It was a Christian, not a Muslim, who bombed the Alfred P. Murrah Federal Building in Oklahoma City, even though the police initially went after Muslim and Hindu doctors who were busy trying to help the victims. Also the incident in Harris's story did not occur in just any place, but in Israel, where the anger of the young man had less to do with his religion than with the oppression of his people, the Palestinians, by the Israelis under whom he and his family live.

Stenger acknowledges that recently many representatives of religion (i.e., Christians and Jews) have been coming out for interfaith tolerance and mutual acceptance. But he claims that there are no grounds for tolerance within these religions themselves. Rather tolerance emerges only when religion has been beaten down by secular humanism and so acknowledges

24. Harris, *The End of Faith*, 1–10.

the need for tolerance because their own intolerance is being discredited. Stenger is evidently unacquainted with statements within the Qu'ran itself that Jews and Christians should not be afraid because they can be redeemed in their own faiths, that there should be no compulsion in matters of religion, and that God is the source of the plurality of religions.[25]

The Vatican declaration on non-Christian religions affirmed the goodness of Hinduism, Buddhism, Islam, and Judaism based on what they saw as their own religious principles, not because they were "broken down" by secularism. The many projects of interfaith cooperation, such as the Global Ethic of the World Parliament of Religion, the Forum on Religion and Ecology and the Interfaith Theological School in Claremont, California, also understand their work as coming out of their religious principles.

But, even more problematic, Harris does not recognize the diversity of forms of intolerance and exclusivism that have to do with racism, ethnicity, class hierarchy, and sexism, and that have nothing to do specifically with religion, except insofar as religion has been a part of all human cultures until recently. Anthropologists have shown that human groups from earliest times have a tendency to see their own group as normatively human and others as different and less acceptable. Language study has explored the way that many indigenous people use the word for their group as equivalent to "human," making the other groups other than human.

Early law codes of the Ancient Near East from the second millennium BCE began to differentiate class and gender hierarchy, and to endorse slavery. American law until the 1950s endorsed the inferiority and secondary status of Blacks and Indians. The separation of races in South Africa was discontinued only in the 1990s. All of these forms of discrimination appear unknown to Sam Harris, who sees all irrationality and violence as religion-based. Although I certainly would agree that we need to overcome intolerance and violence to others based on a negation of their humanity, we need to recognize the cultural diversity of its sources. We cannot assume that religion is the sole culprit, or that religion has no positive resources of offer to overcome it.

However the confusion and simplistic thinking of these writers, who see themselves as speaking for a scientific view of truth, dismissing religion as unscientific and irrational, is not entirely their fault. It also has something to do with the way educated and critical religious studies typical of most theological schools have failed to be communicated on the popular

25. See Qur'an 2:62; 5:69; 2:256; and 5:48.

level. This has to do not only with theology but also with biblical studies. For more than a hundred years theological schools have pursued the latest developments in scriptural studies in a way that has left behind historical literalism. Scripture is understood much more as literary productions created to express visions of meaning and hope, rather than as literal descriptions of events.

But this now well-developed way of reading Scripture has not been communicated to believers in the churches. Church denominations have not created catechetics for children and young adults in the churches that introduce them to the methods of critical biblical studies. This means that students who come to theological schools go through a shock when they discover how their teachers read Scripture. Most of them adjust to this, but when they, in turn, go out to serve the churches, they too come to speak of God, Jesus, and Scripture in a way that can be taken as literal, even though they themselves may no longer think in this way. Thus a kind of conspiracy of silence, and the two-level understanding of theology and Scripture that results, creates a gap between the assumptions of progressive theological schools and the uneducated literalism of the churches.

The churches are paying for allowing this two-level thinking to exist between the theological schools and the popular culture of churches. The backlash of literalist fundamentalism in the popular culture of the churches has invaded the discourse of politics and is a major cause of right-wing anger against the educated elites of universities. These scientific writers critiquing popular religion are basically responding to the discourse of this popular culture and are themselves largely unaware of how Scripture and theology is discussed in progressive theological schools. Clearly there needs to be better communication between science and religion, but this needs to start with better communication *within* religion between the educated classes in the theological schools and the popular culture of the churches.

5

Crises of the Mental Health System
Mind, Brain, and the Finite Self

In 1976 our son David graduated from Gonzaga High School, a Jesuit school in Washington DC. He appeared troubled and conflicted. Although regarded as bright by his teachers, he was pronounced to be not working up to his potential. Since he had skipped two grades in grade school and was only sixteen, it seemed good to delay his going to college and to give him another year of preparatory studies. Friends we knew had spent a sabbatical in Cambridge, England, and had sent their daughter to the University of Cambridge preparatory college. David also had a cousin studying at the university, so this seemed to be a good place for an extra year.

This decision turned out to be a mistake, although David set off for England with great enthusiasm. But at Cambridge he fell in with a group of young men and women, some from Africa and the Arab world, who were using hash and psychedelic drugs. David had at least two LSD experiences where he went berserk. He was spending little time in classes. In January his advisor informed us that he should leave. David's younger sister, Mimi, recalls that when he returned home, he seemed different. She felt that something was wrong with him. Believing that he needed more time to "get himself together," we sent him for some months to study Spanish in Cuernavaca, Mexico (a town with which he was familiar, since our family had spent several summers there in the past), and to take a summer course at the University of California at Santa Cruz. Again these opportunities did not work out well. David was unable to concentrate in the class, spent time walking around the campus, and had a run-in with the police that landed him in jail. His father had to come out to California to bail him out.

The Mental Health System and David's Decline

In the fall of that year we began to connect David and the family with family therapy at a local hospital, based on the then-current assumption that psychological problems were based on family conflicts. David also met with an individual therapist. David began to act out violently in the home. It became evident to us that we needed to find another place for him to live, since he was creating a hostile family environment that was bad for the development of our youngest child, Mimi, who was still in high school.

We tried out several promising "therapeutic communities" on the East Coast, which did not work out for long, either because David did not cooperate with the program there, or else because the community was closing for lack of funds. We then discovered Kahumana, a therapeutic community in Hawaii, where David went in 1987. He stayed there for only two years. He was then placed in the public mental health system in a Hawaii, and stayed in the state for eight years. When these arrangements deteriorated to the point that it appeared David would become homeless and end up being jailed, he was sent to the YMCA in Elgin, Illinois, close to where we were living in Evanston, Illinois. When that didn't work out, we began another round of placements in board-and-care homes and therapy in the Chicago area.

We tried to get him to work in the Threshold program in Chicago, reputedly one of the best therapeutic programs for the mentally ill in the nation. David had started there in the 1980s but had dropped out. This time he was living in a board-and-care in walking distance from its main downtown center. He walked over there several times but seemed unable to go in and enter the program. Those who were at the door seemed to intimidate him. Thresholds seemed to expect an initiative that David lacked.

David had a number of chaotic experiences with very deficient board-and-care homes, in which he injured himself several times by throwing himself down stairs. He would be put in a hospital and then in a nursing home to recover. We continually kept in touch with him, following him around to the various places where he landed in greater Chicago, taking him out for day trips and trying to keep him stimulated with activities. But he seemed stuck at a very low level of functioning. The medications that he was being given did not seem to alleviate his most aggravating symptoms: insistent nagging voices. In 2002 I retired from teaching at Garrett-Evangelical Theological Seminary in Evanston, Illinois. We entered a retirement community, Pilgrim Place, in Claremont, California. We determined to take David with us and to continue to try to help him as best we could.

David was enthusiastic about moving to California and asked if the place he was going would have a swimming pool. We said no, but Pilgrim Place had one where he could swim. But he was immediately disappointed by the board-and-care home a few blocks from our home where he was to live, even though it was a small and pleasant facility. He isolated himself and would not speak to the other residents. He quickly got himself thrown out by the director for bad behavior and was placed in another board-and-care about half an hour away.

There he lasted about four years before being finally ejected by a long-suffering director for trashing his room. We again found him other board-and-cares where he stayed for a while, with intermediate periods in the hospital. Nothing seemed to really help him improve. Most discouraging was his pattern of passivity. Although we continually tried to do things with him—from going to museums, shopping trips, and out for meals, to walks in the mountains, swimming, and playing tennis—he took no initiative. We had the sense that we were simply entertaining him, to no real effect on him taking responsibility for his own life.

Writing a Book with David

One of David's few areas of self-initiated activity was writing. Much of this has become incomprehensible over the years, with long strings of rhyming words and phrases, but some parts have interesting insights. Some of his poetry, particularly in his earlier years, seemed pretty good. Although David had been diagnosed as schizophrenic in his early twenties (in 1982), it was only much later (in 2005) that I began to think about writing a book about our experiences with David's schizophrenia and the limitations of the mental health system as we had experienced it. I thought also that this would be a piece into which I could incorporate some of David's own writing. I sought to draw him into discussing his own experiences and included these as verbatim accounts. I also included some of his poetry and parts of some of his essays. In this way I hoped the book would give David something of his own voice. The book was published by Fortress Press in 2010 as *Many Forms of Madness: A Family's Struggle with Mental Illness and the Mental Health System*. David was listed as coauthor.

This book has been received very well. I have been sent many communications from people who have read the book and felt it was a very helpful account both of our experiences and, in many cases, of their own family problems with mental illness and the health system. I have been asked to join the Board of the local Pomona Valley chapter of the National Alliance on Mental Illness (NAMI), and the book has been promoted by the national board of NAMI. One result the book has not had, however, is helping to bring to our attention better resources to help David. I had hoped that someone reading the book or hearing me speak about it might tell me of some better programs or approaches to therapy that would be more useful for David than what we have been able to find. So far this has not happened. I am still looking.

Some who have read the book *Many Forms of Madness* have claimed to be surprised by it. They saw this as a totally different kind of book from what I had written before. Some have said that they see it as very courageous to speak frankly about these experiences. It does not seem courageous to me, only sadly true. It is much more explicitly autobiographical than other books I have produced (other than this one), but I do not see it as totally different from my other work. As is evident from this present book, everything I have written has autobiographical roots. I expect that this is the case with all academic writings. An author is drawn to write on something because it represents crucial issues of conflict and meaning for her. But academics usually don't reveal what those concerns are and how they have come about in their own lives.

Like my other writings, my work on mental illness is rooted in family experiences, but it also reflects what I see as deep issues of social injustice. Historically the mentally ill have been an abused population. Their treatment in mental hospitals has been deplorable, and continues to be so. Although US society has been willing to put up some funds to pay for the medication and care of the mentally ill, this willingness is and has always been based on a minimum level that will "warehouse" and sedate the mentally ill, not on a more rounded basis for recovery. The dependence on medication in preference to social development has become very problematic and may even be a source of brain damage, a topic I will discuss later in this chapter.

My book on mental illness starts with a detailed account of David's illness and our efforts to help him. I wrote the original version of this account to give to therapists, since those who treat David generally claim to want to know something of his history. What I have discovered is that very few of them want anything more than the barest details of his medical history that they can take in in one minute in order to prescribe "meds." They don't really want to learn his story in fuller detail. During the past thirty years I have offered to share this account with many therapists, but only three have shown an interest in reading it. One is the director of a local clinic; another is the director of a board-and-care home where David was living, and the third is the social-services director of a health-care facility where he was staying.

The book goes on from this biographical beginning to four chapters on some of the ideological and practical problems with the mental-health system. The second chapter discusses the way "symptoms" are defined by the official manual of psychic disorders. I then explore the history of conflicting theories of what causes schizophrenia. Is it understood as social or biological, as being based in mind or body? The abusive treatment of the mentally ill in institutional systems is the topic of the fourth chapter. I then look at the inadequacies of the housing and general living arrangements for those diagnosed. The final chapter tries to say something about how we might be able to improve this system, if we really cared. All of this is very much the pattern of all my books and articles. I ask: What is the problem? How has injustice been created by inadequate or false ideologies? How can we improve the system with better thinking and acting? This book is not an exception, but reflects the main lines of my writing. It simply talks about a topic few people want to discuss.

David's Further Decline

When I finished writing the book, *Many Forms of Madness*, in 2009 David seemed fairly stable. He was living five minutes from us. I was spending a lot of time with him, several hours four days a week. We attended a biweekly aerobics class at the Pomona YMCA. It was a vigorous workout, but he seemed to do well. We also swam, played tennis, and took walks in the mountains. It was good exercise for both of us. Then for no apparent reason, his behavior began to fall apart. He returned to doing flips (sudden somersaults at home or in public places), an activity he had adopted in the past seemingly as a way of staving off inner tension and harassment by voices. These actions caused him to break several objects in the facility where he was living: a water cooler, a table, a gate in the patio. This institution, whose staff was not trained for the mentally ill, and who were not friendly to David, sent him to the hospital and sent us a bill for the damage.

I assumed he would get the usual two weeks in the hospital, and then hopefully we could find him a more appropriate board-and-care in the Los Angeles area not too far from us. I knew some in the Pasadena area and gave the social worker the names and contact information. Instead, for more than two years, David was sent through a cycle of two-to-three-week stays in a very inadequate psychiatric hospital and then released to nursing homes. At this date he has been sent to a total of twelve nursing homes in all sections of the Los Angeles area. These nursing homes are for the elderly or incapacitated, with most of the residents bedridden or in wheelchairs. It should have been evident to the social workers at the hospital that a physically fit fifty-year-old was not a candidate for these types of facilities.

David would last from a day or two to a couple of weeks at these nursing homes, soon acting inappropriately (such as by throwing his food tray or by leaving to walk the streets) only to be sent back to the hospital. We continually appealed to the social workers at the hospital that he needed to be in a board-and-care, not a nursing home, but they ignored us. Meanwhile David became more and more catatonic and withdrawn, barely speaking to us or anyone else, staying in his bed night and day. Although he had never been suicidal, he stopped eating for periods of time and seemed to be trying to die.

At one point an adequate board-and-care was found for him about thirty minutes from our home, with access to nice parks and activities. David's psyche seemed to return to something more like his more communicative self, although he appeared damaged physically and psychologically, lacking the same physical strength and mental ability that he had had two years before. Clearly these hospital stays had nothing to do with helping him recover. The director of this board-and-care and staff seemed insightful, and we were hopeful that an adequate place had been found.

But this situation has also not worked out. He was sent to a nursing home for an infected eye. This took a long time to clear up. When he seemed to be becoming physically well and psychologically communicative, the director of the board-and-care came to visit him. He accused David of being incontinent, although the staff of the medical facility claimed was not the case. David was offended and refused to talk to him. His mental state then fell apart, and he again became noncommunicative and refused to take any medications. The facility finally sent him to a community hospital in central Los Angeles. We visited him there and were alarmed by the chaotic state of this facility. When we called two days later to check on him, we were told he was not there. They seemed to have lost him, at first having no records that he had been there and then claiming that he was at the previous facility, which was not the case.

Finally, after a great deal of insistence from us, one person in medical records told us that he was at the "Van Nuys facility," although with no proper phone or address for this place. After some research, we finally found where he was (at a community hospital in Van Nuys), only to be told that because of "confidentiality" they would not confirm if he was actually there or tell us anything about how he was doing. This is a pretense we have encountered before, in which laws about the rights of the mentally ill to "confidentiality" are used to deny us any information about him. What we gathered, however, was that he was withdrawn and refusing to talk, take medication, sometimes even to eat.

He then was released to yet another nursing home for the elderly. Here too he was at first withdrawn and hostile, although gradually becoming more communicative. He seemed to stabilize there, and ended up living there for almost nine months. My daughter Becky began to visit him, and we established a pattern in which we took him out on Sunday, and she did so on another day of the week. We got him a membership at a nearby YMCA and would take him there to swim and for walks in a nearby park. Although there was no real development of initiative on his part, this worked for many months.

But then in June of 2012 this arrangement fell apart, Becky and I went on a trip to Africa for three weeks. Although we arranged to have David taken out by some students, the nursing home director didn't understand this and refused to let him go out with them. He became angry and struck out at the staff and was thrown out. He was sent again to a hospital, then to a nursing home in Pasadena and now has been transferred to a more open care facility. But his future continues to be in grave doubt. We keep on trying to reach out to him, but David's behavior and the inadequacies of the mental-health facilities keep us in a constant state of crisis.

The Mental Health System
and the Question of Medication

This dilemma has renewed for us (for Herman Ruether and myself) the basic question of what schizophrenia (or any other mental illness) is, and what causes it. Despite all the research and the confident statements that have been made about this over the years, it is evident that this is still very much an unresolved question. The definitions of this illness in the standard handbook of the American Psychiatric Association, the *Diagnosic and Statistical Manual of Mental Disorders*, basically describes a concatenation of symptoms, not any real definition of causes.

American culture over the last two hundred years has gone through a continual back-and-forth between psychosocial and biological theories of the causes of mental illness. In the colonial period, some saw mental illness as an expression of sin and demonic possession, while others saw it as an imbalance in the humors of the body. Chaining and beating were seen as the way to take care of the first problem, while bloodletting was believed would take care of the second problem.

The early nineteenth century saw a movement to strike off the chains of the mentally ill in abusive prisons and the call for their moral treatment in supportive communities of refuge in sylvan settings. But these asylums soon grew into large, underfunded, and abusive hospitals. The idea of moral treatment was abandoned by its theoreticians for biological theories of the causes of mental illness. Some claimed it was caused by brain lesions, although no evidence existed in autopsies for the existence of such lesions. Methods were devised to shock the brain into behaving. These took such forms as sudden immersions in water, shock treatments, and finally lobotomy, or actual removal of the frontal cortex of the brain.

Henry Cotton, who ruled the Trenton State Hospital of New Jersey from 1907 to 1930, was sure mental illness was caused by bacterial infections of the teeth, tonsils, and colon. He proceeded to remove the teeth of patients, followed by their tonsils, colons, gall bladders, the cervices and ovaries for women, and men's penises. Despite continual protests and the high level of deaths, with little evidence of recoveries, such operations continued at the hospital until 1960.

The 1950s and '60s saw rising criticism of the oppressive treatment of patients in large mental hospitals. At that same time Thorazine was invented, the first chemical medication for mental illness. This was said to alleviate the "imbalance" of chemistry in the brain. Straightway a theory was proposed that mental illness was caused by the imbalance of brain chemistry, which Thorazine was then correcting, although there was no evidence that such imbalance existed prior to giving this medication.

The 1960s and '70s also saw major challenges to this emerging biomedical model of mental illness. The antipsychiatry movement popularized the idea that mental illness did not really exist. Calling someone insane was simply a way of labeling deviant, creative people. Physical treatments, such as shock therapy and particularly lobotomy, were strongly criticized. At the same time Freudian and other types of psychoanalytic talk therapy were popular and became the way that the affluent dealt with their problems, although such therapy was out of the reach of poorer people. The training of psychiatrists in universities focused on work in the schools of psychoanalysis.

Meanwhile further research on neuroleptic medications, such as Thorazine, raised questions about the brain-chemistry theory of the cause of mental illness, uncovering evidence that such chemicals actually caused imbalances in brain chemistry rather than curing it. But there was little widespread response to this research. Rather, by the 1980s a powerful alliance of big pharmaceutical companies and established academic psychiatry training was emerging. This alliance sought to reestablish a purely biomedical view of causes and cures for mental illness. Those who questioned this were discredited.

Some therapists who wanted to supplement medications with more social and environmental ways of helping the mentally ill recover were marginalized and defunded. It became established dogma in the psychiatric world that researchers who questioned the efficacy of medication were unscientific, while patients who resisted medication because of their debilitating side effects lacked "self-insight," into the reality of their illness. The prime task of any person diagnosed with mental illness was to become "medication compliant," accepting whatever pills were dished out to them, even if they caused stupefaction, dizziness, and tremors (or, as David has put it, even if they "make you stupid").

Today a purely biomedical model of mental illness reigns supreme in American psychiatry, in hospitals, clinics, nursing homes, and board-and-care facilities, as well as among practicing psychiatrists and in the public media. Insurance and government funds pay for the fifteen-minute, once-every-two-months visit to a psychiatrist to review and adjust medication, not to talk in any depth to the patient (now called a consumer). Social therapies are expensive and not funded by insurance. Few opportunities for work, exercise, or meaningful therapy exist.

Hospitals and group homes often have schedules posted on their walls of the round of activities they offer, but in our experience much of this doesn't actually happen, or few go to what does happen. A weekly list of foods to be served at meals is also posted prominently but does not correspond closely to what is actually served. For example, potato salad may be posted, but potato chips served. Green salad or fresh fruit may be posted, but none served. Passive TV watching is the main activity. The TV is often left on without monitoring, with loud and violent programs that seem inappropriate for the mentally ill. Dishing out the medication as prescribed is the main medical function. Other illnesses, such as a severe cold, are often ignored. David went for months with a dripping infection on his elbow before we could get the doctors to pay attention to it. No chores by the patients are expected. Passive compliance with the regimen is what is valued.

The mental hospital has ceased to be a place of long-term care, and instead has become the place mostly for a two-week stay in times of crisis. Supposedly their role is to stabilize the mentally ill person in times of relapse and then pass them along to the group home. But this short stay of two weeks has little to do with how the patient has actually progressed during this stay. Rather it reflects the time limit of the funding. Little thoughtful analysis is given to the person's overall state of mental, not to mention physical, health. Rather the mental hospital functions more as a temporary dumping place for a person whose behavior has made them unacceptable in the group home.

The hospital social worker's main role is to find another place to send the mentally ill person. There is no follow up relation of the social worker to this person. The exception to this pattern is the mental health system of the state of Hawaii, where a social worker is assigned permanently to a patient and maintains this relation no matter where the patient is sent within the state. Hawaii is the only state in the United States where this happens, as far as we know. If the hospital psychiatrist is doing any reevaluation of the patient's mental health and assigning appropriate medication, it is very difficult for family members, such as ourselves, to find out what this is. Psychiatrists seldom answer phone calls or communicate with the family, although there are some pleasant exceptions. This is the discouraging picture that we have seen in the mental health system, as we have experienced it over the last two decades.

Even more worrying than the stupefying nature of the mental health system is the renewed questioning of the efficacy of medications. Several recent books have raised this challenge, the most comprehensive by psychiatric researcher Robert Whitaker, *Anatomy of an Epidemic: Magic Bullets,*

Psychiatric Drugs, and the Astonishing Rise of Mental Illness.[1] Whitaker focuses on the effects of psychotropic medications and their overuse in the American treatment of the mentally ill.

Whitaker opens the book with documentation of the astonishing increase of the mentally ill in the United States in the last forty years. In 1955 there were 355,000 people with psychiatric diagnoses in mental hospitals. Many had a mild first episode, recovered completely after a few months, and were never hospitalized again. In 2008 the numbers had skyrocketed to forty million, fourteen million of whom are permanently disabled, continuously rehospitalized and have deeply impaired mental and psychical conditions. The numbers continue to expand among younger and younger populations. Children are diagnosed as hyperactive at four and given medication for this; soon their diagnosis is changed to bipolar, and they are put on medication permanently. What has happened?

Whitaker sees the problem as a combination of three factors: the overuse of psychotropic, anti-anxiety, and antidepression medication, their aggressive promotion by an alliance of big drug companies and establishment psychiatry in their pay, and a false account of how these drugs actually work. He begins with a critique of Thorazine. As mentioned before, this drug was first developed in the 1950s. It was originally used as a sedative to numb patients going into surgery. It then began to be used in mental asylums to pacify the agitated. In this role it was hailed as providing a "chemical lobotomy."

From this limited role it was remarketed in the late '50s as a "miracle cure" for schizophrenia. Researchers began to do studies to find out how it worked. These "neuroleptic" (neuron-grabbing) drugs were shown to work by shutting down the dopamine nerve pathways between the neurons, thus inhibiting communication between them. From this evidence the hypothesis arose that schizophrenia was caused by excessive dopamine transmission, thereby generating voices, fantasies, and hallucinations. The drug, by inhibiting dopamine, was correcting this excess and thus creating a chemical balance.

---

1. Robert Whitaker, *Anatomy of an Epidemic: Magic Bullets, Psychiatric Drugs, and the Astonishing Rise of Mental Illness* (New York: Crown, 2010). Marcia Angel reviews Whitaker's book, as well as two other critical books on the current state of psychiatry: Daniel Carlat, *Unhinged: The Trouble with Psychiatry—A Doctor's Revelations about a Profession in Crisis* (New York: Free Press, 2010); and Irving Kirsch, *The Emperor's New Drugs: Exploding the Antidepressant Myth* (New York: Basic Books, 2010) in the *New York Review of Books*, June 23, 2011, and July 14, 2011.

Further research, however, failed to prove that prior to taking the medication there had been an excess of dopamine. Rather, several researchers argued, what happens is that Thorazine represses the transmission of dopamine that was previously normal, and the brain compensates by generating more dopamine to try to restore normality. This means that when a person stops taking this medication, dopamine becomes excessive, generating agitation. This agitation was interpreted by the psychiatric profession as a relapse caused by the disease, necessitating a return to taking the medication, which was now seen as a lifelong necessity. The dogma appeared in psychiatric circles that the only way for a person with a diagnosis of schizophrenia to be stabilized was to take such neuroleptic drugs permanently, despite their discomforting side effects.

This same demand for permanent consumption of medications came to be applied to anti-anxiety and antidepression medications that were being developed. These drugs also worked by repressing neuron-transmitters, causing compensation by the brain, which then results in chaotic effects once the medications are stopped. Again the conclusion was that taking these medications could never be stopped. Going off medications was the sure route to relapse. What was not explored is the possibility that drug-created repression of the neuron-transmitters and the brain-generated compensation meant that withdrawal from the meds needed to happen slowly so the brain could restore the original balance which the medication, not a prior existing disease, was responsible for disturbing.

This demand for more and more widespread and permanent use of medications was fed by the alliance of psychiatry with pharmaceutical companies. Big pharma has become the major funder of the psychiatric profession and its professional organization, the American Psychiatric Association. The National Institutes of Health, the government-based representative of health, had become a tool of this same alliance. Alternative critical research showing problems with these theories or promoting alternatives to them was not widely reported: their authors were discredited. Thus the biomedical interpretation of the causes of mental illness due to neuron-transmitter deficiency, and the need to take such neuron-grapping medications for the rest of one's life, became the overwhelmingly dominant message and practice.

This model of psychiatry is being promoted worldwide. Ethan Watters's 2010 book, *Crazy Like Us: The Globalization of the American Psyche*,[2]

2. New York: Free Press, 2010.

shows that many cultures have had different ways of dealing with mental illness. This has been seen as an understandable stage in a person's development, and the person experiencing such an episode is kept in the family and community. Episodes tend to be short with full recovery. But US influence is promoting the American model of mental illness as the scientific view. The result is the use of medication as the first response, greater separation of the mentally ill from society, and more severe and longer-term debilitation. Needless to say, American pharmaceutical companies are major actors in the promotion of this American approach, and they are the ones who stand to gain from the expanding global market for their drugs.

The results of this promotion of lifelong use of psychiatric medications in increasingly complex cocktails are both the skyrocketing numbers of the mentally ill and their more chronic debilitation. More and more people are made permanently dependent, unable to work or function minimally in society. Supported at poverty level by Medicare and SSI (Supplementary Security Income), they live with worsening physical and mental conditions, with evidence of loss of cognitive capacity. Studies of those on long-term medication have shown that they suffer from shrinking frontal lobes in their brains; in other words, their treatment may be causing significant brain damage. The life expectancy of those with mental illness has been reduced by an average of twenty years, many dying in their midfifties. The average life expectancy is fifty-three.

For Whitaker, this situation is a case of massive medical malfeasance, a major social crime of medically induced debilitation of millions of people in the United States and around the world. Whitaker's solution is twofold. First, the stranglehold of "big pharma" on psychiatry must be broken. The truth of how neuroleptic medications work and don't work needs to be told and widely understood. Second, an alternative approach to the treatment of the mentally ill needs to be developed.

For Whitaker, this alternative approach needs to include a more cautious use of medications. These should not always be the first response to a psychotic episode. Other social methods should be tried, such as discussion therapy, supportive community, and physical exercise. While some medications may have a place in many cases, they need to be used more minimally and with an effort to move quickly beyond their use. This approach has been shown in other countries, such as Finland, to be much more effective than the American way. However, this alternative will be resisted by the pharmaceutical establishment and its disciples, who are the economic beneficiaries of the expanding use of medication. But surely the purpose of the psychiatric profession, like any branch of medicine, is to heal, not to get rich.

What Whitaker says about the effects of these drugs and the way that they have been promoted to create lifetime use, resulting in permanent dependency and evidence of reduced cognitive capacity, closely parallels our own experience with David. Although we have not had an opportunity to test his loss of brainpower and its relation to shrinking frontal lobes, his behavior seems to show that this is likely the case. His declining ability to think, read, and communicate since his twenties, when he began to take these medications, makes it seem like something of the kind has happened to him. This is extremely depressing to us. By cooperating with what the psychiatric profession has not just recommended but demanded of him, we have perhaps facilitated a process by which he has been deeply damaged.

The psychiatric profession would doubtless insist that this has been caused by his "brain disease" itself. But the distressing reality is that we don't know for sure which of these two views is true. There is a deep conflict between a minority of critical thinkers who speak out of careful research and concern, and a self-interested psychiatric establishment that refuses to consider this challenge. There is no one we know in the psychiatric world who has read Whitaker and other such critical books and is prepared to discuss them with us. As parents, we are caught between these contradictions, with no resources for testing which is true or how to find adequate alternatives to help our son, who is clearly being debilitated by the dominant system.

Mind, Brain, and the Self

David's mental deterioration under a regime of psychomedications raises the question of the nature of the self. Earlier psychoanalysis focused on the complexity of the mind, the conscious and unconscious self as that was shaped by social conflicts in family relationships. Delving deeply into the earlier stages of these conflicts allowed repressed memories to become conscious and to resolve these conflicts in the achievement of a mature self. Current psychiatry has abandoned any interest in the history and development of the self. Mind is an epiphenomenon of the brain. Imbalances of brain chemistry cause delusions, fantasies and hearing voices. Balancing this chemistry by medication will banish these feelings. If someone like

David goes into withdrawal and stops eating and speaking when locked in a repressive environment, the environment itself is ignored as a cause of the problem. Tinkering with the medication is all that is needed. Current biomedical theory views the brain as a mechanism to be adjusted chemically. It is profoundly contemptuous of the complexity of the self.

As parents we remember David as a bright, humorous, curious, and creative emerging teenager. What has happened to that self, who at times can barely communicate, who sometimes stares at us with hostile eyes, who has lost skills of sustained reading, who writes strings of rhyming words that are not sentences? Is that self still there? At times he seems to return to a more normal self. Has brain damage caused it to shrink? Could it be partly restored in a more stimulating and supportive environment?

We know that when we die, the brain ceases to function. Traditional Christian religion thought there was a separable soul, a spiritual-ontological self that left the body, hovering over it for a short while and then returning to its heavenly home; or perhaps passing through some stages of punishment to purge it of its sins, until it could return to union with God in heaven.

Today the existence of this immortal, separable self is in question for me. I see the mind as based on the finite contingencies of brain and body in its social and historical context, but not simply reduced to chemistry. A complex consciousness that seeks meaning, interacts in relationships, and generates creative processes is the mental interiority of the bodily self, driving it into activity in the world around it. How does this become diminished when frontal brain lobes are shrunk by assaults of drugs that repress neuron-transmitters? What is happening when one week David seems totally incoherent, uninterested in getting out of bed, and yet the next week some of his complex, questing, and humorous self seems again to be present? How can something of his creative self be salvaged and redeveloped?

The brain-chemistry view of the causes of mental illness is fundamentally reductionist. It fails to reckon with the dynamically organic reality of the relationship between the mental and the somatic in which thought, experience, and learning constantly interact with and change brain chemistry. It is not simply that brain chemistry determines mental processes, but mental processes have an effect on brain chemistry. As a group of researchers on the development of adolescent psychosis put it,

> The first alternative we propose is that *many* (and perhaps *most* or even *all*) *of the biological differences seen in the brains of people*

suffering from psychosis are produced by psychotic symptoms. Thus biological differences would be a biological response or implementation of a psychotic mental state. This changes the direction of causality round so that the symptoms of psychosis can be viewed on a par with the biological in determining the cause of the condition . . . Another more satisfactory proposal is: *the biological and psychological work in a reciprocal and iterative fashion* . . . symptoms produce changes in the brain and . . . these in turn shape the form of the symptoms. These would not be discrete actions but ongoing and reciprocal interchanges.[3]

An example of severe environmental stress causing changes in brain chemistry, and ongoing psychosis, is posttraumatic stress disorder (PTSD). This is a severe anxiety disorder that can develop after exposure to terrifying events that threaten or cause great physical harm to oneself or others around you. People with PTSD display pathological changes in the neurological wiring of the brain as a result of shocks of extreme fear and psychic trauma. There is no evidence that some "brain chemistry disorder" caused this psychosis, but the psychosis was the result of the psychological, environmental trauma. Although war-related trauma is the best-know example of this PTSD, other traumatic and life-threatening events are also known to cause it, such as violent personal assault, including sexual assault, being kidnapped and taken hostage, natural and manmade disasters, automobile accidents, and being tortured.[4]

A great deal of new research from the 1990s has emphasized the plasticity of the brain and the reciprocal interaction of mind and brain. It has become clearer how environmental experiences and learnings interact with neurological pathways of brain chemistry. Some of this work was pioneered by Viennese Jewish psychiatrist Eric Kandel, who fled the Nazis with his family as a child. Kandel's training in neuroscience and psychoanalysis, as well as the shocks he had experienced in his early life from the Nazis, led him to ask how learning changes the brain. He experimented on the Aplysia, a large sea snail, to show this connection. The brain of the Aplysia has only twenty thousand cells, compared to one hundred billion in mammals.

---

3. Chris Harop and Peter Trower, *Why Does Schizophrenia Develop at Late Adolescence?: A Cognitive-Developmental Approach to Psychosis* (Hoboken, NJ: Wiley, 2003), 14, 16.

4. A good study of PTSD is Rachel Yehuda, *Psychobiology of Post-Traumatic Stress Disorder: A Decade of Progress,* Annals of the New York Academy of Sciences (Boston: Blackwell, 2006).

By shocking the snail on its head or tail, Kandel was able to see how the brain cells changed as the animal learned to avoid the shocks. He found that the synapses between the neurons could readily and systematically change in response to stimuli. "In the Aplysia you can see with your eyes that the connections change. When an animal remembers something for the long term, it grows new synaptic connections."[5]

Kandel's pioneering article, "A New Intellectual Framework for Psychiatry," lays out the interactive relationship between environmental learning and changes of brain chemistry.[6] Neuroscientist Norman Dodge says of this article: "Kandel's work demonstrates that the common metaphor that compares the mind with a computer with unmodifiable hardware (the brain) and malleable software (thoughts, memories) is wrong. Rather thoughts can actually change the structure of the brain, the software modifies the hardware."[7]

This recognition of the complex interactions between environmental experience and brain chemistry means that psychiatry needs to go beyond the false dualisms of mind versus brain, social versus biological causes, psychotherapy versus medication. The debate between psychosocial versus biological causes of mental illness needs to be transcended by the development of a biopsychosocial view. More complex interactions between mind and brain need to become part of psychiatric practice. Sometimes psychotherapies that retrain cognition and behavior can more effectively help recovery from an episode of mental illness than medications, whose actual workings are not well known. Even physical exercise has been shown in many cases to help better in recovery than medication.

The brain is far more organically developmental than a reductionist brain-chemistry approach to mental illness has recognized. This has long been recognized medically. I remember a case in 1955 when the son of one of my mother's friends was severely injured in the Korean War. The left side of his brain was severely damaged, and he lost the ability to speak. He was given treatment in the hospital that retrained the right side of his brain as the base for speech. He recovered his ability to speak, but lost the mathematical and scientific learning in which he had previously excelled, yet discovered new talents for aesthetic and artistic creativity.

5. Quoted in Charles Barber, *Comfortably Numb: How Psychiatry Is Medicating the Nation* (New York: Pantheon, 2008), 194.

6. *American Journal of Psychiatry* 155 (April 1998) 457–69.

7. Quoted in Barber, *Comfortably Numb*, 195.

As a teenager I was fascinated by this information shared with me by my mother and her friend. Later I took a class with James Ashbrook, pioneer on the question of theology and the left and right sides of the brain.[8] There I learned that the left side of the brain is more the seat of verbal and mathematic ability, and the right side of the brain the seat of aesthetic and musical ability. Damaging the left side of his brain apparently lessened his previous skills in the area of mathematics, but developing the right side of his brain tapped into heretofore undeveloped artistic skills.

Although I am no scientist, to understand this complexity of the brain, this experience from my childhood early made me aware of the complex organic plasticity of the human brain and its ability of develop and change in response to new learnings and experiences. This recognition gives hope that mentally ill people, including those damaged by medication, are not fixed in a retrograde state, but there are possibilities for the redevelopment of their brain functions, if we take a more appropriate and creative view of mind-brain interrelation. One example of a new therapy that seeks to rebuild the damaged brains of the mentally ill is Cognitive Enhancement Therapy (CET).

Cognitive Enhancement Therapy is based on a recognition that those with schizophrenia suffer from significant brain damage or reduced activity in the frontal cortex. Unlike Whitaker's view, CET does not assign blame for this to long-term use of medications. Rather this reduced activity in the frontal cortex of the brain is seen as a neurodevelopmental disorder caused by the disease itself. But this disorder is seen as correctable, rather than as an irreversible deterioration. CET advocates affirm that "the brain has a natural capacity to repair developmental delays and trauma. This is called *neuroplasticity*. This healing activity is more likely to occur when interventions induce people to use their brains. CET is designed to do this."[9]

CET is a program that takes place for three and a half hours once a week for fifty-five weeks. This program combines computer-based cognitive exercises, psychoeducational group discussion, and individual coaching. The results of this program have shown that after a year, individuals attain significant improvement in mental capacities. This includes processing speed in thinking, motivation and initiative, attention and concentration,

8. James B. Ashbrook, *The Brain and Belief* (Bristol, IN: Wyndham Hall, 1988).

9. Center for Cognition and Recovery, and CET Cleveland. *CET: Cognitive Enhancement Therapy; An Overview of the Evidence-Based Practice* (booklet). Online: http://cetc-leveland.org/Shared%20Documents/CET%20Booklet%20updated%20Oct%202012.pdf/.

working memory, verbal memory, problem solving, cognitive flexibility, and mental stamina. Social cognition is also improved. This includes perspective taking on the relation of self and others, role flexibility and humor, or appreciation of achieving personal goals of the self and others. Self-management of mental and physical health and acceptance of responsibility for one's disability are also improved.

CET is not behavior therapy, in the sense of helping people change the *content* of their thought and behavior, such as changing negative views of the self into positive views. Rather the exercises and discussions aim to enhance the internal agility of mental processes themselves. If one becomes more competent in the actual processes of thinking, a variety of personal and social capacities are improved. For example, by improving one's actual ability to concentrate in reading a book, one's sense of well-being is improved. The effects of these improvements in cognitive ability have proved long lasting. These improvements are maintained after thirty-six weeks and continue to develop over time.

Is this the happy solution to David's loss of cognitive capacity? Probably not, at this time. Those eligible have to be in what is called a "recovery phase of treatment." This means being in a stage of acceptance of functioning in a group and taking responsibility for working through the exercises, discussing them in relation to oneself. David, unfortunately, is not anywhere near what I could call such as recovery phase of his illness. To approach this stage would mean a revolution in his sense of motivation, which so far has eluded all our efforts to help him. Without his willingness to take responsibility for himself, all such efforts are frustrated. But CET at least offers the hope that cognitive functioning of damaged brains is possible, if the mentally ill who suffer from this damage are able to make this motivational turn. How does that motivational turn come about?

One example of a psychiatric movement that has grappled with what it means to move to a "recovery" stage of mental illness is the Village in Long Beach, California. The Village is an integrated service center that helps the mentally ill move to recovery and become able to live and work in their community. The Village puts major emphasis on helping one get a job and manage one's own housing. It offers supportive counseling that includes medication. Medication is not seen as essential but rather as an adjunct to learning how to manage one's own life and health. Medication is negotiated between the psychiatrist and the individual. The psychiatrist presents several options for medication, explains the effects of each, and allows the person to decide what he or she will take or not take.

Mark Ragins, the resident psychiatrist at the Village, sees its vision as a transformative journey for himself. To arrive at this vision he had to unlearn the way he was taught to see the mentally ill in his psychiatric education: "As a psychiatrist I had been taught to manage serious mental illness with a set of assumptions that if articulated would sound something like this: 'People with chronic mental illness are permanently disabled. Medicate them and forget them. They are weak and need to be taken care of. They can't hold down jobs. They have no significant role to play in society. The possibility of them leading a meaningful life is slight. Their prognosis is hopeless.'"[10]

For Ragins, coming to a vision of recovery was like a conversion experience. He realized he was confusing recovery and cure. A person with major mental illness may never be cured, in the sense of having all the symptoms disappear, but one can learn to manage illness in a way that allows them to take charge of life. The process of entering into recovery involves four stages. The first stage is *hope*. The person with mental illness needs to shake off passivity and dependency. Hopelessness is not simply a symptom of the disease; rather it is inculcated through the mental health system itself, which demands a passive compliance. Hope means discovering some idea of something one wants to do to make a better life for oneself, even if it is a small step, like deciding to keep oneself clean and brush one's teeth regularly. It means taking some responsibility for oneself.

The next step is *empowerment*. People are empowered by receiving access to information and opportunities and, above all, by support in taking risks and beginning to believe they have the capacity to do something more than they are presently doing. This is a view that goes directly against the policy of the mental health system, which believes that a person must not take risks since this will lead to failure and relapse. The Village, by contrast, encourages people to try something they have decided to do, even if they do not feel fully "ready." It promises to continue to support them if they fail. Failure itself can be seen as a learning experience that can help a person find out how to succeed next time.

The third step is *self-responsibility*. From hope and empowerment a person begins to take more and more responsibility for his or her own life. This is an ongoing process by which one gets over dependency and blaming others and learns to take charge of improving oneself. The final stage is

---

10. Mark Ragins, *A Road to Recovery* (Los Angeles: The Mental Health Association of Los Angeles County, 2002), 2.

finding a *meaningful role in life*. This does not necessarily mean becoming a successful and well-paid professional. A person may discover a role as an unpaid cook for a homeless shelter. It means finding a meaningful place in a community of relationships.[11]

The Village has a good track record of helping people regarded as hopeless to help themselves and begin to enter this process of recovery. Its vision is a healthy one, in contrast to the mentality of much of the mental health system, which inculcates unhealthy dependency and hopelessness. This is my wish for David, a wish that still eludes us, but one on which I refuse, against all odds, to simply give up, as long as he and I are still alive.

11. This account summarizes the narrative of Ragins's book: ibid. See Rosemary Radford Ruether, *Many Forms of Madness: A Family's Struggle with Mental Illness and the Mental Health System* (Minneapolis: Fortress, 2010), 172–75.

6

Ecology, Feminism, and Spirituality for a Livable Planet

For more than forty years ecology has been an integral part of my concern for planetary justice. As I mentioned in chapter 1, in 1972 I read summaries of the Club of Rome report, *Limits to Growth,* and was deeply impressed. It became evident to me that the current capitalist-industrial growth model of the economy promoted by the West could not be expanded to include the poor of the world. Rather, this model of growth was itself based on impoverishing the majority of the people of the world and depleting the natural resources of the planet. There needed to be a fundamental reconstruction of this whole system of relation of human peoples to each other and to the earth.

Some groups in American society sought to respond to this challenge by advocating serious reduction in the ways we used fossil fuels. Jimmy Carter was president, and he signaled the seriousness of the issue by putting solar panels on the roof of the White House, turning down the heat, putting on a sweater, and advocating fifty-five-mile-an-hour speed limit on American highways. This simple change in driving speed helped cut oil demand by more than a sixth in a decade.[1] But big oil companies and ideologists of economic growth fought back, and Carter was ridiculed for his efforts. In 1980 Ronald Reagan was elected; he quickly ended limits on driving speed and took the solar panels off the White House. We were assured that there

---

1. Bill McKibben, *Earth: Making a Life on a Tough New Planet* (New York: Time Books, 2010), 95

were no limits to growth. "There are no limits to the carrying capacity of the earth," economist Larry Summers opined.[2]

Some real progress might have been made if concerted action had started in the 1970s, led by the United States. Instead the issue was rejected and the data showing human responsibility for climate change derided. This rejection continues today in 2012. With some leadership from the new president, Barack Obama, Congress passed a weak bill to cut back fuel emissions in 2009. But this bill was stalled in the Senate, under pressure from lobbyists from big oil and big coal. With no new pressure from the president, the Senate in 2010 walked away from the bill altogether.

Crises in the Planetary System

At this writing, in 2012, there is evidence of deep changes in the climate and crises in all global systems, from rising temperatures worldwide to more erratic weather. Floods, droughts, heat waves, and stronger hurricanes are everywhere evident. Climate changes that profoundly alter the sustainability of the planet for the human economic system and its growing population are no longer a future threat; they are now an established reality. As environmentalist Bill McKibben puts it in his decisive book, *Earth: Making a Life on a Tough New Planet* (2010), we have already lost the planetary system that sustained human life, its agricultural system, and civilization for ten thousand years. We now have a "tough new planet" that will make it much harder to survive. We will need to make deep changes in our systems of life and our ways of thinking in order to live at least somewhat decently in this new reality.

I will summarize some of these changes in the planet that have moved from threat to reality in the last forty years. There is clear evidence of rising temperature worldwide. In 2010 nineteen nations reported all-time high temperatures; in Pakistan the temperature reached 128 degrees Fahrenheit. The year 2010 ended the warmest decade for which we have records.[3] Since warmer weather holds more moisture than cooler air, this also creates more rain, not gentle steady rain, but rather precipitous rain that creates floods, washing away housing and crops. There were "once in a thousand years" storms creating devastating floods across the globe. In Pakistan the flooded Indus River displaced thirteen million people and destroyed

2. Ibid.
3. Ibid., 214.

much of the country's infrastructure. This continues even as I write at the end of September 2012. Over-one-hundred-degree heat has persisted for months in the United States from coast to coast in the summers of 2011 and 2012. In 2011 from New York to Chicago this was followed by heavy thunderstorms and floods, while the summer of 2012 saw chronic droughts threatening the basic food crops.

A basic cause of this rising temperature is the burning of fossil fuels: oil, natural gas, and coal. The earth receives its energy in the form of sunlight. A naturally occurring layer of greenhouse gases allows the sunlight to be absorbed by the earth and its vegetation. This sunlight is then reflected back at longer heat waves. Greenhouse gases absorb some of this heat. A delicate balance of these gases has kept the temperatures (averaging 57.2 degrees) within a range that has allowed life to flourish for ten thousand years—the years of growing human civilization. But when greenhouse gases increase in the atmosphere due to burning fossil fuels, more of the sun's heat is retained and temperatures rise. Over the last two hundred years since the rise of burning of fossil fuels, carbon dioxide (CO_2) has risen about 25 percent and nitrous oxide about 19 percent. From 280 parts per million, CO_2 had risen to 386 parts per million by 2008. This period saw a rise of global temperature by 1.4 degrees Fahrenheit. If a check on greenhouse emissions does not take place in the twenty-first century, this could rise by as much of 5.4 degrees Fahrenheit by midcentury.[4]

These changes of temperature are larger at the Arctic and Antarctic poles, as much as 9 degrees' change by the early twenty-first century. This is causing rapid melting of polar ice caps. After the summer of 2007 there was 22 percent less ice than the year before. The Arctic ice cap was 1.1 million square miles smaller than in any year before in recorded history. This melting has continued in the subsequent summers of 2008, 2009, 2010, 2011, and 2012. Antarctica is also losing ice rapidly.[5] The melting of polar icecaps removed the albedo (reflection) effect of the white ice and snow cover, absorbing the heat waves into the water, rather than reflecting them back, thereby increasing the rise in temperature. As the permafrost melts, methane is released into the atmosphere, increasing the load of greenhouse gases in the atmosphere.

4. See Dinyar Godrej, *The No-Nonsense Guide to Climate Change* (Oxford: New Internationalist Publications, 2001), 37–43.

5. McKibben, *Earth*, 4, 5.

Ice is not only melting at the poles. The great glaciers of the Himalayas, the mountain ranges of the Andes in Latin America and the Sierras in the United States are also melting. These are the sources of the great rivers that water these continents, their people and agriculture. Without this water it will be impossible for the billions of these people to survive. Melting ice caps also raise sea levels, threatening a flooding of major cities situated by ocean coasts, and endangering the existence of low-lying islands.

Oceans are also changing in other ways. The carbon dioxide poured into the atmosphere is also increasing the acid level of the oceans' waters by 30 percent. This is destroying shellfish that cannot make thick enough shells in this acid water. Phytoplankton, the nutrient that is the basis of marine life, is being destroyed. Coral reefs are dying off rapidly and may be mostly gone by midcentury. These coral reefs are the basis of much ecological diversity and protective shelters around islands and coastal areas. Warmer oceans also generate stronger hurricanes. Between 1995 and 2008 there were 111 hurricanes formed in the tropical Atlantic, 75 percent more than in the previous thirteen years, and these tended to be stronger and more long lasting.[6]

These deep changes in the way the planet works in terms of heat and water for human livelihood are exacerbated by a rising human population. In 1804 human population hit one billion. One hundred and twenty-four years later, in 1927 it had doubled to 2 billion. But it took only another forty-seven years for the population to double again to four billion in 1974. It took only thirteen years for it to expand to five billion in 1987 and twelve years to expand to six billion in 1999. Despite efforts worldwide to lower the birth rate, such as the Chinese one-child policy, another twelve years saw human population cross the line to seven billion in 2011.

This expanding population aggravates the effects of human production, consumption, and waste on the planet. Although not producing and consuming at the level of the wealthiest nations, such as the United States, many developing nations aspire to something like this Western lifestyle. In the United States there are 842 cars for every 1000 persons in a national population of 311 million. In China, with a population more than four times larger, or 1,339 million, car ownership has expanded dramatically. In 1990 there were only one million cars in China, but in 2010, twenty years later, this has expanded to 168 million cars. Chinese cities have deeply

6. Ibid., 8.

polluted air, and many Chinese put on breathing masks before venturing outside.

This expanding population is putting the capacity of global agriculture to feed the world's population under severe pressure. Between 1950 and 1984 world population doubled, but the production of basic grains, the foundation of the human diet, expanded 2.6 times. But since 1988 production of basic grains has been static or in decline as water becomes more scarce. With growing droughts and continuous farming, soil is eroded, creating desert-like conditions. Whether increasing food production will feed the expanding human numbers is in severe doubt. But this is exacerbated by the extreme misdistribution of wealth, making it difficult for poorer people to buy food. Western, affluent people have an abundance and diversity of foods at their fingertips, while poorer people have both inadequate amounts and lack nutritional diversity.

The food-production system developed by the West and promoted globally depends on large farms, the use of petroleum-based fertilizers and pesticides, heavy irrigation, and machine cultivation. These methods pollute the soil, injure animal and human health, and deplete water sources. Industrial agriculture uses huge amounts of fossil fuels both for fertilizer and pesticides and mechanized plowing and picking, and also for long-distance transportation of food. It is estimated that the food US citizens eat typically travels an average of thirteen hundred miles from farm to family table. Often this trade results in the same foods passing each other, such as the United States sending grain to India, while India sends grain to the United States.[7] Packaging adds additional pollution and waste along the way. Seeds are monopolized by large agricultural firms, and farmers are made dependent on these firms.

This industrial agricultural system has been seen as necessary to produce the expanded food supply needed to feed the world, but this is becoming increasingly doubtful. More local systems, which multicrop on the same land, use local agricultural and animal wastes for fertilizer and distribute locally have been shown to actually be able to produce more food per acre than the huge monocrops of industrial farming.[8] As we confront what it means to survive on this "tough new planet," the industrial

---

7. See Andrew Kimbrell, ed., *Fatal Harvest Reader: The Tragedy of Industrial Agriculture* (Washington DC: Island Press, 2002), 289, 257.

8. McKibben, *Earth*, 168.

agricultural system is a major piece of the present global system that needs to be rethought.

Ideologies of Domination of Nature

To explore the responses we must give to this crisis of the planet, we need to ask how this system of abuse of the planet has developed over human history. How have the ideologies and practices of domination of the planet been shaped? How do we need to reshape our culture to change these ideologies and practices? These patterns go back a long way. We need to see them as part of the emergence of patriarchy at least seven millennia ago.

With the emergence of patriarchy in the fifth millennium BCE there also developed law codes that defended this hierarchy of ruling class over peasants and slaves, men over women. For example, in the Code of Hammurabi (1727 BCE) a series of laws deals with violence by members of the ruling aristocracy toward women of different classes who are pregnant:

> If a seignor (nobleman) struck another seignor's daughter and caused her to have a miscarriage, he shall pay ten shekels for her fetus.
> If that woman has died, they shall put his daughter to death
> If by a blow he has caused a commoner's daughter to have a miscarriage, he shall pay five shekels of silver.
> If that woman has died, he shall pay half a mina of silver.
> If he struck seignor's female slave and caused her to have a miscarriage, he shall pay two shekels of silver.
> If that female slave has died, he shall pay one-third mina of silver.[9]

The presuppositions of these laws are clear. The females are always referred to in relation to their male owners, father or slave master. There is a hierarchy of social class in terms of the value of the females and their fetuses. The fetus of a nobleman's daughter is worth ten shekels, a commoner's five and that of a slave woman two shekels. The life of a nobleman's daughter is invaluable and is paid for by the life of the perpetrator seignor's daughter. The fact that she had nothing to do with the violence is irrelevant. Her life is taken as equivalent property of her father. A commoner's daughter is worth half a mina of silver, and a slave woman's life is worth a third

---

9. "Code of Hammurabi," in James B. Prichard, ed., *Ancient Near Eastern Texts Related to the Old Testament*, 3rd ed. (Princeton: Princeton University Press, 1969), 175.

of a mina of silver. Presumably these payments go to the father or slave master, not to the woman or to her mother.

Greek philosophy was likewise built on a hierarchy of class and gender. This hierarchy presupposes a dualism of mind over body. In Plato's *Timaeus*, reality originally consisted of a dualism of an eternal, intellectual world of Ideas and the gods, and unformed matter. The Creator shaped matter into the universe by looking to the eternal ideas as intellectual models. He then shaped the energy or world soul to move the universe. From the remaining energy after he had infused the world soul into the universe, the Creator shaped individual souls, which he placed in the stars to contemplate the eternal Ideas. Then he incarnated them into bodies shaped by the planetary gods. The task of the soul is to live a good moral life and keep itself from being corrupted by the base passions that arise from the body. If it succeeds in doing so, it will return to its immortal star to enjoy a "blessed and congenial existence." But if it fails to do so, it will be reincarnated into a woman; if in that lower state it does not desist from evil, it will become "some brute."[10] Thus in Plato the dualism of mind and matter is expressed by the hierarchy of male over female over animal. A hierarchy of classes is also assumed in other Platonic dialogues: ruling class over warriors and peasants.

Similar assumptions govern Aristotle's thought. For Aristotle, the ruling-class Greek male is the natural ruler who exemplifies the principle of rationality that governs the body and material existence. Women, lower-class people, and Orientals are "natural slaves," or expressions of that bodily existence governed by the rationality of the male ruling-class culture: "The male is by nature superior and the female inferior; the one rules and the other is ruled: this principle extends to all mankind. Where there is such a difference as that between soul and body or between men and animals (as is the case of those whose business is to use their bodies and who can do nothing better) the lower sort are by nature slaves, and it is better for them as for all inferiors that they should be under the rule of a master."[11]

Christianity inherited and passed along this pattern of thought in which the spiritual, intellectual world was positioned outside and above the physical, material world of nature. The social hierarchies of gender, class, and race are seen as graded expressions of this hierarchy of mind

---

10. Plato, *Timaeus*, in *The Dialogues of Plato*, B. Jowett, ed., 2 vols. (New York: Random House, 1937), 2:23.

11. Aristotle, *Politics* 1254b.

over body. With the expansion of Western European power into colonial domination of indigenous peoples of the Americas, Africa, and Asia in the sixteenth and seventeenth centuries, Aristotle's *Politics* was revived as the model for viewing the European male colonizer as the natural master and the colonized people as natural slaves.

Seventeenth-century European thought saw the development of an ideology of the natural world as "dead matter" to be dominated by the rational mind of the master class. This ideology banished the remaining elements of a more organic view of nature that still existed in the Greek and medieval worlds, in which the universe as animated by a "world soul" of similar spiritual nature to human souls. This view of nature as dead matter is found in the early modern science of Descartes and Newton. For Descartes the thinking mind, found only in (male intellectual) humans, is transcendent and stands over against matter, which by nature is dead, without soul or spirit, moving mechanically according to the laws of causality. For Newton, matter is reducible to small, hard atomic particles, or atoms, moving in a spatial void because of the laws of force and gravity.[12]

This new view of a mechanical universe of dead matter knowable and to be ruled by the transcendent minds of European male intellectuals becomes the paradigm for a view of nature reduced to resources, appropriated as power and wealth by the ruling elites of Europe. Although more recent science has changed this view of primal matter as reduced to small, hard particles to a view of the atom as whirling matrices of energy, the mechanical view of the relation of humans to nature still governs the psychological culture of modern science and technology. The world around us is inanimate stuff that (elite male) humans can possess and use at will for their power and enrichment. Women, workers, and colonized people are reduced to tools of this domination and use of nature.

Ecofeminist Critiques of the Domination of Nature

From the 1980s to today there have emerged many responses to this patriarchal ideology of domination of nature that seek to recover, both an animate nature in interrelation with humans, and human mutuality with one another across gender, race, and class relations. This is called ecojustice, or ecofeminism, when the emphasis is on gender symbolism and relations. I

12. See Rosemary Radford Ruether, *Gaia & God: An Ecofeminist Theology of Earth Healing* (San Francisco: HarperSanFrancisco, 1992), 196–97.

will mention here a few major representatives of this movement and their thought and practice.

Starhawk, an American neopagan thinker and activist, is a major leader of ecojustice advocacy. Starhawk sees the basic conversion from patterns of domination to those of mutuality as a shift from power *over* to power *within* and power *with*. Power *over* is the basic model of patriarchal societies. Elite males dominate women, subjugated races, and classes, and the nonhuman world. Power *within* expresses the process by which dominated people shake off control by others and their internalized subjugation and realize their own inner power and goodness. Power *with* is the development of ways to share power with one another in community by mutual empowerment.[13]

Starhawk works as a trainer for nonviolent protest actions against global agents of domination, such as the World Trade Organization. She sees the model for nonviolent action and transformation of relations as represented by permaculture gardening. In permaculture, the gardener must attune her- or himself to the changes of the seasons, the patterns of the land, and the interrelation of soil, plants, insects, and animals in the local context, in order to bring forth the most flourishing growth. One does not impose power from above using monocultures of plants foreign to the land.

For Starhawk, violent ways of treating the earth and violent ways of treating other humans are similar, and both are inherently unstable. Such violence does not nurture the natural energies of the others, and it demands continual force to be maintained. The present economy is based on deepening impoverishment of the peoples and the lands of the earth for the enrichment of the superrich. Ecological crisis is found as this way of treating the others becomes more and more contradictory.

Starhawk suggests five principles for creating an alternative, regenerative global economy. These are: 1) a shift from fossil fuels to renewable energy, such as solar and wind energy, 2) a return to human labor rather than reliance on machines, 3) continual recycling of the waste side of production and consumption as fertilizer and material for new production, 4) the cultivation of biological and cultural diversity, rather than the present focus on monocultures, and 5) greater efficiency or doing more with less use of resources.[14]

13. Starhawk, *Dreaming in the Dark: Magic, Sex, and Politics* (Boston: Beacon, 1982), 1–15.

14. Starhawk, *Webs of Power: Notes from the Global Uprising* (Gabriola Island, BC: New Society, 2002), 244–45.

Another leading ecojustice thinker is Indian organizer Vandana Shiva. Shiva's first major book was *Staying Alive: Women, Ecology, and Development*.[15] She has written numerous other books along the same lines, critiquing the global system of development and its ideologies. Shiva was trained as a physicist and critiques the ideology of Western science, as well as its model of development. She sees both of these as "projects of patriarchy." Western developmentalism picks up when colonialism left off and is a neocolonial continuation of it. It is basically engaged in the exploitation and plunder of Third World labor and their lands. This exploitation is rooted in and justified through the distorted epistemology of Western science. In this epistemology the Western male knower is abstracted into a transcendent space outside nature, while reducing nature to dead matter pushed and pulled by mechanical force. Thus Western science "kills" nature by denying its possession of self-generating organic life.

This subjugation of nature is linked to the way Western developmentalism views native women. Women's work in cultivating the land is seen as unproductive, to be pushed aside for the mechanization of farming in the hands of male landowners. Thus developers fail to see that native women traditionally play a key role in sustainable cultivation of the land through connecting humans and animals, forests and crops. Women tend the animals, feeding them fodder from forests and the waste leaves and stalks of the crops. They harvest and prepare the food for the family, and convert animal dung into fuel and fertilizer. They gather herbs from forests as medicines and maintain the green cover of fields and waterways, caring for the waterways and providing clean water for families. These multiple roles of women in traditional agriculture Shiva sees as modeling an expression of a sustainable relationship between people and land that needs to be rediscovered and redeveloped.

Shiva looks to popular Hinduism for a vision of ecological theology. She lifts up the Hindu principle of *Shakti*, the female-identified creative energy of nature, together with its male form *Purusha*, that together produce nature (*Prakriti*) as a model. *Prakriti* has been traditionally understood as a Goddess, the basic female power of the universe. Shiva sees Hinduism in this popular expression, despite its official patriarchalism, as venerating women as the active principle of the maintenance of life.

Another key ecofeminist thinker is Brazilian theologian Ivone Gebara. Gebara worked in the 1980s in a Brazilian liberation theology-oriented

---

15. Delhi: Kali for Women, 1989.

Catholic theological school preparing priests for ministry through service to the poorest rural and urban peoples. When the seminary was abruptly closed and its faculty fired with the advent of a new conservative bishop, Gebara realized that the earlier perspective of liberation theology, despite its commitment to the oppressed, ignored women entirely. Gebara began to rethink her theological perspective, calling her new outlook ecofeminism.[16]

Gebara sees ecofeminist theology as a fundamental paradigm shift in theological thinking. Instead of just trying to add women into a hierarchical universe culminating in a male deity outside creation, ecofeminism deconstructs the patriarchal model of the universe and its methodology of thought. This means deconstructing the whole pattern in theological thought of male over female, mind over body, transcendent over immanent, with God as a transcendent male Ego outside and ruling over creation. This means starting with experience—female experience of daily life—rather than with abstract ideas located in heaven. From this experience of daily life, one does not aim at eternal truths. Rather one aims to discern the network of relations that link us to people around us, in our families, in our societies, in the earth and natural life around us, discerning finally how all of this is interconnected in life systems of the universe.

One of Gebara's major projects of deconstructing and reconstructing a basic Christian theological symbol is her writing on the meaning of the Trinity.[17] For Gebara, the Trinity is not about three transcendent male persons residing in a transcendent space together outside the universe. Rather the Trinity is a way of expressing the dynamics of life in interconnected creativity. Creative energy is a dialectical process. By nature creative energy ramifies into diversity while interconnecting in relationships, which then ramify into new diversity. The universe has been created and continues to be created through the dialectical process of creative energy ramifying, interconnecting, and diversifying again. This Trinitarian process is not all benign. There is within it a dynamic relation of life and death, creativity and vulnerability. Death is an integral part of the finitude and renewal of life, not foreign to it.

16. For Gebara's theological journey from liberation theology to ecofeminism, see her autobiography, *Las Aguas de Mi Pozo: Reflecciones sobre Experiencias de Libertad* (Montevideo: Doble Clic, 2005).

17. Ivone Gebara, "The Trinity and Human Experience: An Ecofeminist Approach," in Rosemary Radford Ruether, ed., *Women Healing Earth: Third World Women on Ecology, Feminism and Religion*, Ecology and Justice (Maryknoll, NY: Orbis, 2005), 13–23.

But this aspect of natural evil in the finite life process is different from what we might call sin or destructive evil. Perniciously destructive evil comes about when humans try to resist their own limits and finitude and to monopolize power and resources to perpetuate themselves by subjugating other people and land around them. The construction of systems of dominating and exploitative power of some humans over others and over the nonhuman world has been endlessly repeated in human history since the rise of the plow, warfare, slavery, and social hierarchy. We are now living in an extreme crisis of these systems of distortion of human relations to each other and to nature that has grown global. This system needs to be dismantled and an alternative constructed that is more just and sustainable. This will not result in paradise but rather, at best, in a society in which we can live more justly and healthily with our fellow human beings and with the natural world within our finite limits.

Another important ecofeminist thinker seeking to reconstruct the basic paradigm of Christian thought is theologian Catherine Keller. Keller has written a major trilogy of theological reconstruction. In her first book, *From a Broken Web: Separation, Sexism, and Self*,[18] she rethinks the basic way masculine and feminine have been constructed in Western thought as separate and complementary. She constructs a new paradigm of mutual selves in relationship. In her second book *Apocalypse Now and Then*,[19] she surveys the way the idea of the end of the world has been seen as the crisis and transformation of creation. She seeks an alternative model of transformative moments within human historical process, rather than a crisis and decisive end of it.

Keller's third book, *Face of the Deep: A Theology of Becoming*,[20] addresses our foundational model of the creation of the world. The Hebrew author of Genesis 1 describes God as shaping creation from a watery darkness, dividing light from darkness, the waters above from the waters below, and the dry land from the sea. But the Christian church fathers became uneasy with the idea that there was preexisting stuff before God's creative work. They invented the doctrine of *creatio ex nihilo* (creation from nothing) to abolish this preexisting reality. Yet in Christian thought this primal

18. Catherine Keller, *From a Broken Web: Separation, Sexism, and Self* (Boston: Beacon, 1986).

19. Catherine Keller, *Apocalypse Now and Then: A Feminist Guide to the End of the World* (Boston: Beacon, 1996).

20. Catherine Keller, *Face of the Deep: A Theology of Becoming* (London: Routledge, 2003).

chaotic reality has a tendency to return as demonic, often female-gendered, monsters to be abolished by God again and again. Keller claims that Christian theology is compulsively "tehomophobic" (fearful of darkness and chaos).

Keller seeks to redefine the theology of creation by embracing, rather than abolishing, primal chaos. She shapes a theology of becoming between being and nothing, that also questions that "dominology" of church and state that seeks absolute power over the chaotic "other." Her Trinitarian vision of becoming interconnects *tehom* ("chaos"), *elohim* ("god/s") and *ruach elohim* ("breath of God"). *Tehom* and *elohim* are interacting energies in which what *is* appears in ever new and creative forms, without absolutes of beginning and end. In this creative space the *ruach elohim*, God's breath, can hover, empowering us to begin again and again.[21]

Africa has also been a fecund source of ecojustice and ecofeminist movements, but more as practical actions rather than as grand theories to reconstruct Western thought. I mention two such movements here. One is the Greenbelt movement founded by Kenyan feminist environmentalist Wangari Maathai, who won the Nobel Peace Prize for her work. Maathai saw the terrible problems being created in her country by deforestation, and she organized a movement of rural women to grow trees in their yards and plant them around their neighborhoods. From 1977 to 1999 over twenty million trees were planted from six thousand locally created tree nurseries. The project of reforestation expanded to other issues: food security (by redeveloping locally grown and consumed foods), water harvesting, and political and economic organizing to oppose land grabbing and violation of human rights by the powerful elites in alliance with foreign corporations. Maathai's movement has spread beyond Kenya to other African countries, and she became a world-renowned leader awarded the Nobel Prize for her work.

In Zimbabwe pastoral leader Marthinus Daneel created the Association of African Earthkeeping Churches (AAEC) that brought together indigenous religious leaders and African indigenous Christian churches around the project of reforestation as well as water renewal. The AAEC developed tree-planting eucharists conducted outdoors in the bush. The assembled worshipers drew on Christian and indigenous Shona religious

---

21. See my summary of Keller's thought, and these other ecofeminists in "Ecofeminist Thea/ologies and Ethics," in Rosemary Radford Ruether, *Integrating Ecofeminism, Globalization, and World Religions*, Nature's Meaning (Lanham, MD: Rowman & Littlefield, 2005), 91–129

traditions to ask forgiveness from the divine spirits for abusing and de-
foresting the land. After this ritual the group fans out to plant trees and
care for the watersheds. These churches teach local communities to care
for the land, renew water sources, and develop sustainable agriculture.[22]
These ecofeminist responses to the ideologies and practices of domination
of nature give use some important guidelines for the needed responses to
the crisis of the planet today. But they are radicalized by the changes that
have already afflicted our earth.

Building an Alternative System of Survival
on a Tough New Planet

In the tough new planet that we are in the process of creating through fossil
fuel emissions, resulting in rising temperatures and more erratic storms
and water availability, the growing of food is becoming more difficult for
farmers in many parts of the world. Large industrial agriculture is becoming less useful as a way of producing adequate food for a growing world
population. Droughts in much of Africa and across Australia and the United States wither crops, and sudden storms wipe them away. As always, these
crises affect the poorest people most severely: these have less land, and so
lack resources for the seeds, pesticides, fertilizers and machines promoted
by Western food production.

However, even as these systems are falling into crisis, local farmers
in many parts of the world are discovering alternatives, often alternatives
that go back to earlier methods of agriculture with new sophistication. The
emphasis of this new agriculture is a return to local production for local
consumption. This means smaller farms with a great variety of crops produced in interconnection with each other, small herds of animals or flocks
of chickens that produce fertilizer, and composting of organic wastes.
More people are employed in sowing, weeding, and harvesting, rather than
displacing rural workers by machines. The big monocrops of industrial
agriculture, petroleum-based pesticides, and fertilizers and toxic wastes
produced by large crowds of animals raised in pens are discarded for more
organic methods.

22. See Marthinus Daneel, "Earth-Keeping Churches at the African Grassroots," in
Rosemary Radford Ruether and Dieter Hessel, eds., *Christianity and Ecology*, Religions
of the World and Ecology (Cambridge: Harvard University Press, 2000), 531–52.

This return to more local, organic farming also proves better able to sustain crops in storms. Hurricanes in Honduras and Nicaragua in 1998 dropped three feet of rain in twenty-four hours, flooded local rivers, and wiped out every bridge and secondary road. Seventy percent of the crops were wiped out. But a study of 1800 farms after the storm showed that small farmers using sustainable practices suffered far less damage than neighbors using conventional methods. Greater topsoil, moisture, and diversity of crops allowed these more organic farms to suffer less soil erosion as a result of the storms.[23]

Bill McKibben, in the concluding chapter of his book, titled "Lightly, Carefully, Gracefully," details the redevelopment of this kind of small diverse organic farming in his home state of Vermont.[24] He cites the case of Tom Gilbert, founder of the Highlands Institute, who composts dead livestock. He also collects and composts food waste from surrounding schools, farms, and restaurants, providing fertilizers for many surrounding farms. Some of Gilbert's compost goes about a mile down the road to the gardens, where High Moving Seeds grows its produce. This is one of the largest organic seed companies in the nation. It provides a great range of seeds for vegetables.

One of the farmers buying this seed in the nearby town of Craftsbury is Peter Johnson, who is pioneering year-round farming in New England by using solar greenhouses. He had figured out how to make his greenhouses mobile, moving them around across the fields eleven months a year. John runs a CSA farm that supplies boxes of food to local subscribers. Johnson has calculated that he is able to supply this fresh locally grown food for about 20 percent less than the same products (but less fresh and nutritious) would cost in the supermarket.

Some of High Moving's seeds also go to a nearby company of Vermont Soy, which gives it to a small group of local Vermont farmers who produce soybeans, which in turn become tofu and soymilk in a small factory. Some of the soymilk is turned into furniture varnish. This small company is doing well economically and sees itself as having expanding markets for its products in Boston and New York. For McKibben, these interconnected producers of composts, seeds, year-round food, soymilk, and tofu are striking examples of how a new kind of local organic agriculture is beginning to flourish in his neighborhood.

23. See McKibben, *Earth*, 181.

24. Ibid., 159–80

Community-supported agriculture (CSA) is not only found in Vermont. It is a movement that began in England and in Japan. CSA connects farms with consumers in their area. CSAs consist of small farms of twenty to two hundred acres that grow a variety of crops by organic or biodynamic methods. They are supported by direct subscriptions by members, who pay the farm on a yearly or biyearly basis and receive a box of fresh seasonal foods weekly within a few days of actual harvesting. By intercropping or crop rotation and using natural fertilizers and pesticides, such farms avoid the toxic effects on food, soil, and water of industrial agriculture. There is a minimum of food waste since CSA farms avoid storage and long-distance shipping of their products, a major problem of industrial agriculture. There are about a thousand community-supported farms in the United States, most of them in New England, the Upper Midwest, and the Pacific Coast states. The farmers are generally younger than the average farmer in the US, well educated, and socially conscious. About 40 percent are women.

One good example of CSA is Full Belly Farm in Guinda, California, north of the Bay Area.[25] Full Belly Farm began in 1984 with a partnership of four men and women. It is a two-hundred-acre certified organic farm growing over eighty different crops, including a variety of vegetables, fruits, and nuts. It also has a flock of chickens, a herd of sheep, and several cows and uses these animals for fertilizer and soil renewal. It plants green cover crops that fix nitrogen and provide organic fertilizer for the soil, as well as habitat for beneficial insects.

Full Belly Farm has 650 subscribers who receive boxes of fresh food weekly that are delivered to pick-up places in their neighborhoods. It also employs thirty-five year-round workers who receive a living wage and medical insurance, plus help with housing. These workers, together with the partner-owners who also do manual labor, have provided a stable, committed workforce. Full Belly also sells its food in farmers' markets and to restaurants who value its fresh produce. It promotes its vision through study interns who work on the farm and by school presentations and visiting school groups. An annual Harvest Festival also acquaints the public with its way of growing and marketing food sustainably.

Community Supported Agriculture and other small organic farms reverse the population trends in Western and global agriculture. For more than a hundred years social development in the West and in the Third World has been based on taking workers off the farms into urban production and

25. See Ruether, *Integrating Ecofeminism, Globalization, and World Religions*, 152–53.

services. Fewer and fewer people living on farms and more and more in cities has been the worldwide pattern. Farm workers are replaced by machines, and seasonal pickers are badly exploited. CSA farms like Full Belly show that increased numbers of farm workers can be employed full time and enjoy a decent livelihood. Farm work is no longer seen as the bottom of the job hierarchy to be left behind by the educated, but is itself an educated and socially concerned occupation.

In addition to Community Supported Farms, there has been a great increase in urban and suburban gardens in cities like New York and San Francisco. More and more people are producing food for their own families and also selling it in their neighborhoods. San Francisco recently passed new laws encouraging this neighborhood food production and taking away laws that limited its local marketing. In my own community, Pilgrim Place, we have over a two hundred fruit-bearing trees and many vegetable plots. We have a weekly farmers' market to sell this produce. The profits go to a fund for emergency medical needs of our members.

Redeveloped agriculture needs to be matched by redeveloped energy production. This means turning from the focus on burning fossil fuels, which has brought us our present crisis, to sustainable energy production: solar, wind, and hydropower. This shift also means a turn from vast centralized production and transportation of energy to more local methods. This is being resisted by the big energy companies who have been the major funders of efforts to discredit the reality of the climate crisis. Nuclear power plants are not going to provide the main alternative, although they continue to be promoted. But the toxic wastes created by nuclear production, and their instability in the face of major earthquakes and storms, which are increasing with climate change, have decisively challenged the creed that this is the way to go. This had been clearly shown by the damaged nuclear plants in Japan's earthquakes and storms of March 2011.

The first step away from the present wasteful system is conservation and greater efficiency. Humans need to use much more carefully the energy we presently have. We need more efficient cars that get more mileage per gallon of fuel. We also must curb toxic emissions from automobiles and insulate all buildings to use much less energy. These are ways of using much less energy than in our current systems. Moving to alternative forms of transportation, bicycles and public transportation, rather than the private car, will become more attractive as the cost of gas rises.

Even in car-dominated Los Angeles there has been a 50 percent increase in bicycle riders, many of them using bicycles to go to work, not just for recreation. This increase in bicycle riders forced the LA City Council to pass a new law protecting bicycle riders from assault and harassment by car drivers.[26] More bicycle lanes are being constructed on major streets and highways.

A combination of greater conservation and efficiency and a switch to alternative non-polluting energy production could provide much of the energy needed in the US and around the world. Bill McKibben cites a 2008 report by the Institute for Local Self-Reliance showing that wind turbines and rooftop solar panels could provide 81 percent of New York's power and two-thirds of Ohio's. Fourteen thousand three hundred percent of its power, far beyond its own power needs, could be generated by windmills alone in North Dakota.[27]

The best way to construct energy systems from sun and wind is locally, even in individual family homes. Solar panels put on a family roof can provide much of the energy of the home. Solar panels produce more energy than is needed so the surplus feeds back into the electric company system. In the community where I live a recently constructed group home has solar panels across the garages, providing some of the energy to fifteen apartments and the administration building. With high-level insulation and many other energy efficient features, this qualifies as a LEED-certified building. (LEED stands for Leadership in Energy and Environmental Design.)

Long transportation lines for energy are cut by local transmission. The costs of energy no longer flow overseas to big oil companies. Although the big oil and electrical companies are resisting this and seeking to undermine this transition, rising costs of the present system are having their effects. China, although still dependent on its large supplies of coal, is preparing for at least a partly post-fossil fuel world by building vast new collections of solar and wind energy systems. By 2010 China had leapt ahead of the West to become the largest producer of both wind turbines and solar panels.[28]

This shift to more locally controlled agriculture and energy production does not, McKibben argues, simply leave us confined to a parochial

26. Ted Chen and Julie Brayton, "More Rights for Bike Riders Approved by LA City Council," NBC LA, aired on July 21, 2011. Online: http://www.nbclosangeles.com/news/local/More-Rights-for-Bike-Riders-Approved-by-LA-City-Council-125925813.html/.

27. McKibben, *Earth*, 188.

28. Keith Bradsher, "China is Leading the Race to Make Clean Energy," *New York Times*, January 30, 2010. Online: http://www.nytimes.com/2010/01/31/business/energy-environment/31renew.html?pagewanted=all&_r=0/.

world. This redevelopment requires both more local and more global consciousness. We may have to physically travel much less as the cost of fuel for cars and airplanes becomes more prohibitive. But we need even more than in the past to understand how our systems of food and energy production and consumption interconnect with our neighbors across the globe. The inexpensive electronic means of communication have arrived at the moment when we need to communicate much more with friends and colleagues, not just across our nation, but across the world.[29] We can begin to hold face-to-face meetings on Skype, rather than getting on planes.

Spirituality for New Communities of Life

With the crisis of the earth system that has supported civilization for ten thousand years and the arrival of a "tough new planet," hotter and more erratic in its weather, we need to change not only the way we have exploited the earth and burned up the fossil fuels buried beneath the soil for three hundred million years, but we need to deeply change the *way we think*, the culture by which we imagine our relationships to one another, to the earth, and to ultimate reality, however we name that. We have never experienced this before, and so we have no adequate models for how we need to think about the new ways we should live together.

For Christians one model for responding to the collapse of a whole world system and the development of a lifestyle for the "end of the old world" was ascetic, monastic spirituality of the third and fourth centuries, CE. For thousands of years the Mediterranean world had been engaged in expanding networks of empires: Egyptian, Babylonian, Assyrian, Hellenistic, and finally the Roman Empire, which knit together a vast power system from England to the borders of India. The third and fourth centuries saw this whole power system begin to collapse and disintegrate.

A remnant of the Roman Empire persisted in Byzantium (Greece and Turkey), but the empire lost its Near Eastern and North African territories to an expanding Islam in the eighth century. In the West the political system of empire disappeared, and with it much of its economic and cultural superstructure. Feudalism developed as a way of tying peasants, landowners, and warriors together locally. Monasticism became the community of spiritual life that also took over the preservation of culture and education.

29. McKibben, *Earth*, 196–204.

The worldview of monasticism was based on the belief that the monastics] were living of the end of the world. Christians saw themselves as living in the last years of human life on earth, awaiting a final intervention of God, the ultimate war between the forces of good and evil, and the establishment of a millennium of redeemed life on earth. This was to be followed by a heavenly transformation of the whole creation.

The present crisis of the planetary system that has sustained human civilization for ten thousand years is both the end of a much longer era of human development and also the end of a much more global reach of that development. How do we think about the impending end of our world, and how we are to live in the new "tough planet" we are entering? Does ascetic, monastic spirituality and community fashioned in the fourth-century provide any clues for the spirituality we need today?

I think there are some clues from that earlier experience that might be helpful. The monastic communities that sprang up in Egypt in the era of Anthony and Pachomius saw themselves as discarding the indulgent consumerism that had distorted the relation of soul and body. After years of fasting and struggle with demonic powers, Anthony emerged from his tomb, not emaciated, but renewed in a healthy body united to spirit. Central also to Egyptian monasticism was rejection of hierarchies of wealth and power. The new communities lived together as equals in a simple way of life, supported by the work of their own hands.

Another aspect of Egyptian monasticism was the new friendship of humans and animals. Monastic Christianity looked back to Genesis 6–9 for an account of the fall that had come about in human life from God's original intention for creation. Originally God created humans in God's likeness and gave them every green plant for food. But when human population increased and wickedness began to accelerate on the earth, God grew angry and sought to wipe out human civilization with a great flood.

But the faithfulness of one man caused God to relent and save his family and pairs of animals with them. But when the human survivors emerged from the ark, God witnessed to a change in the relation of humans and animals after the flood. Before, God had given humans only green plants for food. Now God gave humans the right to kill and eat everything, the birds of the air, the beasts of the earth and the fish of the sea. But now the fear and the dread of humans would be on all these birds, beasts, and fish, manifesting the new violent, corrupted relationship of humans to animals after the flood.

For monastics, their renewed way of human life overcomes this distortion of humans toward animals and allows a return to the more benign relationship to animals before the flood. Humans give up meat eating and return to the vegetarian diet of God's original mandate. In turn animals no longer fear the new redeemed human. Surrendering themselves to complete vulnerability in the barren desert, the monk is fed by birds who drop bread into his cave. The wolf lifts his paw to receive assistance from the monk who removes a painful thorn. This sense of new reconciliation of monk and the natural world culminates in the religious vision of St. Francis of Assisi in the thirteenth century.

> We praise You, Lord, for all Your creatures,
>
> especially for Brother Sun,
>
> who is the day through whom you give us light . . .
>
> We praise You, Lord, for Sister Moon and the stars
>
> In the heavens you have made them bright, precious and fair . . .
>
> We praise You, Lord, for Brother Wind and Air,
>
> Fair and stormy, all weather's moods,
>
> By which You cherish all that You have made.
>
> We praise You for Sister Water,
>
> So useful, humble, precious and pure.
>
> We praise You, Lord, for Brother Fire,
>
> Through whom you light the night.
>
> He is beautiful, playful, robust and strong.,
>
> We praise You, Lord for Sister Earth, who sustains us.
>
> With her fruits, colored flowers and herbs, . . .
>
> We praise You, Lord, for Sister Death,
>
> From whom no-one living can escape.[30]

This beautiful prayer gives us a sense of the whole community of life—including finitude and death—as our extended family, our sisters and brothers whom we love and praise.

Not all monastic spirituality is helpful to us. Much of it is built on hatred and fear of the embodied world, and an effort to escape the body for a spiritual world outside. We need to separate the positive efforts to create egalitarian communities, reconciled to creation, from this legacy of escape

---

30. Saint Francis of Assisi, "Canticle of Brother Sun." Online: http://www.prayer-foundation.org/canticle_of_brother_sun.htm/.

from creation. A spirituality for a new community of life on our tough new planet needs to clearly distinguish between our legacy of exploitation of the natural world for power and profit, and how to enter into a community of life with the plants and animals, wind and water and earth, and to attune our own energies to those of the ecosystems around us.

In the new world we are entering, there is much in those exploitative relations to the natural world that we need to give up. In that sense an element of asceticism or sacrifice must be part of the creation of a new spirituality. But what we need to give up is not about hating the physical world, but about giving up those practices that pollute the natural world, which are killing fish and birds and oppressing the poor among humans. We need to give up the privilege of jumping in private cars to go wherever we want because we know that the emissions we cause by this use of energy is corrupting the air around us. I suspect that air travel for the relatively affluent to fly around the world may no longer be possible in the new world we are entering. Rising prices of fuel will make this option much less available to even to the middle-level wealthy for whom it has been accessible. But how soon it is surrendered altogether is in question. Certainly the present power system will not soon give up this asset.

But many of the ways we need to become more attune to the energies of earth to cultivate food organically and generate energy from sunlight, wind and water will make our daily lives more complex, although more related to our immediate environment. For example, when I prepare dinner, mostly of fruits and vegetables, I carefully separate edible parts from peels, leaves, and seeds. Instead of throwing these in the trash with no concept of their future destiny, I now put them in a jar and then incorporate them in a compost container outside my back door. I bury them under the top levels of the compost as part of a process of turning them into rich soil, which is then dug into the ground to grow a new round of vegetables and fruits. My consumption becomes part of a life cycle: growth, eating, disintegration, composting, renewed soils, and growth again. Preparing food and composting waste becomes part of a spiritual discipline for the renewal of life.

These spiritual disciplines for the renewal of life through composting, renewing soils, growing food, sharing it with neighbors, saving water, and generating energy from solar panels on our roofs, also link us in a new way to our local communities. Some of us, like myself, may have moved into more intentional communities where we are growing food and renewing soils as part of our collective relationship. Others are doing so more in relation to towns or neighborhoods, with whom we are creating new sensibilities of our interconnection. Instead of being abstracted into fragmented selves by big states and national bureaucracies, we are rebuilding local community. From this base we are relating to the larger political and economic systems, in some cases changing the way we relate to these larger systems for more local ways of generating life.

The new world we are entering is frightening. Life will not be as easy for all of us. But life has also become less easy for many poorer people who earlier lived in traditional ways of life that were relatively satisfying. It has become much less easy for shellfish, which cannot form eggs in an acid ocean, and animals whose habitat has been destroyed by encroaching human populations. The new relationships we are entering to survive on our tough new planet need to generate a new sense of responsibility to other humans, other animals, and the ecosystems around us. We need a deep conversion from anthropomorphic to biocentered life. In the process this can bring us a new sense of gratification in our daily life. This is the spirituality and practice by which I am seeking to live my life.

Bibliography

Rosemary Radford Ruether

BOOKS

1967

The Church against Itself: An Inquiry into the Conditions of Historical Existence for the Eschatological Community. New York: Herder & Herder.

1968

Communion Is Life Together. New York: Herder & Herder.

1969

Gregory of Nazianzus, Rhetor and Philosopher. Oxford: Clarendon. Reprint: Lima, OH: Academic Review Press.

1970

The Radical Kingdom: The Western Experience of Messianic Hope. New York: Harper & Row.

1971

El Reino de los Extremistas. Translated by Dafne C. S. de Plou and Adam F. Sosa.Buenos Aires: La Aurora.

1972

Liberation Theology: Human Hope Confronts Christian History and American Power. New York: Paulist. Italian edition, 1976.

1974

Religion and Sexism: Images of Women in the Jewish and Christian Traditions. New York: Simon & Schuster. Reprint, Eugene, OR: Wipf & Stock, 1998.
Faith and Fratricide: The Image of the Jews in Early Christianity. New York: Seabury. German edition, 1980. Reprint, Eugene, OR: Wipf & Stock, 1996.

1975

And Eugene Bianchi. *From Machismo to Mutuality: Essays on Sexism and Woman–Man Liberation.* New York: Paulist.
New Woman, New Earth: Sexist Ideologies and Human Liberation. New York: Seabury.

1977

Mary: The Feminine Face of the Church. Philadelphia: Westminster (London: SCM, 1979).

Mujeres Nuevas, Tierra Nueva.

1978

And Wolfgang Roth. *The Liberating Bond: Covenants Biblical and Contemporary.* New York: Friendship.
And Eleanor McLaughlin. *Women of Spirit: Female Leadership in the Jewish and Christian Traditions.* New York: Simon & Schuster. (Reprint, Eugene, OR: Wipf & Stock, 1998.)

1981

To Change the World: Christology as Cultural Criticism. London: SCM, 1981; New York: Crossroads. (Reprint, Eugene, OR: Wipf & Stock, 1989. Dutch edition, Ten Have, 1981).
And Rosemary Keller. *Women and Religion in America.* Vol. 1, *The Nineteenth Century.* New York: Harper & Row.

1982

Disputed Questions: On Being a Christian. Journeys in Faith. Nashville: Abingdon.

1983

Sexism and God-Talk: Toward a Feminist Theology. Boston: Beacon.
And Rosemary Keller. *Women and Religion in America.* Vol. 2, *The Colonial and Revolutionary Periods.* New York: Harper & Row.

1985

Womanguides: Readings toward a Feminist Theology. Boston: Beacon.
And Rosemary Keller. *Women and Religion in America.* Vol. 3, *1900–1968.* New York: Harper & Row, 1986.
Women-Church: Theology and Practice of Feminist Liturgical Communities. San Francisco: Harper & Row.

1987

Contemporary Roman Catholicism: Crisis and Challenges. Kansas City: Sheed & Ward.

1989

Disputed Questions: On Being a Christian. 2nd ed. Maryknoll, NY: Orbis.

And Herman J. Ruether. *The Wrath of Jonah: The Crisis of Religious Nationalism in the Israeli-Palestinian Conflict.* San Francisco: Harper & Row.

1990

And Marc H. Ellis. *Beyond Occupation: American Jewish, Christian, and Palestinian Voices for Peace.* Boston: Beacon.

1992

And Eugene Bianchi, editors. *A Democratic Catholic Church: The Reconstruction of Roman Catholicism.* New York: Crossroads.

And Naim S. Ateek, and Marc H. Ellis, editors. *Faith and the Intifada: Palestinian Christian Voices.* Maryknoll, NY: Orbis.

Gaia & God: An Ecofeminist Theology of Earth Healing. San Francisco: HarperSanFrancisco.

1993

Gaia y Dios: Una Teología Ecofeminista para la Recuperación de la Tierra. Tlacopac, San Ángel, México: DEMAC.

Sexism and God-Talk: Toward a Feminist Theology. 2nd ed. Boston: Beacon.

Sexismo e Religião: Rumo a Uma Teologia Feminista. Translated by Walter Altmann and Luís Marcos Sander. São Leopoldo: Synodal.

1994

Gaia und Gott: Eine Ökofeministiche Theologie der Heilung der Erde. Luzern: Exodus.

1995

And Thomas Merton. *At Home in the World: The Letters of Thomas Merton and Rosemary Ruether.* Edited by Mary Tardiff. Maryknoll, NY: Orbis, 1995.

Gaia e Dio: Una Teologia Ecofemminista. Brescia: Queriniana.

And Rosemary S. Keller. *In Our Own Voices: Four Centuries of American Women's Religious Writings.* San Francisco: HarperSanFrancisco.

And Douglas John Hall. *God and the Nations.* Minneapolis: Fortress.

New Woman, New Earth: Sexist Ideologies and Human Liberation. With a new preface. 2nd ed. Boston: Beacon, 1995.

1996

Mulheres Curando a Terra. São Paulo, Brazil: Paulinas.

Sei Sabetsu to Kami no Katarikake: Feminisuto Shingaku no Kokoromi. Translated by Rui Kohiyama. Nijuisseiki Kirisutokyo Senso 9. Tokyo: Shinkyo Shuppansha.

Editor. *Women Healing Earth: Third World Women and Feminism, Religion and Ecology.* Ecology and Justice. Maryknoll, NY: Orbis.

1997

W Domu na Całym Świecie: Listy Tomsz Merton I Rosemary Radford Ruether. Translated by Malgorzata Golicka-Jablonska. Warsaw: Verbinum.

1998

Introducing Redemption in Christian Feminism. Introductions to Feminist Theology 1. Sheffield: Sheffield Academic.
Women and Redemption: A Theological History. Minneapolis: Fortress.

1999

Mujeres Sanando la Tierra: Ecología, Feminismo y Religión, Según Mujeres del Tercer Mundo. Santiago, Chile: Sello Azul.

2000

And Dieter Hessel. *Christianity and Ecology: Seeking the Well-being of Earth and Humans.* Religions of the World and Ecology. Cambridge: Harvard University Press.
Christianity and the Making of the Modern Family. Boston: Beacon.

2001

And Rita M. Gross. *Religious Feminism and the Future of the Planet: A Buddhist-Christian Conversation.* London: Continuum.

2002

Editor. *Gender, Ethnicity, and Religion: Views from the Other Side.* Minneapolis: Fortress.
Visionary Women: Three Medieval Mystics. Minneapolis: Fortress.
And Herman J. Ruether. *The Wrath of Jonah: The Crisis of Religious Nationalism in the Israeli-Palestinian Conflict.* 2nd ed. Minneapolis: Fortress.

2005

Goddesses and the Divine Feminine: A Western Religious History. Berkeley: University of California Press, 2005.
Integrating Ecofeminism, Globalization, and World Religions. Nature's Meaning. Lanham, MD: Rowman & Littlefield.

2006

And Marion Grau, edtiors. *Interpreting the Postmodern: Responses to "Radical Orthodoxy."* New York: T. & T. Clark.

2007

America, Amerikkka: Elect Nation and Imperial Violence. Religion and Violence. London: Equinox.

Editor. *Feminist Theologies: Legacy and Prospect.* Minneapolis: Fortress.

2008

Catholicism Does Not Equal the Vatican: A Vision for Progressive Catholicism. New York: New Press.

And Lisa Isherwood, editors. *Weep Not for Your Children: Essays on Religion and Violence.* Religion and Violence. London: Equinox.

2009

Christianity and Social Systems: Historical Constructions and Ethical Challenges. Lanham, MD: Rowman & Littlefield.

2010

Many Forms of Madness: A Family's Struggle with Mental Illness and the Mental Health System. Minneapolis: Fortress.

2012

Women and Redemption: A Theological History. 2nd ed. Minneapolis: Fortress.

BOOK SYMPOSIA

1964

"The Difficult Decision: Contraception." In *The Experience of Marriage: The Testimony of Catholic Laymen,* edited by Michael Novak, 69–81. New York: Macmillan.

"A Question of Dignity, a Question of Freedom." In *What Modern Catholics Think of Birth Control,* edited by William Birmingham, 233–40. New York: New American Library.

1965

"Catholicism and Catholicity." In *The Generation of the Third Eye,* edited by Daniel Callahan, 186ff. New York: Sheed & Ward.

1967

"Birth Control and the Ideals of Marital Sexuality." In *Contraception and Holiness,* edited by Thomas Roberts, 72–91. New York: Herder & Herder.

"Ministry in the Church of the Future." In *Secular Priests in the New Church,* edited by Gerald Sloyan, 232–49. New York: Herder & Herder.

1969

"The Free Church Movement in Contemporary Roman Catholicism." In *New Theology*, No. 6, edited by Martin Marty and Dean Peerman. New York: Macmillan, 1969. (Reprinted from *Concilium* [Spring 1968].)

"Preface." In *Can These Bones Live?: The Failure of Church Renewal*, edited by Robert S. Lecky and H. Elliott Wright. New York: Sheed & Ward.

1970

"Education in the Sociological Situation, U.S.A." In *Does the Church Know How to Teach?: An Ecumenical Inquiry*, edited by Kendig Cully, 79–100. New York: Macmillan.

"Theological Anti-Semitism in the New Testament." In *The Death of Dialogue and Beyond*, edited by Sanford Seltzer and Max Stackhouse, 86–104. New York: Friendship.

1971

"Beyond Confrontation: The Therapeutic Task." In *The Berrigans*, edited by William van Etten Casey and Philip Nobile, 113–21. New York: Praeger.

"Government Coercion and One-Dimensional Thinking." In *The Population Crisis and Moral Responsibility*, edited by Philip Wogaman, 167–73. Washington DC: Public Affairs.

1974

"The Believers' Church and Catholicity in the World Today." In *Confusion and Hope: Clergy, Laity, and Church in Transition*, edited by Glenn Bucher, 113–24. Philadelphia: Fortress.

"Male Clericalism and the Dread of Women." In *Women and Orders*, edited by Robert Heyer, 1–13. Deus Books. New York: Paulist.

"L'orizzonte messianico della chiesa e della societa." In *Teogogia dal Nordamerica*, edited by Dean Peerman and Rosino Gibellini. Brescia: Queriniana.

1975

"Anti-Judaism Is the Left Hand of Christology." In *Jewish/Christian Relations*, edited by Robert Heyer, 1–9. New York: Paulist.

"Beginnings: An Intellectual Autobiography." In *Journeys: Theological Autobiographies*, edited by Gregory Baum, 34–56. New York: Paulist.

"Toward a New Covenantal Theology." In *Disputation and Dialogue: Readings in the Jewish-Christian Encounter*, edited by Frank Ephraim Talmage, 320–29. New York: Ktav.

1976

"From Misogynism to Liberation." In *Transcendence and Mystery*, edited by Earl P. C. Brewer. New York: IDOC, 1976.

"Una nuova donna per una nuova terra! donna, ecologia e rivoluzione sociale." In *Vecchi e Nuovi Dei*, edited by Rocco Caporale, 389–409. Turin: Valentino.

"Ordination: What Is the Problem?" In *Women and Catholic Priesthood*, edited by A. M. Gardiner, 30–34. New York: Paulist.

"'Response' Feminist Theology Panel," and "Letter of Rosemary Ruether to Sergio Torres and the Planners of the Conference." In *Theology in the Americas*, edited by Sergio Torres and John Eagleson. Maryknoll, NY: Orbis.

"Theological Brief: Life Everlasting." In *Christian Theology: A Case Method Approach*, edited by Robert A. Evans and Thomas D. Parker, 255–61. Harper Forum Book. New York: Harper & Row.

1977

"America as Babylon: Reflections on Rev. 13." In *Flesh and Spirit: Gamaliel*.

"Anti-Semitism and Christian Theology." In *Auschwitz: Beginning of a New Era; Reflections on the Holocaust*, edited by Eva Fleishner, 79–92. New York: Ktav.

"Home and Work: Women's Roles and the Transformation of Values." In *Woman, New Dimensions*, edited by Walter J. Burkhardt, 71–83. New York: Paulist.

"The Ministry of the People and the Future Shape of the Church." In *Toward AD 2000: Emerging Directions in Christian Ministry*, edited by John I. Durham, 81–93. Southeastern Studies 1. Wake Forest, NC: Southeastern Baptist Seminary.

"The Person and Work of Christ: Contemporary Understandings and Applications." In *Case Studies in Christ and Salvation*, edited by Jack Rogers et al., 141ff. Philadelphia: Westminster.

"The Relevance of Martin Luther King for Today." In *Essays in Honor of Martin Luther King, Jr.*, edited by John H. Cartwright, 64–81. Evanston, IL: Leiffer Bureau for Social and Religious Research, Garrett-Evangelical Theological Seminary.

"Women Priests and Church Tradition." In *Women Priests*, edited by Leonard Swidler and Arlene Swidler, 234–37. New York: Paulist.

1978

"Rich Nations, Poor Nations: Towards a Just World Order in the Era of Neo- Colonialism." In *Christian Spirituality in the United States: Independence and Interdependence*, edited by Francis A. Eigo, 59–91. Proceedings of the Theology Institute of Villanova University. Villanova, PA: Villanova University Press.

"Sexism and God-Talk: Two Models of Relationship." In *Process and Relationship: Issues in Theology, Philosophy and Religious Education*, edited by Iris V. Cully et al., 75–81. Birmingham, AL: Religious Education Press.

"You Shall Call No Man Father: Sexism, Hierarchy, and Liberation." In *Women and the Word: Sermons*, edited by Helen G. Crotwell, 92–99. Philadelphia: Fortress.

1979

"The Faith and Fratricide Discussion." In *Anti-Semitism and the Foundations of Christianity*, edited by Alan T. Davies, 230–56. New York: Paulist.

"Kvinnornas befrielse i ett historiskt och teologiskt perpektiv" and "Fortryck och befrielse an kvinnan inom den kristna teologin." In *Halva Himlen ar var*, edited by Gorel Janarv et al. Kriss-serien. Stockholm: Gummessons.

"Motherearth and the Megamachine." In *Womanspirit Rising*, edited by Carol Christ and Judith Plaskow, 43–52. New York: Harper & Row.

"Patristic Spirituality and the Experience of Women in the Early Church." In *Western Spirituality: Historical Roots, Ecumenical Routes*, edited by Matthew Fox, 140–63. Notre Dame, IN: Fides/Claretian.

1980

"The Bible and Liberation." In *The Bible and Our Future*, 8–17. WSCG Conference, Haugtun, Norway, 11–17 August, 1979. Geneva: World Student Christian Federation.

"Cristologia e Femminismo: Un Salvatore maschile puo aiutare le donne?" In *La sfida del Femminismo alla Teologia*, edited by Mary Hunt and Rosino, 126–40. Gibellini. Brecia: Queriniana.

"A Feminist Perspective on Religion and Science." In *Faith and Science in an Unjust World*, edited by Roger Shinn, 55–58. Geneva: World Council of Churches.

"Is a New Consensus Possible?" In *Consensus in Theology?: A Dialogue with Hans Küng and Edward Schillebeeckx*, edited by Leonard Swidler, 63–68. Philadelphia: Westminster, 1980.

1982

"Christology and Jewish-Christian Relations." In *Jews and Christians after the Holocaust*, edited by Abraham Peck, 25–38. Philadelphia: Fortress.

"Introduction." In *Threatened with Resurrection: Prayers and Poems of Julia Esquivel*, 9–13. Elgin, IL: Brethren.

"Liberation Theology." In *Contemporary American Theology*, edited by Diane W. Ferm, 141–46. New York: Seabury.

"Toward an American Socialism: The Search for a Just Economic Order." In *The Right Time: The Best of Kairos*, edited by David B. Parke. Boston: Skinner House.

"Woman as Oppressed, Woman as Liberated in the Scriptures." In *Spinning a Sacred Yarn: Women Speak from the Pulpit*, 181–86. New York: Pilgrim.

1983

"The Feminist Critique of Religious Studies." In *A Feminist Perspective in the Academy*, edited by Elizabeth Langland and Walter Grove. Chicago: University of Chicago Press.

"Sexism, Religion and Social and Spiritual Liberation of Women Today." In *Beyond Domination: New Perspectives on Women and Philosophy*, edited by Carol C. Gould, 107–22. New Feminist Perspectives Series. Totowa, NJ: Rowman & Allanheld.

"Triple Oppression: Sex, Class and Race." In *God and Human Freedom: A Festschrift in Honor of Howard Thurman*, edited by Henry J. Young, 33–43. Richmond, IN: Friends United Press.

1984

"Envisioning Our Hopes: Some Models of the Future." In *Women's Spirit Bonding*, edited by Janet Kalven and Mary Buckley, 325–35. New York: Pilgrim.

"Feminist Theology." In *The Dictionary of Christian Theology*, edited by Alan Richardson and John S. Bowden, 210–12. London: SCM.

"Feminist Theology and Spirituality." In *Christian Feminism: Vision of a New Humanity*, edited by Judith Weidman, 9–32. San Francisco: Harper & Row.

"Mariology." In *The Dictionary of Christian Theology*, edited by Alan Richardson and John S. Bowden. London: SCM.

1985

"The Biblical Vision of the Ecological Crisis." In *Teaching and Preaching Stewardship*, edited by Nordan Murphy, 202–9. New York: NCC Press.

"Feminism and Peace." In *Women's Consciousness, Women's Conscience: A Reader in Feminist Ethics*, edited by Barbara Andolsen et al., 63–74. Minneapolis: Winston.

"Feminist Interpretation of the Bible: A Method of Correlation." In *Feminist Interpretation of the Bible*, edited by Letty M. Russell, 111–24. Philadelphia: Westminster.

"The Interrelatedness of Oppression and Efforts for Liberation: A Feminist Perspective." In *Doing Theology in a Divided World*, edited by Virginia Fabella and Sergio Torres, 65–71. Maryknoll, NY: Orbis, 1985.

"Theology as Critique and Emancipation from Sexism." In *The Vocation of the Theologian*, edited by Theodore Jennings, 25–36. Philadelphia: Fortress.

1986

"The Conflict of Political Theologies in the Church: Does God Take Sides in Class Struggle?" In *Churches in Struggle: Liberation Theologies and Social Change in North America*, edited by William Tabb, 18–31 New York: Monthly Review Press.

"Covenant and People in the Christian Tradition, Church, Synagogue and Nation." In *The Life of the Covenant: The Challenge of Contemporary Judaism; Essays in Honor of Herman E. Schaalman*, edited by Joseph Edelheit, 183–94. Chicago: SCJ.

"Differing Views of the Church." In *Authority and Community in Conflict*, edited by Madonna Kolbenschlag, 96–107. Kansas City, MO: Sheed & Ward.

"Feminist Liturgical Movement." In *A New Dictionary of Liturgy and Worship*, edited by J. C. Davies, 240–41. London: SCM.

"Foreword." In *Sanctuary: The New Underground Railroad*, by Renny Golden and Michael McConnell, viff. Maryknoll, NY: Orbis.

"Inclusive Language." In *A New Dictionary of Liturgy and Worship*, edited by J. C. Davies. London: SCM.

"John Paul II and the Growing Alienation of Women from the Church." In *The Church in Anguish: Has the Vatican Betrayed Vatican II?*, edited by Hans Küng and Leonard Swidler, 279–83. New York: Harper & Row.

Through the Eyes of a Woman: Bible Studies from the Experience of Woman, edited by Wendy S. Robins, 37–38, 63. Geneva: World YWCA.

"Women-Church: Emerging Feminist Liturgical Communities." *Popular Relig-ion: Concilium: Religion in the Eighties*, edited by Norbert Greinacher and Norbert Mette, 52–61. Edinburgh: T. & T. Clark.

1987

"Androcentrism." In *The Encyclopedia of Religion*, edited by Mircea Eliade et al., 1:272–76. London: Macmillan.

"Asceticism and Feminism: Strange Bedfellows." In *Sex and God: Some Varieties of Women's Religious Experience*, edited by Linda Hurcombe, 229–50. London: Routledge & Kegan Paul.

"The Call of Women in the Church Today." In *Women of Faith in Dialogue*, edited by Virginia Ramey Mollenkott, 77–88. New York: Crossroad.

"Christianity." In *Women in World Religions*, edited by Arvind Sharma, 207–33. McGill Studies in the History of Religions. Albany: SUNY Press.

"Feminism and Jewish-Christian Dialogue: Particularism and Universalism in the Search for Religious Truth." In *The Myth of Christian Uniqueness: Toward a Pluralistic Theology of Religion*, edited by Paul Knitter and John Hick, 137–48. Faith Meets Faith. Maryknoll, NY: Orbis.

"Foreword." In *Children of Palestinian Refugees vs. the Israeli Military: Personal Accounts of Arrest, Detention and Torture*, compiled by Dina Lawrence and Kameel Nasr. Lafayette, CA: BIP Publications.

"Foreword." In *The Inside Stories: Thirteen Valiant Women Challenge Their Church*, v–xii. New London, CT: Twenty-Third Publications.

"The Future of Feminist Theology in the Academy." In *Trajectories in the Study of Religion: Addresses at the Seventy-Fifth Anniversary of the American Academy of Religion*, edited by Ray L. Hart, 163–74. Scholars Press Studies in Religious Thought and Scholarship. Atlanta: Scholars.

"Spirit and Matter; Public and Private: The Challenge of Feminism to Traditional Dualism." In *Embodied Love: Sensuality and Relationship as Feminist Values*, edited by Paula Cooey et al., 65–76. San Francisco: Harper & Row.

"Theologizing from the Side of the Other: Women, Blacks, Indians, and Jews." In *Faith That Transforms: Essays in Honor of Gregory Baum*, edited by Mary Jo Leddy and Mary Ann Hinsdale, 62–81. New York: Paulist.

1988

"Catholics and Abortion: Authority and Dissent." In *Abortion and Catholicism: The American Debate*, edited by Patricia B. Jung and Thomas A. Shannon, 320–26. New York: Crossroad.

"Gender Equality and Social Change: Feminism and Redemptive Transformation of Society." In *The World Community in Post-Industrial Society*. Vol. 1, *Changing Families in the World Perspective*, edited by the Christian Academy, 197–203. Seoul: Wooseok.

"Matthew 23:1–12: Unwandlung von Macht zu Dienst." In *Feministisch Gelesen*, edited by Eve Renate Schmidt et al., 170–78. Stuttgart: Kreuz, 1988.

"Sexism as Ideology and Social System: Can Christianity Be Liberated from Patriarchy?" In *With Both Eyes Open: Seeing beyond Gender*, edited by Patricia A. Johnson and Janet Kalven, 148–64. New York: Pilgrim.

"Voluntary Associations." In *A Catholic Bill of Rights*, edited by Leonard Swidler and Herbert O'Brien, 54–56. Kansas City, MO: Sheed & Ward.

"War and Peace in the Christian Tradition." In *A Council for Peace*, edited by Hans Küng and Jürgen Moltmann , 17–24. Concilium, Religion in the Eighties. Edinburgh: T. & T. Clark.

1989

"The Feminist Critique in Religious Studies." In *Religious Issues and Interreligious Dialogues: An Analysis and Sourcebook*, edited by Charles Wei-hsun Fu and Gerland E. Spiegler, 91–104. New York: Greenwood.

"Foreword." In *Justice and Only Justice: A Palestinian Theology of Liberation*, by Naim Ateek, xi–xiv. Maryknoll, NY: Orbis.

"Homophobia, Heterosexism, and Pastoral Practice." In *Homosexuality in the Priesthood and in Religious Life*, edited by Jeannine Grammick, 21–35. New York: Crossroad.

"Introduction." In *The Israeli Army vs. the Palestinian People: Personal Accounts of Human Rights Violations in the West Bank and the Gaza Strip*, edited by Dina Lawrence, 3–6. Lafayette, CA: BIP Publications.

"Religion and Society: Sacred Canopy vs. Prophetic Critique." In *The Future of Liberation Theology: Essays in Honor of Gustavo Gutiérrez*, edited by Marc H. Ellis and Otto Maduro, 172–76. Maryknoll, NY: Orbis.

"Sexism and God-Language." In *Weaving the Visions: Patterns in Feminist Spirituality*, edited by Carol Christ and Judith Plaskow, 151–62. San Francisco: Harper & Row.

"Toward an Ecological Feminist Theory of Nature." In *Healing the Wounds: The Promise of Ecofeminism*, edited by Judith Plant, 145–50. Philadelphia: New Society.

"The Western Religious Tradition and Violence against Women in the Home." In *Christianity, Patriarchy, and Abuse: A Feminist Critique*, edited by Joanne Carlson Brown and Carole Bohn, 31–41. New York: Pilgrim.

1990

"Black Women and Feminism: The US and South African Contexts." In *A Black Theology of Liberation*, by James Cone, 174–84. 20th anniversary ed. Maryknoll, NY: Orbis.

"Catholicism, Women, Body and Sexuality: A Response." In *Women and Sexuality: Studies on the Impact of Religious Teachings on Women*, edited by Jeanne Becher, 221–32. Geneva: WCC Publications.

"Eschatology and Feminism." In *Lift Every Voice: Constructing Christian Theologies from the Underside*, edited by Susan Brook Thistlethwaite and Mary Potter Engel, 111–24. San Francisco: Harper & Row.

"The Liberation of Theology from Patriarchy." In *Feminist Theology: A Reader*, edited by Ann Loades, 138–47. London: SPCK.

"The Place of Women in the Church." In *Modern Catholicism: Vatican II and After*, edited by Adrian Hastings, 260–66. London: SPCK.

Questions of Faith: Contemporary Thinkers Respond (interviews), edited by Dolly K. Patterson, 48–49, 58–59, 79–80, 82–83, 110. Philadelphia: Trinity.

"Religion and Science in an Unjust World." In *John Paul II on Science and Religion: Reflections on the New View from Rome*, edited by Robert Russell et al., 95–98. Vatican City: Vatican Observatory Publications.

"Women's Body and Blood: The Sacred and the Impure." In *Through the Devil's Gateway: Women, Religion, and Taboo*, edited by Alison Joseph, 7–21. London: SPCK.

1991

"The Adversus Judaeos Tradition in the Church Fathers: The Exegesis of Christian Anti-Semitism." In *Essential Papers on Judaism and Christianity in Conflict: From Late Antiquity to the Reformation*, edited by Jeremy Cohen, 174–92. Essential Papers on Jewish Studies. New York: New York University Press.

"Catholic Women in the Era of Vatican II." In *Thoughts on Feminism*. Special issue, Catholic *Commission on Intellectual and Cultural Affairs Annual* 10:134–45.

"False Messianism and Prophetic Consciousness: Toward a Liberation Theology of Jewish-Christian Solidarity." In *Judaism, Christianity, and Liberation: An Agenda for Dialogue*, edited by Otto Maduro, 83–95. Maryknoll, NY: Orbis.

"Foreword." In *The Hour of the Poor, the Hour of Women: Salvadorean Women Speak*, by Renny Golden, 9–10. New York: Crossroad.

"Imago Dei, Christian Tradition and Feminist Hermeneutics." In *Image of God and Gender Models in Judaeo-Christian Tradition*, edited by Kari Borresen, 258–81. Oslo: Solum.

"The Task of Feminist Theology." In *Doing Theology in Today's World*, edited by Thomas McComiskey and John Woodbridge, 359–76. Grand Rapids: Zondervan.

"Women's Home Rule." *The Best of Resurgence*, edited by John Button, 311–14. Hartland, Devon, UK: Green Books.

1992

"Feminist Hermeneutics, Scriptural Authority and Religious Experience: The Case of Imago Dei and Gender Equality." In *Radical Pluralism and Truth: David Tracy and the Hermeneutics of Religion*, edited by Werner G. Jeanrand and Jennifer L. Rike, 95–106. New York: Crossroad.

"Feminist Theology and Interclass/Interracial Solidarity." In *Struggle for Solidarity: Liberation Theologies in Tension*, edited by Lorine Getz and Ruy Costa, 49–62. Minneapolis: Fortress.

"Feminist Theology in Global Context." In *Knowledge, Attitude & Experience: Ministry in Cross-Cultural Perspective*, edited by Young-Il Kim, 37–45. Nashville: Abingdon.

"Introduction." In *Georgia Harkness: For Such a Time as This*, by Rosemary S. Keller, 23–30. Nashville: Abingdon.

"Patriarchy and the Men's Movement: Part of the Problem or Part of the Solution?" In *Women Respond to the Men's Movement: A Feminist Collection*, edited by Kay Leigh Hagan, 13–18. San Francisco: HarperSanFrancisco.

"Spirituality and Justice: Popular Church Movements in the United States." In *A Democratic Catholic Church: The Reconstruction of Roman Catholicism*, edited by Rosemary Radford Ruether and Eugene Bianchi, 189–206. New York: Crossroads.

1993

"Birth Control and Ideals of Marital Sexuality." In *Dialogue about Catholic Sexual Teaching*, edited by Charles Curran and Richard McCormick, 138–52. Readings in Moral Theology 8. New York: Paulist, 1993.

"Can Christology Be Liberated from Patriarchy?" In *Reconstructing the Christ Symbol: Essays in Feminist Christology*, edited by Maryanne Stevens, 7–29. New York: Paulist.

"Can Christology Be Liberated from Patriarchy?" In *Contemporary Reflections on the Faith of Our Mothers and Fathers*, edited by M. Mani Chacko, 25–48. Madras, India: Gurukul Theological Seminary.

"Ecofeminism: Symbolic and Social Connections between the Oppression of Women and the Domination of Nature." In *Ecofeminism and the Sacred*, edited by Carol J. Adams, 13–23. New York: Continuum.

"Feminist Critique and Revisioning of God-Language." In *A Reader in Feminist Theology*, edited by Prasanna Kumari, 18–31. Women's Studies Series 2. Madras, India: Gurukul Seminary Press.

"Feminist Theology in Global Context." In *Contemporary Reflections on the Faith of Our Mothers and Fathers*, edited by M. Mani Chacko, 25–48. Madras, India: Gurukul Theological Seminary.

"Men, Women and Beasts." In *Good News for Animals?: Christian Approaches to Animal Well-Being*, edited by Charles Pinches and Jay B. McDaniel, 12–13. Ecology and Justice Series. Maryknoll, NY: Orbis.

"Theological and Ethical Reflection on the Shoah: Getting beyond the Victim-Victimizer Relationship." In *Contemporary Christian Responses to the Shoah*, edited by Steven L. Jacobs, 167–93. Studies in the Shoa 6. Lanham, MD: University Press of America.

1994

"Christianity and Women in the Modern World." In *Today's Women in World Religions*, edited by Arvind Sharma, 267–302. McGill Studies in the History of Religions. Albany: State University of New York.

"Deflecting in Place: Reflections on Women's Spiritual Quest and New Support Groups." In *Defecting in Place: Women Claiming Responsibility for Their Own Spiritual Lives*, edited by Miriam Therese Winter et al., 248–52. New York: Crossroad.

"Ecofeminism." In *Ecological Prospects: Scientific, Religious, and Aesthetic Perspectives*, edited by Christopher Chapple, 158–68. Albany: SUNY Press.

"Ecofeminism and Theology." In *Ecotheology: Voices from South and North*, edited by David Hallman, 199–204. Geneva: WCC Publications.

"Homophobia, Heterosexism, and Pastoral Practice." In *Sexuality and the Sacred: Sources for Theological Reflection*, edited by James B. Nelson and Sandra P. Longfellow, 387–96. Louisville: Westminster John Knox.

1995

"Feminist Metanoia and Soul-Making." In *Women's Spirituality, Women's Lives: Women and Therapy*, edited by Judith Ochshorn and Ellen Cole, 33–44. New York: Haworth.

"Foreword." In *I Am a Palestinian Christian*, by Mitri Raheb, vii–x. Minneapolis: Fortress.

"Grace in the Midst of Failings." In *Common Era: Best New Writings on Religion*, edited by Stevan Scholl, 161–67. Ashland, OR: White Cloud.

"Imago Dei, Christian Tradition and Feminist Hermeneutics." In *The Image of God and Gender Models in Judaeo-Christian Tradition*, edited by Kari Borresen, 267–91. Minneapolis: Fortress.

"Making the Earth Whole Again." In *Nourishing the Soul: Discovering the Sacred in Everyday Life*, edited by Anne Simpkinson et al., 261–70. San Francisco: HarperSanFrancisco.

"Marge Tuite, Prophet and Martyr." In *Pilgrims and Seekers: Saints without Pedestals*, by Mary An Luke, 125–30. Erie, PA: Pax Christi.

"Theologische vindplaastsen voor de genezing van de aarde." In *God Opnieuw Gedacht: Verantwoordelijkheid voor de schepping in feministisch perspectief: theologische essays voor Catharina Halkes*, edited by Johanna Jaeger-Sommer, 219–30. Baarn: Ten Have.

1996

"Christian Anthropology and Gender." In *The Future of Theology: Essays in Honor of Jürgen Moltmann*, edited by Miroslav Miro et al., 241–52. Grand Rapids: Eerdmans, 1996.

"Christian Understandings of Human Nature." In *Religion, Feminism & the Family*, edited by Anne Carr and Mary S. Van Leeuven, 95–110. The Family, Religion, and Culture. Louisville: Westminster John Knox.

"Christology." In *An A to Z of Feminist Theology*, edited by Lisa Isherwood and Dorothy McEwan, 26–27. Sheffield: Sheffield Academic.

"Ecofeminism: First and Third World Women." In *Women Resisting Violence: Spirituality for Life*, edited by Mary John Mananzan, et al., 27–38. Maryknoll, NY: Orbis.

"Ecofeminism: Symbolic and Social Connections between the Oppression of Women and the Domination of Nature." In *This Sacred Earth: Religion, Nature, and Environment*, edited by Roger S. Gottlieb, 322–33. New York: Routledge.

"Ecumenism and the Ordination of Women: Roman Catholic Feminist Reflections." In *The Call to Serve: Biblical and Theological Perspectives on Ministry, in Honour of Bishop Penny Jamieson*, edited by Douglas A. Campbell, 228–38 Sheffield: Sheffield Academic.

"Healing the World: The Sacramental Tradition." In *Feminist Ethics and the Catholic Moral Tradition*, edited by Charles E. Curran et al., 560–85. New York: Paulist.

"One of the Great Truth-Tellers." In *Apostle of Peace: Essays in Honor of Daniel Berrigan*, edited by John Dear, 41–46. Maryknoll, NY: Orbis.

"Patriarchy." In *An A to Z of Feminist Theology*, edited by Lisa Isherwood and Dorothy McEwan, 173–74. Sheffield: Sheffield Academic.

"Prophetic Tradition and Liberation of Women: Promise and Betrayal." In *Let Justice Roll: Prophetic Challenge in Religion, Politics, and Society*, edited by Neal Riemer, 59–70. Religious Forces in the Modern Political World. Lanham, MD: Rowman & Littlefield.

"The Unrealized Revolution: Searching the Scripture for a Model of the Family." In *Christian Perspectives on Sexuality and Gender*, edited by Elizabeth Stuart and Adrian Thatcher, 442–50. Grand Rapids: Eerdmans.

1997

"Theological Resources for Earth-Healing: Covenant and Sacrament." In *The Challenge of Global Stewardship: Roman Catholic Responses*, edited by Maura A. Ryan and Todd David Whitmore, 54–66. Notre Dame: University of Notre Dame Press.

1998

"The Church Isn't a Democracy, but Shouldn't It Be?" In *Rome Has Spoken: A Guide to Forgotten Papal Statements and How They Have Changed through the Centuries*, edited by Maureen Fiedler and Linda Rabben, 91–100. New York: Crossroad.

"Ecofeminism: Religion, Gender Hierarchy, and Environment." In *Traditional and Modern Approaches to the Environment in the Pacific Rim: Tension and Values*, edited by Harold Coward, 89–104. Albany: SUNY Press.

"Gender Equity and Christianity: Pre-Modern Roots, Modern and Post-Modern Perspectives." In *Faith and Praxis in a Post-Modern Age*, edited by Ursula King, 60–74. London: Cassell.

"Introduction." In *Ethics for a Small Planet: New Horizons on Population, Consumption and Ecology*, by Daniel C. Maguire and Larry L. Rasmussen, xi–xv. SUNY Series in Religious Studies. Albany: SUNY Press.

1999

"Becoming a Feminist." In *An Invitation to Christian Spirituality: An Ecumenical Anthology*, edited by John R. Tyson, 454–57. New York: Oxford University Press.

"Foreword." In *Liberating Christ: Exploring the Christologies of Contemporary Liberation Movements*, by Lisa Isherwood, vii–viii. Cleveland: Pilgrim.

"The Holocaust: Theological and Ethical Reflections." In *The Twentieth Century: A Theological Overview*, edited by Gregory Baum, 76–90. Maryknoll, NY: Orbis.

"Justice and Reconciliation." In *Holy Land, Hollow Jubilee: God, Justice, and the Palestinians*, edited by Naim Ateek and Michael Prior, 116–21. London: Melisende.

"Liberation Theologies and African Women's Theologies." In *Black Faith and Public Talk: Critical Essays on James H. Cone's "Black Theology and Black Power,"* edited by Dwight N. Hopkins, 167–77. Maryknoll, NY: Orbis.

"Prayer for the Earth." In *Prayers for a Thousand Years: Blessings and Expressions of Hope for the New Millennium*, edited by Elizabeth Roberts and Elias Amidon, 201. San Francisco: HarperSanFrancisco.

"The Theological Vision of Letty Russell", in *Liberating Eschatology: Essays in Honor of Letty M. Russell*, edited by Margaret Farley and Serene Jones, 16–25. Louisville: Westminster John Knox.

"Women-Church: An American Catholic Feminist Movement." In *What's Left?: Liberal American Catholics*, edited by Mary Jo Weaver, 46–66. Bloomington: Indiana University Press.

"Women-Church: Reimagining Immanence and Transcendence." In *The Annual Review of Women in World Religions*, Vol. 5, edited by Arvind Sharma and Katherine Young, 80–89. Albany: SUNY Press.

2000

"Church, Feminism, and Family." In *God Forbid: Religion and Sex in American Public Life*, edited by Kathleen M. Sands, 93–103. Religion in America Series. Oxford: Oxford University Press.

"From Private Struggle to Public Thought." In *Selving: Linking Work to Spirituality*, edited by William Cleary 32–34. Milwaukee: Marquette University Press.

"God of Possibilities: Immanence and Transcendence Rethought." In *The Bright Side of Faith*, edited by Ellen van Wolde, 45–54. Concilium, 2000/4. London: SCM.

"Searching Scripture for a Model of the Family." In *Voices of the Religious Left: A Sourcebook*, edited by Rebecca T. Alpert, 231–38. Philadelphia: Temple University Press.

"Sex in the Catholic Tradition." In *The Good News of the Body: Sexual Theology and Feminism*, edited by Lisa Isherwood, 35–53. New York: New York University Press.

"A Tale of Two Books: My Journey into Israeli-Palestinian Issues." In *They Came and They Saw: Western Christian Experiences in the Holy Land*, edited by Michael Prior, 69–76. London: Melisende.

2001

"Christian Feminist Theology." In *Daughters of Abraham: Feminist Thought in Judaism, Christianity, and Islam*, edited by Yvonne Yazbeck Haddad and John L. Espositio, 65–68. Gainesville: University Press of Florida.

"Ecofeminism: Healing Ourselves, Healing the Earth." *Gender Mosaics: Social Perspectives; Original Readings*, edited by Dana Vannoy, 406–14. Los Angeles: Roxbury.

"Feminist Theology in Global Context." In *The Wisdom of Daughters: Two Decades of the Voice of Christian Feminism*, edited by Reta Halteman Finger and Kari Sandhaas, 91–94. Philadelphia: Innisfree.

"Foreword." In *Gem: The Life of Sister Mac, Geraldine MacNamera*, by Eleanor Stebner, 9–12. Out of the Ordinary. Ottawa: Novalis.

"Foreword." In *Red Thread: A Spiritual Journal of Accompaniment, Trauma, and Healing*, by Jennifer Atlee-Loudon, 9–13. Washington DC: EPICA.

"Gender, Ecology and the Crisis of Religions in the New Millennium." In *Religion in the New Millennium: Theology in the Spirit of Paul Tillich*, edited by Raymond F. Bulman and Frederick J. Parrella, 63–77. Macon, GA: Mercer University Press.

2002

"The Emergence of Christian Feminist Theology." In *The Cambridge Companion to Feminist Theology*, edited by Susan Frank Parson, 3–22. Cambridge Companions to Religion. Cambridge: Cambridge University Press.

"An Intellectual Autobiography." In *Shaping a Theological Mind: Theological Context and Methodology*, edited by Darren C. Marks, 103–14. Burlington, VA: Ashgate.

"Methodologies in Women's Studies and Feminist Theology." In *Methodology in Religious Studies: The Interface with Women's Studies*, edited by Arvind Sharma, 179–206. McGill Studies in the History of Religions. Albany: SUNY Press.

"The War on Women." In *Nothing Sacred: Women Respond to Fundamentalism and Terror*, edited by Betsy Reed, 3–9. New York: Thunder's Mouth Press.

2003

"American Empire and the War against Evil." In *Spiritual Perspectives on America's Role as Superpower*, 165–76. Woodstock, VT: Skylight Paths.

"Christology and Patriarchy." In *Thinking of Christ: Proclamation, Explanation, Meaning*, edited by Tatha Wiley 122–34. New York: Continuum.

"Ecofeminism." In *Feminism and Theology*, edited by Janet M. Soskice and Diana Lipton, 23–33. Oxford Readings in Feminism. New York: Oxford University Press.

"The Feminist Liberation Theology of Dorothee Soelle." In *The Theology of Dorothee Soelle*, edited by Sarah K. Pinnock, 205–20. Harrisburg, PA: Trinity.

2004

"Rosemary Radford Ruether." In *Transforming the Faiths of Our Fathers: Women Who Changed American Religion*, edited by Ann Braude, 73–84. New York: Palgrave Macmillan.

"The Spiritual Feminine in the New Testament and Patristic Christianity." In *Dem Tod nicht glauben, Sozialgeschichte de Bibel*, edited by Frank Crüsemann et al., 579–99. Gütersloh: Gütersloher, 2004.

2005

"Feminist Theologies in Latin America." In *Feminist New Testament Studies: Global and Future Perspectives*, edited by Kathleen O'Brien Wicker et al., 159–70. Religion/Cutlure/Critique. New York: Palgrave Macmillan.

"Foreword." In *Girl Friend Theology: God Talk among Young Women*, by Dori Baker, vii–viii. Cleveland: Pilgrim.

"Women in Christianity." In *Christianity: The Complete Guide*, edited by John Bowden, 1230–43. London: Continuum.

2006

"The Post-Modern as Pre-Modern: The Theology of D. Stephen Long." In *Interpreting the Postmodern: Responses to "Radical Orthodoxy,"* edited by Marion Grau and Rosemary Radford Ruether, 76–90. New York: T. & T. Clark.

2007

"Augustine: Sexuality, Gender and Women." In *Feminist Interpretations of Augustine*, edited by Judith C. Stark, 47–68. Re-reading the Canon. University Park: Pennsylvania State University Press.

"The Biblical Vision of Ecojustice." In *Earth and Word: Classic Sermons on Saving the Planet*, edited by David Rhoads, 251–58. New York: Continuum.

2008

"Catholicism." In *The Hope of Liberation in World Religions*, edited by Miguel A. De La Torre, 13–34. Waco, TX: Baylor University Press.

"Ecofeminist Thea\ologies and Ethics: A Post-Christian Movement?" In *Post-Christian Feminisms: A Critical Approach*, edited by Lisa Isherwood and Kathleen McPhilips, 39–52. Aldershot, UK: Ashgate.

"Religion, Reproduction, and Violence against Women." In *Weep Not for Your Children: Essays on Religion and Violence*, edited by Rosemary Radford Reuther and Lisa Isherwood, 7–25. London: Equinox, 2008.

2009

"The Possibilities of Creating Church: A Personal Reflection." In *Prophetic Witness: Catholic Women's Strategies for Reform*, edited by Colleen M Griffith, 25–33. New York: Crossroad.

2010

"Antisemitism," "Patriarchy," "Woman, Theological Views about." In *The Cambridge Dictionary of Christianity*, edited by Daniel Patte. Cambridge: Cambridge University Press.

"The Politics of God in the Christian Tradition." In *Radical Religion: Contemporary Perspectives on Religion and the Left*, edited by Benjamin J. Pauli, 95–104. Lanham, MD: Rowman & Littlefield.

"Modern and Post-Modern Voices: Rosemary Radford Ruether." In *The Gospel among Religions: Christian Ministry, Theology, and Spirituality in a Multi-Faith World*, edited by David R Brochman and Ruben L. F. Habito, 99–103. Maryknoll, NY: Orbis.

"Talking Dirty: Speaking Truth: Indecenting Theology." In *Dancing Theology in Fetish Boots: Essays in Honour of Marcella Althaus-Reid*, edited by Lisa Isherwood and Mark D. Jordan, 254–67. London: SCM.

2011

"Critical Connections in Religion: An Intellectual Autobiography." In *True Confessions: Feminist Professors Tell Stories Out of School*, edited by Susan Gubar, 270–84. New York: Norton.

ARTICLES AND REVIEWS

1963

"Marriage, Love and Children." *Jubilee* 11/8:17–20.

"The Sacramental and Charismatic Ministries and the Theology of the Laity." *Frontline* 1/3 (Winter).

1964

Review: "Woman and Man." *Cross Currents* (Summer).

"Women, Birth Control, and the Church." *Frontline* 2/3 (Winter).

1965

"The Church Is a Happening." *Cross Currents* (Spring).

"Crisis in Los Angeles." *Continuum* 2/4:652–62.

"Is Roman Catholicism Reformable?" *Christian Century*, Sept 22, 1152–54.

"Loisy: History and Commitment." *Continuum* 3/2:152–67.

"Report from Edwards, Mississippi." *Claremont Courier*, August 18.

1966

"Celibacy." *Christian Century*, October 19.

"Communion under Both Species." *National Catholic Reporter*, September 14.

"Post-Ecumenical Christianity." *Ecumenist* 5 (Nov–Dec) 3–7.

"Query to Dan Sullivan" (On Bonhoeffer, *Creation, and Fall*). *Continuum* (August).

"Vahanian: The Worldly Church and the Churchly World." *Continuum* 4/1.

1967

"Basic Eucharist for Small Groups." *Continuum* 5/3.

"The Becoming of Women in Church and Society." *Cross Currents* 17:418–26.

"Divorce." *Commonweal*, April 14.

"Modernism." *National Catholic Reporter*, December 6.

"Symposium on Women." *Commonweal* 85, January 27, 446–58.

"The Visual Arts for the Church of the Present." *The Living Light* 4/2 (Summer).

1968

"Are Women's Colleges Obsolete?" *The Critic* 17 (Oct–Nov) 61–63.

"Creating New Kinds of Religious Communities." *National Catholic Reporter*.

"Dialogue at a Distance." *Brethren Life and Thought*.

"The Free Church Movement in Contemporary Roman Catholicism." *Continuum* 6 (Spring) 41–52.

"The Left Hand of God in the Theology of Karl Barth." *Journal of Religious Thought* 9:3–26.

"Post-Ecumenical Christianity." *Ecumenist* (Nov–Dec).

"Schism in Consciousness in the Church." *Commonweal*, May 31.

"St. Stephen's Educational Program." *Living Light* 5/1 (Spring).

"Theological Anti-Semitism in the New Testament." *Christian Century*, February 14, 191–98.

1969

"Black Realists—White Idealists." *National Catholic Reporter*.
"Black Theology." *America*, June 14.
"Celebrating Life in the Cathedral of Death." *National Catholic Reporter*, December 17.
"Confrontation and Communication." *Christian Century*, September 10.
"Credibility of the Church" (Review of G. Baum). *Salesian Studies*.
"Easter on Fourteenth Street." *National Catholic Reporter*.
"A Head in Biafra; A Heart in Catonsville." *National Catholic Reporter*.
"In the Wakes of Two Pastoral Letters." *National Catholic Reporter*.
"The Larkes and the Changing Seasons." *National Catholic Reporter*.
"The Liberal/Radical Dilemma." *National Catholic Reporter*, August 27.
"Ministry and the Eschatological Ethic." *Cross Currents* 18:149–58.
"The New Church." *Commonweal*, April 4.
"The New Left." *Soundings* 52/3.
"New Wine, Maybe New Wineskins, for the Church." *Christian Century*, April 2, 445–49.
"On Sharing the Sacred Sauna." In *National Catholic Reporter*.
"Parousia Now or Later." *National Catholic Reporter*.
"Pastoral Education for New Communities." *Theology Today* 26:187–94.
"The People with No Names." *National Catholic Reporter*.
"A Perspective on Radical Ecclesiology." *Dialog* 8:209–13.
"Pin Police Badges on Black Militants." *National Catholic Reporter*.
"The Radical Tradition and the Historical Church." *Ecumenist* (July–August).
"The Radical and the Mediator." *America*, November 29.
"The Virginity of Mary and the Brothers of Jesus: The Collision of History and Doctrine." *Continuum* 7 (Spring) 93–105.

1970

"Baum/Ruether Dialogue." *National Catholic Reporter*, March 18.
"The Believer's Church and Catholicity in the World Today." Believer's Church Conference, Chicago, June 1970. *The Chicago Theological Register* 60/6 (Sept) 1–9.
"Black and White Power Subreption" (Review of J. R. Washington). *National Catholic Reporter*, January; also in *Journal of Religious Thought* (Spring).
"Christ as the Saving Protest" (review of B. Häring, *A Theology of Protest*). *National Catholic Reporter*, June 5.
"A Christocentric World History" (review of A. T. van Leeuwen). *Commonweal*, December 4.
"Criteria for Abortion." *Voice* (March). Also in *Liturgy* (1970).
"The Discussion Continues" (Berrigan). *Commonweal*, September 4, 431.
"Ecumenism Today." *The Lamp* (January) 8, 27–28.
"Education in Tandem: White Liberal, Black Militant." *America*, May 30, 582–89.
"Finding Meaning in Science Fiction" (review of L. & S. Rose, *The Shattered Ring*). *National Catholic Reporter*, November 6, 12.
"The Left-Wing Tradition." *Commonweal*, January 16.

"Letter to Catholic Radicals—After the Action—What?" *National Catholic Reporter*, October 2.

"Love Your Enemies as Rebellion." *Fellowship* (July) 7ff.

"The Magic of Holden Village." *Lutheran Forum* (May) 14–15.

"A New Political Consciousness." (Mythology and Counter-Mythology in the Making of a Revolutionary Consciousness) *Ecumenist* (May–June) 61–64.

"On Bigger and Better Ways of Not Giving Up the Barque." *The Lamp* (April) 27–28.

"Perspectives sur les Mouvement Revolutionnairs aux Etats-Unis." *Freres du Monde* 6:86ff.

"Peter Yakovlevich Chaadayev: Philosophical Letters and Apology of a Madman." *Journal of the History of Philosophy* 8:494–96.

"The Search for Soul Power in the White Community." *Christianity & Crisis* (May) 83.

"Theology for the Liberated Churches" (Review of J. P. Brown). *National Catholic Reporter*, February 11.

"Truthfulness—The Future of the Church" (review of H. Küng). *Salesian Studies* (Winter).

"The Underground Church." *Lutheran Forum* (Jan).

"An Unexpected Tribute to the Theologian." *Theology Today* 27:332–39.

"The White Left in the Mother Country." *Commonweal*, November 6, 142–45.

"Women's Liberation in Historical and Theological Perspectives." *Soundings* 43/4:363ff.

1971

"A Black Theology of Liberation" (review of J. H. Cone). *Journal of Religious Thought* 28 (Spring–Summer).

"Christian Origins and the Counter Culture." *Dialog* 10 (Summer) 193–200.

"Communitarian Socialism and the Radical Church Tradition." *Ecumenist* 9/4:52–57.

"Convergence: (Liberal Reform Groups in Roman Catholicism)." *National Catholic Reporter*, October 8, 7.

"J. Edgar Hoover Has Brought Us Together." *World View* 14/3:8.

"Male Chauvinist Theology and the Anger of Women." *Cross Currents* 21/2 (Spring) 173–84.

"Mother Earth and the Megamachine." *Christianity & Crisis* (Dec 13). Reprinted as "Screwing Mother Earth." *Movement* 15 (Apr–May 1974) 37–39.

"Les Ordres Religieux qui Desparaisseut et la nouvelle Communaute Humaine." *IDOC* 41 (March) 22ff.

"A Radical Liberal in the Streets of Washington." *Christianity & Crisis* 31/12:144–46.

"The Reformer or the Radical." *Bulletin: Gettysburg Seminary* 51/1:22ff.

"Sad Songs of Zion beside the Waters of Babylon." *Event*; Baccalaureate, Claremont, June, 1971.

"The Search for a Useable Future" (review of M. Marty). *Journal of Ecumenical Studies* 8:841–42.

"A Second Look at Secular Theology." Review of *The Age of the Person in the 20th Century*, by Dietrich Von Oppen. *Journal of Religion* 51:206–15.

"I Tramonto Degli Ordini Religiosi." *IDOC* 5/1:33–34.

"The Vanishing Religious Order and the Emerging Human Community." *Christian Century*, April 7, 425–26.

"Who'll Investigate the Investigators?" *World View* 14/5:9.

1972

"Black Liberation and Women's Liberation." *Sisterhood* 2/1:3–4

"Christian Anti-Semitism—The Dilemma of Zionism." *Christianity & Crisis* 32/6:91–94.

"In What Sense Can We Say That Jesus Is the Christ?" *Ecumenist* 10:14–19.

"Judaism and Christianity: Two Fourth-Century Religions." *Studies in Religion* 2:2–10.

"A Liturgy from the Lands of Burning Children." *Christianity & Crisis* 32/11.

"Outlines for a Theology of Liberation." *Dialog* 11:252–57.

"Paradoxes of Human Hope: The Messianic Horizon of Church and Society." *Theological Studies* 33:235–52.

"The Reformer and the Radical in the Sixteenth Century." *Journal of Ecumenical Studies* 9:271–84.

"The Spirituals and the Blues" (review of J. H. Cone). *National Catholic Reporter* (Sept 29) 15.

1973

"Continuing Reform After Vatican II" (tribute to Archbishop Roberts on his 80th birthday). *The Month* (March) 93–96.

"The Cult of True Womanhood." *Commonweal* 97/6:127–31.

"The Ethic of Celibacy." *Commonweal* 97/17:390–93.

"Male Clericalism and the Dread of Women." *Ecumenist* 11/5:65–69.

"The Messianic Horizon of Church and Society." *Concilium* 1/9:136–43.

"Monks and Marxists: A Look at the Catholic Left." *Christianity & Crisis* 33/7:75–79.

"One More Time" (letter on celibacy). *Commonweal* 93/5:99–119.

"The Personalization of Sexuality." *Christianity & Crisis* 33/6:59–62.

"The Pharisees in First-Century Judaism." *Ecumenist* 11:1–7.

"Revolutionaries' Faith" (review of E. Bianchi). *National Catholic Reporter*, February 16, 14.

"Sexism and the Theology of Liberation." *Christian Century*, December 12, 1224–29.

"Sexism and Theology of Liberation." *Drew Gateway* 42/2:138–48.

"The Task of the Church in Contemporary America." *Dialog* 12:284–88.

"Theology by Sex." Review of *Beyond God the Father*, by Mary Daly. *New Republic*, November 10, 24–26.

"Women's Liberation, Ecology and Social Revolution." *WIN*, October 4, 4–7.

1974

"Anti-Judaism is the Left Hand of Christology." *New Catholic World* (Jan–Feb) 12–17.

"Anti-Semitism and the State of Israel—Some Principles for Christians." *Christianity & Crisis* 33/20:240–44.

"Anti-Semitism in Christian Theology." *Theology Today* 30:365–82.

"Better Red Than Dead." *Ecumenist* 26:10–14.

"Crisis in Sex and Race: Black Theology vs. Feminist Theology." *Christianity & Crisis* 34/6:67–73.

"A Further Look at Feminist Theology." *Christianity & Crisis* 34/11:139–43.

"God Talk: Three Recent Books on Religion." Review of *Jesus Now*, by Malachi Martin; *Is God a White Racist*, by William Jones; and *God is Red*, by Vine Deloria, Gosset and Dunlap. *New Republic* (Jan 5 & 12) 25–26.

"The Ministry of the Laity." *Notre Dame Journal of Education* 5/1:70–77.

"Notre Dame Statement." *Commonweal* 100/7:61–62.

"Ordination: Witness against Evil." *National Catholic Reporter*, October 11, 7.

"The Persecution of Witches: A Case of Ageism or Sexism?" *Christian Century* 34/22, December 23, 291–95.

Review of *God in Public: Political Theology beyond Niebuhr*, by William R. Coats. *Christianity & Crisis* 34/22:298–300.

Review of *The Gospel and the Land: Early Christian and Jewish Territorial Doctrine*, by W. D. Davies. *Journal of Religious Thought* 31:78–79.

"Rich Nations/Poor Nations and the Exploitation of the Earth." *Dialog* 13/3:201–7.

"Sexism and Ministry." *Pax Christi* 1/3:12–18.

"The Suffering Servant Myth." *Worldview* 17 (March) 45–46.

"White or Black" (review of *Getting Ready: The Education of a White Family in Inner City Schools*, by Lois Mark Stalvey). *New Republic*, April 20, 29–30.

"Woman in Christian Tradition" (review of G. H. Tavard). *Religious Education* (July–Aug) 505–17.

"Women in a Man's Church." *The Witness*. Special issue (August) 7–9.

1975

"The First and Final Proletariat: Socialism and Women's Liberation." *Soundings* 58/3:311–28.

"The Foundations of Liberation Languages: Christianity and Revolutionary Movements." *Journal of Religious Thought* 32/1:74–85.

"Home and Work: Women's Roles and Transformation of Values." *Theological Studies* 36:647–60.

"Whatever Happened to Theology?" *Christianity & Crisis* 35/8:109–10.

"Women, Ecology and the Domination of Nature." *Ecumenist* 14/1:1–5.

And Herman Ruether. "Zionism and Racism." *Christianity & Crisis* 35/21:307–11.

1976

"The Bible and Social Justice." *Ecumenist* 14/2:24–27.

"Christology and Feminism." *Occasional Papers: United Methodist Board of Higher Education* 1/13 (December 25).

"Cult of True Womanhood." *The Movement* 23:13–16.

"Individual Repentance Is Not Enough." *Explor* 2/1:47–52.

"Integrates Theologies." Review of *Blessed Rage for Order, The New Pluralism in Theology*, by David Tracy. *National Catholic Reporter*, April 9, 25.

"Male Clericalism and the Dread of Women." *The Movement* 24:16–18.

Monks and Marxists (pamphlet). *The Holy Bible*, 17–20.

"The Next President . . ." *World View* 19/4:7.

Reply to Paul Van Buren. *N.I.C.M. Journal for Jews and Christians in Higher Education* 1/2:25–37.

Report: "Catholic Women and Ordination." *Christianity & Crisis* 36/1:12.

"The Two Faces of America." *Christianity & Crisis* 36/13:180–88.

"What Is the Task of Theology?" *Christianity & Crisis* 36:121–25.

"Women and Priesthood: Historical and Social Perspective." *Concilium* 3 (Jan) (French, German, Spanish Dutch, and Italian).

"Women at Mari" (review of B. F. Batto). *Anglican Theological Review* 58:229–30.

1977

"Martin Marty's Mythical Moonscape." *Journal of Current Social Issues* 14/2:10–13.

"Prayer—Authentic Marriage of Contemplation and Social Witness." *New Catholic World* 220:22–23.

Review of *The Burden of Freedom: Americans and the God of Israel*, by Paul Van Buren. *Interpretation* 31:322–24.

Review of *Quest for Wholeness in Female Experiences*, by Penelope Washbourne. *New Review of Books and Religion* 1/ 9 (May).

Reviews of *Down to Earth*, by John de Sutge; *The Mary Myth*, by Andrew Greeley; *The Virgin*, by Geoffrey Ashe. *New Review of Books and Religion* 1/10 (June 10) 9–10.

"Time Makes Ancient Good Uncouth: The Catholic Report on Sexuality." *Christian Century*, August 3–10, 682–85.

"Working Women and the Male Work Day." *Christianity & Crisis* 37:3–8.

1978

"The Biblical Vision of the Ecological Crisis." *Christian Century* 22:1129–32.

"Chicago Statement of Concern: A Symposium." *Commonweal* 105/4:112–13.

"Did Jesus Have Women Apostles?" *Across* (Easter) 14ff.

"The Expectation of the Third Age of the Spirit." *Explor* (Spring) 66–74.

"God Talk after the End of Christendom?" *Commonweal* 105/12:369–74.

"Israel and the Land." *Christianity & Crisis* 38 (June 12).

Review of *Early Christianity and Society*, by R. M. Grant. *Christian Century* (Apr 26) 449–50.

Review of *The Exclusion of Women from Priesthood*, by I. Raming. *Theology Today* 34:454–57.

"The Sexuality of Jesus: What Do the Synoptics Say?" *Christianity & Crisis* 38/9:134–37.

"St. Paul and Sarah Grimke: Two Models of Liberation of Women." *Soundings* 61/2:168–71.

1979

"Consciousness Raising at Puebla." *Christianity & Crisis* 39 (Apr 2).

"Liberation Mariology." *The Witness* 62/10:15–18.

"The Other Side of Marriage." *AD* 8/6:8–9.

"A Religion for Women, Sources and Strategies." *Christianity & Crisis* 39:307–11.

Review: "Jesus the Jew and Israel and the Palestinians." *Christian Century* 96/8:254–55.

Review of *The Feminine Dimension of the Divine*, by Joan Chamberlain Englemann. *Spirituality Today* (Winter) 71–73.

Review of *The Gnostic Gospels*, by Elaine Pagels. *Chicago Sun-Times*, December.

1980

"Asking the Existential Questions: How My Mind Has Changed." *Christian Century*, April 2, 374–78.

"Goddesses and Witches: Liberation and Countercultural Feminism." *Christian Century*, September 10–17, 842–47.

"Is a New Christian Consensus Possible?" *Journal of Ecumenical Studies* 17:63–68.

"Liberation Mariology." *The Other Side* (May) 17–21.

"The Ministry of the People and the Future Shape of the Church." *NICM Journal* (Spring) 8–17.

"Politics and the Family." *Christianity & Crisis* 40 (Sept 26).

Review of *The Spiral Dance*, by Starhawk. *Christian Century*, February 20, 208–9.

"Sister Kane and the Pope." *The Witness* 63, March 3, 14–15.

"Toward a Theology of Ecojustice." *Catholic Rural Life* (Sept).

"Why Males Fear Women Priests." *The Witness* 63/7 (July).

"Why Socialism Needs Feminism and Vice Versa." *Christianity & Crisis* 40/7:103–8.

"Women/Body/Nature: The Icon of the Divine." *Newsletter* (Center for Women and Religion) (Spring) 842–47.

"Women Explore Their Place in the Church." *The Episcopalian* (June) 11–19.

1981

"Basic Christian Communities: Introduction." *Christianity & Crisis* 41/14:234–37.

"The Christian Left in Italy." *The Ecumenist* 19/3:33–38.

"The Femininity of God: A Religious Problem of Our Time." *Concilium* 163 (German, French, Portuguese, Italian, Spanish, Dutch).

"Italy's Third Way on Abortion." *Christianity & Crisis* 41 (May 11).

"What Is Shaping My Theology?" *Commonweal* (Jan).

1982

"Feminism and Patriarchal Religion: Principles of Ideological Critique of the Bible." *Journal for the Study of the Old Testament* 22:54–66.

Review of *Receiving Woman: Studies in the Psychology and Theology of the Feminine*, byAnne Belford Ulanov. *Spirituality Today* (Mar) 87–88.

Review of *Christ in a Changing World: Toward an Ethical Christology*, by Tom F. Driver. *Christian Century*, April 7, 418–20.

Review of *Christian Realism and Liberation Theology: Practical Theologies in Creative Conflict*, by Dennis McCann. *Review of Books and Religion* (July) 10.

Review of *Poems of Anger and Love*, by Collins, Golden, and Esquivel. *Christianity and Crisis* 42/19:38–40.

1983

"The Call of Women in the Church Today." *Studies in Formative Spirituality* 4/2:243–52. (Reprinted from *Listening* [Fall 1980] 241–49.

"Courage as a Christian Virtue." *Cross Currents* 33/1:8–16.

"The Crisis of the Two Americas." *Circuit Rider* (March) 4–6.

"The Family in a Dim Light" (Review of books on the family by Kramer, Berger, and Berger and Dally) *Christianity & Crisis* 43/11:263–66.

"Feminism and Peace." *Christian Century* 100/25, September 7, 771–76.

"Interview: Tony Clarke-Sauer." *The Witness* 66/3:8–9, 17.

Review of *Christ, the Experience of Jesus as Lord*, by E. Schillebeeckx. *Religious Studies Review* 9/1:42–44.

Review of *Reweaving the Web of Life: Feminism and Nonviolence*, by P. McAlister. *Christianity & Crisis* 43/1:18–20.

Review of *Woman, Church, and State*, by M. J. Gage. *Journal of Church and State* 358–59.

"Scripture and the Family: An Unrealized Revolution." *Christianity and Crisis* 43/17 (Oct 31) 399–404.

"Theology from the Side of the Other." *Soundings* 5/6:6–7.

"Women, Where Are They Going?" *Christianity & Crisis* 43/50:111–16.

1984

"Abortion, Capturing the Middle Ground." *Christianity and Crisis* 44/2:285–86.

"Church and Family in Scripture." *New Blackfriars* 4–14.

"Church and Family in the Medieval and Reformation Periods." *New Blackfriars* (Feb) 74–86.

Comment on Harvey Cox, *After the Secular City*. *Christianity and Crisis* 44/2:40–41.

"The Family in Late Industrial Society." *New Blackfriars* (April) 170–79.

"Feminism, Church, and Family in Late Industrial Society." *New Blackfriars* (May) 202–12.

"Feminism, Church and Family in the 1980s." *American Baptist Quarterly* 3/1:21–30.

"Religion and the Making of the Victorian Family." *New Blackfriars* (March) 110–18.

Review of *Pure Lust: Elemental Feminist Philosophy*, by M. Daly. *Unitarian Universalist World*, June 15, 14.

"Symposium, *In Memory of Her: A Feminist Theological Reconstruction of Christian Origins*, by Elisabeth Schüssler Fiorenza." *Horizons* 1/2:146–50.

1985

"Catholics and Abortion: Authority and Dissent." *Christian Century*, October 3, 859–62.

"Christians and Cubans: A Renewal of Faith." *Christianity & Crisis* 45/13:329–33.

"Feminist Theology in the Academy." *Christianity & Crisis* 45/3:57–62; also in *Journal of the American Academy of Religion* 53/3.

"For Whom, With Whom, Do We Speak Our New Stories." *Christianity & Crisis* 45 (May 13) 183–85.

"The Liberation of Christology from Patriarchy." *Religion in Intellectual Life* 2/3 (1985) 116–28; also in *New Blackfriars* (July-August) 324–25; and in *Svensk Teologist Kvartalskrift* (Aug 6) 97–105.

"Prophetic Tradition and the Liberation of Women." *Drew Gateway* 55/2–3.

"The Sisters of Charity and the Vatican: Differing Views of the Church." *Probe* 23/2:5–6; also in *New Blackfriars* 392–401.

1986

"Community of Resistances and Solidarity: A Feminist Theology of Liberation." Sharon Welch, *Grail* 2/1 (March) 125–27.

"Crises and Challenges in Catholicism Today." *America* (March 1) 152–58.

"Feminist Spirituality and Historical Religion." *Harvard Divinity School Bulletin* (Feb-Mar) 5–7, 11; also in *Religion and Intellectual Life* (Winter) 7–20.

"Feminist Theology: What Is It? Why Is It Necessary?" *U.U. World* (Sept 15) 1, 8.

"Recontextualizing Theology." *Theology Today* 43:22–27.

Review of *Bread Not Stone: The Challenge of Feminist Biblical Interpretation*, by E. Schüssler Fiorenza. *Journal of the American Academy of Religion* 54 (Spring) 141–43.
Review of *New Catholic Women*, by Mary Jo Weaver. *The Tablet* 12 (July) 732.
"Zapping Greenham's Women." *Christianity & Crisis* 46/11 (Aug 11) 265–66.

1987

"Bishops Challenged on Peace Pastoral." *Pax Christi* (Summer 1987) 14–16.
"Female Symbols, Values and Context." *Christianity & Crisis* 47 (Jan 12) 460–64.
"From the Ecclesia of Patriarchy to a Community of Liberation." *Probe* 15/2:1–3.
"Invisible Palestinians in Israel." *Christian Century* (July 1–8) 587–91.
"Is There a Place for Feminists in the Christian Church?" *New Blackfriars* (Jan) 2–24.
"Response to Rita Gross: The Three-Yana Journey in Tibetan Vajrayana Buddhism." *Buddhist–Christian Studies* 7:117–27.
Review of *The Lady and the Virgin: Attitude and Experience in Twelfth-Century France Journal of the American Academy of Religion* 44/3:282–83.
"Women-Church: What Is It? Where Is It Going?" *The World Journal of the UUA* 1/2 (Mar–Apr) 4–7.

1988

"Catholic Bishops and Women's Concerns." *Christianity & Crisis* 48 (May 16) 177.
"The Catholic Bishops' Pastoral on Women: A Flawed Effort." *Conscience* 9/3.
"Has There Been a Reagan Revolution in Theology: A Symposium." *Christian Century* (Mar 16) 280–81.
"Il Sacerdozio e Universale: Il Ministero e della Chieza." *CNT Quaderni* (Dec) 30–31.
"Listening to an Arab Christian Theologian." *Holy Land* (Winter) 208–14.
"Listening to Middle Eastern Christians." *New Blackfriars* (May) 204–9.
"Listening to Palestinian Christians: A Challenge to Biblical Traditions." *Christianity & Crisis* 48/5:113–15.
"Models of God: Exploring the Foundations." *Religion and Intellectual Life* 5/3:19–23.

1989

"Brain and Gender: The Missing Data." *Christian Century* (Mar 8) 263–64.
"Can Israel Save Its Soul?" *The Witness* 72/5 (May) 10–12.
"Christian Churches and the Intifada." *American–Arab Affairs Journal* 30:72–76.
"Cristiani palestinesi: Una Sfida alla Tradizione biblica." *Gioventu evangelica* (Feb) 8–10.
"The Development of My Theology." *Religious Studies Review* 15/1:1–2.
"Does Feminism Have a Stake in Immortality?" *IDOC International* (Nov/Dec) 18–29.
"Ecumenism in Central America." *Christianity & Crisis* (July 10) 208–12.
"Feminist Critique and Revisioning of God-Language." *The Way* 27/2:132–43.
"Liberation Theology: New Friends, Old Enemies." *Christianity & Crisis* 49/9 (June 12) 181–82.
"The Liberation of Women in the Work Place." *International Christian Digest* 3/6 (July/ Aug) 17–20.
"The Manuscript in My Drawer." *The Critic* (Summer) 29–30.
"Mary's Pence: Promoting Women's Ministries." *Cross Currents* (Spring) 97–102.

"Prochoice Is Prolife: Winning the Propaganda War for Reproductive Rights." *Conscience* 10/5.

Reviews of *Beyond Power*, by Marilyn French; *The Chalice and the Blade*, by Riane Eisler; *The Creation of Patriarchy*, by Gerda Lerner. *Daughters of Sarah* (May/June) 2–3.

"Salvadorean Refugees Come Home." *Christian Century* (Sept 27) 851–53.

"To Preserve and Protect Democracy." *Sojourners* 18/2:19.

"Uppity Women and Authentic Ecumenism: The Ordination of Barbara Harris to the Episcopacy." *The Witness*, 42/4:16–17; reprinted in *The Guardian*, May 15, 39.

"The War on Palestinian Education." *Christianity & Crisis* 49:54–55.

"What Liberal Ministers Should Know about Sexist America." *The Wild Goose* 1/1 (Sept) 13–21.

1990

"Brutalidad Creciente contra los Palestinos." *Correo Del Sur*, Cuernavaca, Mor. Mexico, (Jan 7).

"Christian Zionism Is Heresy." *Journal of Theology for Southern Africa* 69 (Dec) 60–64.

"Creation Spirituality: The Message and the Movement." *Creation* 11/6 (Nov/Dec) 20–23, 37.

"Feminist Theology in Global Context." *In God's Image* (Dec) 4–7.

"Intifada: New Forms of Resistance." *Christianity and Crisis* 50:409–10.

"Is Feminism the End of Christianity: A Critique of Daphne Hampson's *Theology and Feminism*." *Scottish Journal of Theology* 43:390–400.

"Jewish-Christian Relations in the Theology of Paul Van Buren." *Religious Studies Review* 16/14:320–23.

"Kwart eeun na het Tweede Vaticaans Concilie: Kerk op een Kruispunt." *De Barzuin* 73/46:7–12.

"Matthew Fox and Creation Spirituality." *Catholic World* (July/Aug) 168–72.

"Prophets and Humanists: Types of Religious Feminism in Stuart England." *Journal of Religion* 70:1–18.

"Religion and Science in an Unjust World." *Center for Theology and the Natural Sciences* (Winter) 3–5.

Review of *Asad of Syria: The Struggle for the Middle East*, by Patrick Seale. *Annals of the American Academy* (Spring) 198.

Review of *Toward Two Societies*, by Andrew Winnick. *Christianity & Crisis* 50/12:277–78.

"Robert Palmer; First the God, Then the Dance." *Christian Century*, February 7–14, 125–26; and *Scripps College Bulletin* (Spring 1990) 29.

"Roundtable: A Dialogue about Women in Buddhism and Christianity." *Journal of Feminist Studies in Religion* 6/2:87–120.

"Standing Up to State Theology: The Global Reach of Christian Zionism." *Sojourners* (January) 30–32.

"Women as Prophetic Word." *Probe* 18/2:1, 6.

"Women, Sexuality, Ecology and the Church." *Jesuit Shalom Center*, Seattle (Spring 1990) 4–22.; also *Conscience* 11/4 (1990).

1991

"Catholic Women in the Era of Vatican II." *Catholic Commission on Intellectual and Cultural Affairs Annual* 10:134–45.

"Dangerous Illusions of Victory." *Christian Century*, March 20–27, 318–19.

"Degevaarlijke illusie van de overwinning." *De Barzuin*, April 12, 5–7.

"Facing Up to Global Repentance." *Christianity & Crisis* 51:244–46.

"Feminist Critique and Revisioning of God-Language." *Gurukul Journal of Religious Studies* 2/1:30–42.

"Feminist Theology in Global Context." In *ATLA Proceedings* 44th Annual Conference of the American Theological Library Association, 130–36.

"Frauen, Männer, und Tiere." *Evangelische Kommentare* 8:474–77.

"The Israeli Peace Movement: Failure and Hope." *COELI International* (Fall) 22–23.

"Le Mouvement Pacifiste Israelien: Echec et Espoir." *Relations* 574 (Oct) 231.

"Redemptive Community in Christianity." *Buddhist–Christian Studies* 11:217–30.

"Religion and War in the Middle East." *Sojourners* (June) 4–6.

"Religion and War in the Middle East." *COELI International* (Summer) 3–7.

"Witness to Hope against a Demonic World." *Sojourners* (Aug–Sept) 22–23.

"Women's Difference and Equal Rights in the Church." *Concilium* 1991/6 (Nov) 11–18 (also in Dutch, German, Italian, French, Spanish, and Portuguese).

1992

"Ahistorical Ideals vs Messy Realities: Response to Jacob Neusner's 'There Has Never Been a Judaeo-Christian Dialogue, But There Can Be One,'" *Cross Currents* 42/2:277–80.

"La Derive Israelienne du Sionisme." *Relations* (June) 152–55.

"Het dubbele gezicht van het Zionisme." *De Barzuin* 28 (Feb) 10–13.

"Ecological Imperialism: 500 Years of Conquest." *Basta* (May) 41–45.

"De hoeksteen onder de Amerikaanse Stembus." *De Barzuin* (Oct 16) 3–5.

"Is Feminism the End of Christianity?: A Critique of Daphne Hampson's *Theology and Feminism*." *Scottish Journal of Theology* 45:282–92.

"Is Zionism Racism?: Ideology and Reality in the Battle for Palestine." *COELI International* 62 (Summer) 25–29.

"Men, Women and Beasts: Relations to Animals in Western Culture." *Between the Species: A Journal of Ethics* 8/3:136–41.

"De Padre is een Vrouw." *De Barzuin* (Oct 30).

Review of, *The Broken Staff: Judaism through Christian Eyes*, by Frank Manuel. *Boston Globe* (June 14) B43.

"Seeking the Better Part." *Sojourners* (Nov) 24–25.

"Socialism and Christian Faith." *Religious Socialism* (Winter).

"Women-church: Theologie et pratique dans les communautes liturgiques feminists." *Echanges* (March) 22–24.

1993

"Anger and Liberating Grace." *The Living Pulpit* 3/4 (Oct–Dec) 6–7.

"The Art of Survival: Feminism in Nicaragua." *Sojourners* (July) 18–23; reprint, *COELI* (Summer) 18–21.

"Behind the Middle East Accord and Looking Ahead." *Christian Century*, September 22–29, 885.

"Christology and Jewish-Christian Relations." *Concilium* 245 (Feb) 171–84 (seven languages).

"Cruise Missiles as Political Therapy." *Sojourners* (Sept–Oct) 5–6.

"De-educating Nicaragua." *Christianity & Crisis* 53/4:93–96.

"Ecofeminism." *Open Eye* 2:35–37.

"In Israel, Invisible Arabs." *Christianity & Crisis* 53:8–9.

"Patriarchy and Creation: Feminist Critique of Religious and Scientific Cosmologies"; "Destroying the Earth"; "Theological Resources for Earth-Healing"; "Before and Beyond Patriarchy." *Feminist Theology* 2:57–112.

"Voorheursoptie voor de rijken: de Bisschopper van Nicaragua hebben liever een kathedraal dan een Volkskerk." *De Bazuin,* June 11, 8–9.

"Watershed for Faithful Catholics." *Conscience* 14/4.

"A Wise Woman: Mothered by One Touched by Wisdom's Spirit." *Christian Century* (Feb 17) 164–65.

"Woman-church." *Relations* (Mar) 50–52.

"Women: First and Last Colony: Female Status and Roles within Class and Race Hierarchy." *Humboldt Journal of Social Relations* 19/2:391–416.

1994

"The Alliance That Fizzled: The Vatican and Islamic Fundamentalists at Cairo." *Conscience* 15/4.

"Can Women Stay in the Church?" *The Witness* (July 1994) 8–11.

"Faith to Face: The Pope's Fallibility in Quashing Debate." *The Guardian* (June 11).

"Hets Versets van Vertrapte Vormen." *De Barzuin* (Sept 30) 12–13.

"Pope's Fallibility in Quashing Debate." *The Guardian* (Nov 11) 1994.

"Solidly Rooted, Ready to Fly" (On my Father). *The Witness* 77/12:8–10.

"Thoughts on Being Cancelled in Rome." *Conscience* 15/3:52–53.

"Why I Stay in the Church." *Sojourners* (July) 15–17.

1995

"Being a Catholic Feminist at the End of the Twentieth Century." *Feminist Theology* 10:9–20.

"The Cycle of Life and Death in Ecofeminist Spirituality." *Creation Spirituality* 11/2:34–38.

"Ecofeminism: Symbolic and Social Connections of the Oppression of Women and the Domination of Nature"; and "Ecofeminism and Healing Ourselves, Healing the Earth." *Feminist Theology* 9 (May) 35–62.

"Ecofeminismo y Teología." *Prometeo* 8 (Spring) 33–37.

"Feminist Metanoia and Soul-Making." *Women and Therapy: A Feminist Quarterly* 16/2–3:33–44.

"Feminist Theology and Soul Making: Women's Spirituality, Women's Lives." *Women and Therapy* 16/2–3:33–44.

"Lessons from Chiapas." *Conscience* 16/4.

"Mary's Role in U.S. Catholic Culture." *National Catholic Reporter,* February 10, 15–17.

"Mixing Faith and Politics: Beyond the Religious Right; Bridging the Gap." *Boston Review* 20/1 (Feb/Mar) 7–8.

"Women and Culture: The Case for Universal Rights." *Conscience* 16/4.

1996

"First- and Third-World Women, Spirituality, and Ecology." *Vox Feminiarum* 1/2:28–33.

"The Image of God's Goodness." *Sojourners* (Jan–Feb) 30–31.
Review of *Jesus: Miriam's Child, Sophia's Prophet*, by Elisabeth Schüssler Fiorenza. *Journal of Biblical Literature* 115:345–47.
"Speaking Truth to Power in the USA in 1996." *COELI* 79 (Fall) 24–27.

1997

"Created Second, Sinned First: Women, Redemption, and the Challenge." *Conscience* 18/1.
"Ecofeminism: First- and Third-World Women." *Ecotheology*, January, 72–83.
"Jesus: Quien Es y No Es para Mi." *Conspirando: Revista Latinoamerano de Ecofeminismo, Espiritualidad y Teología* 22:10–13.
"Judaism and Christianity in Earth's Insights." *Worldviews: Environment, Culture and Religion*, 163/6:163–66.
"Reform Jews and Palestinians: Something in Common." *The Jerusalem Times*, August 1, 5.

1998

"Gender Equity and Christianity: Premodern Roots, Modern and Postmodern Perspectives." *Union Quarterly* 50:47–61.

1999

"Gender and Redemption in Theological History." *Feminist Theology* 21:98–108.
"How Did the Creator Become a White Racist?" *Chicago Tribune* July 18, sec. 1, p. 17.
"Sex and the Body in the Catholic Tradition." *Conscience* 20/4:3–11.

2000

"The Mantra of "Anti-Catholicism": What Is Bigotry?" *Conscience* 21/3.
"Sister of Earth: Religious Women and Ecological Spirituality." *The Witness* (May) 14–17; also in *Trefoil: Southern African Catholic Christianity* (Summer) 15–16.
"Whither Theological Education?" *Dialog* 39:306–9.
"Women and Roman Catholic Christianity." *Catholics for a Free Choice* (Spring 2000) 3–12.

2001

"Resisting the Silence: Reflections on Joan Chittister's Decision to Speak." *Conscience* 22/3.
Review of *Palestinian Women: Patriarchy and Resistance in the West Bank*, by Cheryl A. Rubenberg. *Shofar: Interdisciplinary Journal of Jewish Studies* 21/1 (2002) 147–49.
"The War on Women." *Conscience* 22/4.

2002

"Reflections on Being a Catholic." *Conscience* 23/2.
"Polarization among Christians: Is Dialogue Possible?" *Conscience* 23/3.

2003

"Sexual Illiteracy." *Conscience* 24/2.

2004

"The Choice to Speak Out." *Conscience* 25/3.

"Distortion, Misrepresentation and Caricature: The Vatican's Letter to Women Is Confused about Scripture and Feminism." *Conscience* 25/3.

2005

"Identity and Openness to a Pluralistic World: A Christian View." *Buddhist-Christian Studies* 25/1 (2005) 29–40.

"Letter to Elsa Tamez." *Feminist Theology* 14/1:17–19.

Review of *Women in Christ: Toward a New Feminism*, edited by Michele M Schumacher. *Theological Studies* 66:687–89.

"Teaching Peace in a Time of Impending War." *Feminist Theology* 14/1:21–24.

"Why Do Men Need the Goddess? Male Creation of Female Religious Symbols." *Dialog* 44/3:234–36.

2006

"After Katrina: Poverty, Race, and Environmental Degradation." *Dialog* 45/2:176–83.

"Benedict XVI's First Encyclical: 'God Is Love.'" *Conscience* 27/2.

"Twenty Years of Christian–Buddhist Dialogue." *Turning Wheel*, 31–32.

2007

"A Consistent Life Ethic? Supporting Life after Birth." *Conscience* 28/1.

"For the Good of the Church" (review of C. E. Curran, Loyal Dissent: Memoir of a Catholic Theologian). *Conscience* 28/2.

"Love between Women: A Context for Theology." *Biblical Theology Bulletin* 37:153–60.

2008

"Fictionalizing the Unspeakable" (review of *The Children's Crusade*, by Eugene Bianchi). *Conscience* (Winter) 49.

"Intellectual Freedom and the Catholic University." *Conscience* 29/2:36–37.

"Women, Reproductive Rights and the Catholic Church." *Feminist Theology* 16/2:184–93.

2009

"Are Michael Moore's Films Inspired by His Catholicism?" *Religion Dispatches*, Oct. 5. Online: http://www.religiondispatches.org/dispatches/culture/1889/are_michael_moore_s_films_inspired_by_his_catholicism/.

"The Politics of God in the Christian Tradition." *Feminist Theology* 17:329–38.

"A U.S. Theology of Letting Go." *Episcopal Peace Witness* (Spring) 5, 13.

"Un Viaje Intellectual/Social." *Sabidurias Compartidas: Conspirando* 16:174–76.

2010

"Shalom: The Biblical Vision of Ecojustice." *Church of the Brethren Messenger*, December, 8–11.

2011

"Rosemary Ruether: A Commemorative Issue: Highlights from Her Prolific Writings in *Conscience.*" *Conscience* (June).

NATIONAL CATHOLIC REPORTER COLUMNS

1982

"Women Spirit Bonding." August 13, 15.
"Denominations: Real Divisions in Family." October 15, 13.
"Holocaust, A Rationale for Violence." December 3, 11.
"Jewish and Christian Feminism." December 31, 13.

1983

"Third World Women." February 11, 20.
"God Language Metaphor, Not Fact." March 25, 17.
"Father, Son and Amorphous Female Other: God Language and Theology." May 5.
"Idols Drawn from Verbal Imagery." August 1983.
"Will the Religious on the Left Please Step Down?" September 16, 23.
"Protestant Churches Repair Broken Ties." October 7, 17.
"Give Women a Chance or Else." October 21, 13.
"Roman Church Ignores Pleas of Women Who Seek Ministry." December 9, 13.

1984

"US–Vatican Ties Give Reagan Leverage." February 17, 38.
"Feminists Seek Structural Change." April 13.
"Betzie Hollants Joining Women and Latin Americans." May 11, 12.
"Feminism Must Seek a Solid Design for the Family." June 22, 15.
"Women Religious, More 'Quasi-Clerics' Than 'Laity.'" August 17, 19.
"Dilemmas of Zionism." September.
"Sweden's Feminist Theology." December 7, 12.

1985

"Why the Nuns on Abortion at This Time." January 11, 12.
"The Flaw in the Weave of the Seamless Garment." February 22, 17.
"Buddhists and Christians Work Toward Co-Existence." May 3, 17.
"Meetings but Not of Minds." July 5, 13.
"Some Well-Guarded Secrets of Churches in Cuba." August 30, 14.
"It's Unnatural to Dominate the Earth." September 27, 22.
"Women and Humor." November 15, 12.

1986

"Trickle Down Mystery." January 24, 12.
"The Bane of Infallibility." March 5.

"Celibacy and Asceticism." April 4.
"Was Mary Magdalene a Prostitute?" May 9, 13.
"The Church—A Democracy?" June 20, 15.
"Remembering Marjorie Tuite." August.
"Why Mary Chandler Left the Church She Loves." September 26, 14.

1987

"Women-Church: Neither Over or Under Men." January 23, 15.
"Religion of Survival in the Holy Land." April 10, 12.
"Arab Farmers." June 5, 12.
"Archaeology and Israeli Occupation." July 17, 12.

1988

"Peace Doesn't Mean Putting Palestinians in Their Place." April 8, 14–15.
"Uppity Men Aim at the Altar." May 13, 15.
"America Putting Own Brand on Buddhism." June 17, 15.
"Esalen and Gaza." July 29, 13.
"Thinking in Black and White." September 16, 15.
"Spirituality: Testing the Spirits." October 4, 15.
"Exclusion of Women Distorts the Good News." November 11, 14.
"Matthew Fox and the Vatican." December 2, 13.
"The Bishops' Pastoral, Flawed but Important." December 23, 15.

1989

"In Occupied Territories, Even Happiness Outlawed." January 27, 13.
"Witches and Christianity." March 17, 33.
"Infallibility, Antithesis of Faith." April 21, 1989, 18. Reprint: *Confronti* (May 1989) 19–20.
"It Is Possible: Israeli-Palestinian Art Exhibit." May 20.
"China and US Ideology." June 30, 25.
"Biblical God vs. Idols of Death: The Damascus Document." August 25.
"The Defiance Campaign in South Africa." October 13, 18.
"The American Bishops' Letter on the Middle East." November 17, 10.
"The Devil Can Quote Scripture." December 22, 16.

1990

"Third-World Feminism on the Move." February 2, 13.
"Guatemala and Nicaragua on Closer Inspection." February 23, 17.
"Modern Catacombs in the Guatemalan Mountains." May 4, 20.
"Dear US Bishops, You Insult Our Intelligence." May 18, 16.
"Zionism's Long Range Plans for Soviet Jews in Israel." July 13, 21.
"Holy War or Hypocrisy?" October 5, 18.
"The Temple Mount Massacre." November 16, 22.

1991

"Two Kinds of Ecumenism." January 18, 36.

"War Incurs Odium for US." March 1, 12.

"Hyun Kyun Chung's Minjung Theology for Asian Women." March 29, 21.

"Middle East Peace Must Start with Truthfulness." May 10, 15.

"Bullets to Beatings to Baker: Palestinians Seeking Relief." June 21, 30. Reprint: "De Palestijnen verdwijnen." *De Barzuin*, May 31, 1991, 12–13.

"Peace Doesn't Begin at the Negotiating Table." August 16, 16.

"European Women Envision Theology beyond Patriarchy." October 4, 19.

"Julie Raino Found Her Way to Be Both Priest and Catholic." December 11, 26.

1992

"India's Catholic Women Shaking Off 'Airyfairy' Theology." January 31, 18.

"Holy War Fueled by Rival Faith in the One God." February 2.

"Egyptian Christians in the Arab World." May 1, 18.

"The Church as Occasion of Sin." July 17, 34.

"In These Filipino Churches Only Women Can Be Priests." September 4, 14.

"The Episcopal Myth of Radical Feminism." September 18, 18.

"Jubilee Remission of Debt." Novemer 6.

"The Attack on Catholic Feminists by the Radical Right." December 5.

1993

"New View of Mary: No Improvement on Tradition." January 15, 27.

"Nicaraguan Hierarchy: Preferential Option for the Poor." February 26, 16.

"The Future of Liberation Theology Is Ecumenical." April 9, 16.

"FBI Misfires in Martyrdom Milieu." May 7, 20.

"New Voices, Visions Opening Up Liberation Theology." June 18, 20.

"Women-Church: A Way to Stay while Patriarchy Wears Away." August 13, 22.

"Many Women's Lot Still Poverty and Violence." September 17, 23.

"Recent Handshake Ignored Long Palestinian Plight." October 15, 24.

"What a Bishop Might Tell Her People about the Encyclical." November 12, 18.

"God Doesn't Need Transcendence: We Do." December 17, 18.

1994

"Tourists Must Look beyond the Walls to See the Scars." January 21.

"Women Thrive, Shine Serve in Grail These 50 Years." February 18.

"Identity Politics." March 25, 28.

"Main Steam Media." April 22, 12

"Welfare Reform Punishes the Poor." June 5, 17.

"Pope Ups the Ante on Ordaining Women." July 1, 19.

"Diversity of American Catholic Identity." August 12, 16.

"Vatican Blackout on Theology." September 16, 13.

"Vatican Alliance with Muslims Didn't Materialize in Cairo." October 14, 19.

"Politics of Meanness." December 9, 16.

1995

"Religion and the Subjugation of Women." January 27, 19.

"Maryknoll Nuns: The Salt of the Earth." March 10, 17.

"Turtles and Population." April 7, 16.
"For Powerless, the Contract Is on America." May 19, 15.
"Story of Japanese Haunts US." June 30, 21.
"Apocalyptic and Oklahoma." August 24, 15.
"Family Eschatology." September 8, 16.
——. "Vatican Status at the UN," Oct. 20, 21.
"Mary Moylan: Another Casualty of War." November 10, 14.
"Infallibility: Untenable on Every Ground." December 29, 19.

1996

"Chiapas: Organizational Skills", Jan. 26, 17.
"Israel's Stranglehold on Jerusalem." March 1, 13.
"Palestinian Israelis Taxes, Squeezed." March 22, 14.
"Jewish Settlers in Hebron", April 26, 12.
"Nuclear Weapons: US and Israel." May 31, 12.
"Catholicism in Old Struggle." July 26, 19.
"Miracle of Loaves and Picnic Baskets", September 6, 13.
"Animals Could Teach Us a Lot about Ourselves." September 27, 22.
"Rift with Gutierrez and Peru Women." Oct. 18, 28.
"Fight for Women's Vote, Nation's Identity", November 15, 22.

1997

"Love Prisons More Than Prisoners." January 10.
"Christmas Consumer Habit." February 7, 12.
"Mardi Gras." February 28, 18
"Voices in the Night." April 11, 18.
"Heaven's Gate: A Mingling of Traditions." May 2, 14.
"Yesterday's Illusions: Today's Modest Hope", June 6, 16.
"Problem of a Jewish State: Exclusivism on Both Sides." August.
"Cold War: What We Resist Persists." September 18.
"Best and Brightest Caught between Two Worlds." November 7, 14.
Christianity Gives Family Values a New Spin." December 12, 19.

1998

"Buddhist Conference: They Meet to Count Consumerist Evils." January 30.
"Israel's 50th Anniversary Gala in May Brings no Joy to Palestinian Hearts." March 27, 29,
"Monasticism and Ecology: Hectic Age Ends on a Hint of Harmony." June 19, 26.
"America Must Face Nuclear Guilt." August 14, 20.

1999

"For Feminist Theologians a Good Job is Hard to Find." January 15,
"Charles Davis: He Sought the Truest Meaning of Faith." February 12, 7.
"Don't Waste Cairo's Gain on Population Issues." March 5, 19.
"Clinton's Immorality More Than Sex Life." April 23, 20.
"An Unrealized Promise of Dialogue with Buddhism." June 4, 18.
"US Should Think Twice Before Making Kosovo a Model for Future Wars." July 2, 19.

"Racist Extremists Use Bible Verses to Justify Killing." August 27, 13.
"Christians Are Few in the Holy Land as History, Economics Takes Its Toll." October 2.
"The Puzzle of Pluralism." October 22, 28.
"Only Catholics Can Really Be Protestant." December 10, 20.

2000

"Thought Control Extends its Reach in Lincoln." March 31, 20.
"Diverse Forms of Family Life Merit Recognition." June 16, 19.
"Renewed in the Zone of Truth." August 25, 16
"Segregation, Harassment Mark Palestinian Life." October 20.
"Bombing in the Name of Redemption." December 8.

2001

"No Church Conspiracy against Mary Magdalene." February 9, 17.
"Mandatum Threatens Covenant of Respect." April 27, 17.
"Good Marital Sex Mirrors Love of God." May 25, 18.
"Vatican Favors the Palestinian Homeland." July.
"Question is How to End the Cycle of Violence." Sept. 28, 19.
"Two Spiritualities of Violence." Oct. 26.
"Ecumenical Deals Leave Women Out. " December 14, 16.

2002

"Media Reports Unity in War Effort not Reflected in Reality." January 25, 17.
"Though Poles Apart, Peaceful Coexistence and Dialogue Possible." April 12, 20.
"Destruction of Hope, Goal of Israeli Rampage." May 10, 16.
"Abuse a Consequence of History's Wrong Turn." June 7.
"Good Guys, Bad Guys Politics." September 27, 21.
"Threat of Mass Expulsion Adds to Palestinian Woes." November 29, 18.
"Feminism Must Rediscover Pacifist Roots." December 20, 22.

2003

"Global Capitalism a New Challenge to Theology." February 7, 16.
"Church Needs a Deeper Accountability." March 21, 20.
"Protest Ordinations Ignore Community." May 2, 14.
"Environmental Work in Women's Work." August 15, 20.

2004

"Was the Bush Administration Complicit in 9/11?" January 30, 17.
"US Churches Must Reject Americanist Christianity." April 23, 17.
"Tales of Hope and Resistance from the Holy Land" (Mitri Rabeh book), September 24, 17.
"Sexual Abuse at Abu Graib Stemmed from Pentagon Policy." October 15, 20.

2005

"Neo-conning the Electorate." January 21, 17

"Is Liberation Theology Dead?" April 29, 17
"Suppose This Is a Papal Election Not Received?" June 3, 20.
"The Wrong Response to Terrorism." August 12, 21.
"Marriage between Homosexuals is Good for Marriage." November 18, 20.

2006

"In the Name of Security." June, 15.
"When the Irish Were Mexican." September 1, 18.
"Consistent Life Ethic." November 17, 13–15.

2007

"What the Pope Should Have Said to the Muslim World." January.
"Creativity at the Grass Roots." September 7.
"The Sisters and the Union." October 19, 15.

2008

"The Whys of Holocaust Denial." April 4, 29.
"Damning America, Right and Left." April 18, 17, 20.
"The Lie That Barack Obama Is a Muslim Won't Go Away." October 17, 12, 16.

2010

"Two Views of Valid Women's Ordination Emerge." September 3, 116, 118.